The Future for Investors

ALSO BY JEREMY J. SIEGEL

Stocks for the Long Run

The Future for Investors

WHY THE TRIED AND THE TRUE TRIUMPH
OVER THE BOLD AND THE NEW

JEREMY J. SIEGEL

CROWN
BUSINESS
NEW YORK

Published in the United States by Crown Business,

an imprint of the Crown Publishing Group,

a division of Random House, Inc., New York.

www.crownpublishing.com

CROWN BUSINESS is a trademark and the Rising Sun colophon
is a registered trademark of Random House, Inc.

Library of Congress Cataloging-in-Publication Data

Siegel, Jeremy J.

The future for investors : why the tried and the true triumph
over the bold and the new / Jeremy J. Siegel.—1st ed.

1. Stocks. 2. Stocks—History. 3. Rate of return.

4. Stocks—Rate of return. I. Title.

HG4661.S52 2005

332.63'22—dc22   2004022938

ISBN 1-4000-8198-X

Printed in the United States of America

Design by Robert C. Olsson

10 9 8 7 6 5 4 3

First Edition

To Paul Samuelson, my teacher, and
Milton Friedman, my mentor, colleague, and friend.

CONTENTS

PREFACE

My first book, *Stocks for the Long Run*, was published in 1994 when the U.S. market was midway through its longest and strongest bull market in history. My research showed that over extended periods of time, stock returns not only dominate the returns on fixed-income assets, but they do so with lower risk when inflation is taken into account. These findings established that stocks should be the cornerstone of all long-term investors' portfolios.

The book's popularity led to many speaking engagements before audiences of individual and professional investors. After my presentations, two questions invariably came up: "*Which* stocks should I hold for the long run?" and "What will happen to my portfolio when the baby boomers retire and begin liquidating their portfolios?"

I wrote *The Future for Investors* to answer these questions.

The Great Bull Market of the 1990s

In *Stocks for the Long Run*, I recommended that investors link the equity portion of their portfolio to broad-based indexes of stocks, such as the S&P 500 Index or the Wilshire 5000. I had seen so many investors succumb to the temptation of trying to "time" the ups and downs of the market cycle that I believed a simple, disciplined, indexed approach was the best strategy. I did discuss some techniques that might improve on these indexed returns, but these suggestions were never central to the major thesis of the book.

Although indexation was a very good strategy for investors in the 1990s, by the end of the decade I became increasingly uncomfortable with the valuations that were put on many stocks. I thought frequently of what Paul Samuelson, my graduate school mentor and first American Nobel prize winner in economics, wrote on the cover of *Stocks for the Long Run:*

> Jeremy Siegel makes a persuasive case for a long-run, buy-and-hold invest-ment strategy. Read it. Profit from it. And when short-run storms rock your ship, sleep well from a rational conviction that you have done the prudent thing. And if you are a practitioner of economic science like me, ponder as to when this new philosophy of prudence will self-destruct after Siegel's readers come some day to be universally imitated.

When he wrote this in 1993, stock valuations were near their historical averages, and there was little danger that the market would "self-destruct." But as the Dow Industrials crossed 10,000, and Nasdaq approached 5,000, stock prices relative to either earnings or dividends climbed to higher lev-els than they had ever reached before. I worried that stock prices had reached heights from which they would yield poor returns. It was tempt-ing to urge investors to sell and wait for prices to come back down before going back into stocks.

But when I investigated the market in depth, I found that overvaluation infected only one sector—technology; the rest of the stocks were not un-reasonably priced relative to their earnings. In April of 1999, I took a stand on the pricing of Internet stocks by publishing an op-ed piece in the *Wall Street Journal* entitled "Are Internet Stocks Overpriced? Are They Ever!" It was my first public warning about market valuations.

Shortly before that article appeared, I invited Warren Buffett to speak before the Wharton community. He had not been on campus since he left the Wharton undergraduate program in 1949. He spoke to an overflowing crowd of more than one thousand students, many of whom had waited hours in line to get an opportunity to hear his wisdom on stocks, the econ-omy, and whatever else was on his mind.

I introduced Warren to the audience and detailed his extraordinary investment record. I was particularly honored when, in response to a ques-tion about Internet stocks, he urged the audience to read my *Journal* piece that had been published just a few days earlier.

His encouragement persuaded me to look deeper into the technology stocks that were selling at unprecedented valuations. At that time, technology stocks were all the rage and not only had the market value of the technology sector reached almost one third of the entire S&P 500's market value, but trading volume on Nasdaq for the first time in history eclipsed that on the New York Stock Exchange. I penned another article for the *Journal* in March 2000 entitled "Big Cap Tech Stocks Are a Sucker's Bet." I argued that stocks such as Cisco, AOL, Sun Microsystems, JDS Uniphase, Nortel, and others could not sustain their high prices and were heading for a severe decline.

If investors had avoided technology stocks during the bubble, their portfolios would have held up very well during the bear market. Indeed, the cumulative return of the 422 stocks in the S&P 500 Index that are not in the technology sector is higher than it was at the market peak in March 2000.

Long-term Performance of Individual Stocks

My interest in the long-term returns of individual stocks was piqued by the experience of one of my close friends, whose father had purchased AT&T fifty years earlier, reinvested the dividends, and held all the firms spun-off from Ma Bell. A modest initial investment had turned into a substantial bequest.

Similarly, much of Warren Buffett's success was also attributable to holding good stocks over long periods of time. Buffett has remarked that his favorite holding period is forever. I was curious how investors' portfolios would have performed if they did just that—bought a group of large capitalization stocks and held on to them for many decades.

Computing long-term, "buy-and-hold forever" returns seems like it would be an easy task. But the reality proved otherwise. The returns data on individual stocks available to academics and professionals assumed that all stock distributions and spin-offs were immediately sold and the proceeds reinvested in the parent firm. But this assumption did not match the behavior of many investors, such as my friend's father who purchased AT&T around 1950.

I went back a half century and investigated the long-term returns of the twenty largest stocks trading on the New York Stock Exchange, assuming dividends were reinvested and all distributions were held. To reconstruct these buy-and-hold returns was a time-consuming but ultimately extremely rewarding endeavor. To my amazement, the performance of the "Top Twenty," as I called this group of stocks, beat the returns of an investor who indexed to the entire market, which included all the new firms and new industries.

After that preliminary investigation, I was determined to explore the returns on all the 500 firms that constituted the S&P 500 Index when it was first formulated in 1957. This project yielded the same surprising conclusion—the original firms outperformed the newcomers.

These results confirmed my feeling that investors overprice new stocks, many of which are in high technology industries, and ignore firms in less exciting industries that often provide investors superior returns. I coined the term "the growth trap" to describe the incorrect belief that the companies that lead in technological innovation and spearhead economic growth bring investors superior returns.

The more I investigated returns, the more I determined that the growth trap affected not just individual stocks, but also entire sectors of the market and even countries. The fastest-growing new firms, industries, and even foreign countries often suffered the worst return. I formulated the basic principle of investor return, which specifies that growth alone does not yield good returns, but only growth in excess of the often overly optimistic estimates that investors have built into the price of stock. It was clear that the growth trap was one of the most important barriers between investors and investment success.

The Coming Age Wave

Understanding which stocks did well over the last half century helped me address the first of the two questions that I was frequently asked. To address the other, it was necessary to examine the economic consequences of our rapidly aging population. Having been born in 1945, I long realized that I was at the leading edge of the surge of baby boomers that would soon become a tidal wave of retirees.

Investor interest in the impact of the population trends on stock prices was sparked by Harry Dent, whose 1993 best-seller, *The Great Boom Ahead,* provided a novel explanation of historical stock trends. Dent found that stock prices over the last century correlated well with the population between forty-five and fifty years of age, an age that corresponded to peak consumer spending. On the basis of population projections, Dent predicted that the great bull market would extend to 2010 before crashing when the boomers entered retirement.

Harry Dent and I were invited to speak at many of the same conferences and conventions, although we rarely shared the same platform. I had never before used population trends to predict stock prices, preferring to use historical returns as the best estimate of future returns.

But the more I looked into demographics, the more I believed that population trends were critical to our economy and to investors. Although the United States, Europe, and Japan are getting older, most of the world is very young and these young economies are finally making their presence felt. Thanks to the superb technical ability of Wharton students, I was able to construct a model that integrated international demographic and productivity trends to forecast the future of the world economy.

The results were exciting and quite different from what Dent was forecasting. Rapid economic growth of the developing countries, if sustained, will have a significantly positive impact on the aging economies, mitigating the *negative* consequences of the age wave.

The more I studied the sources of growth, the more I believed that this growth can be sustained due to the communications revolution that enabled vast amounts of knowledge to become available to billions of people worldwide. For the first time, information that in the past could only be accessed at the great research centers of the world suddenly became accessible to anyone with an Internet connection.

The expansion of knowledge abroad had far-reaching consequences. As an academic, I had seen a dramatic increase in the number of talented students from outside the United States. In fact, the number of international students in our Ph.D. programs now clearly outnumbered the Americans. It was clear that in not too many years the West would no longer have a monopoly on knowledge and research. The diffusion of information around the globe had significant implications for investors everywhere.

New Approach to Investing

All these studies had a great impact on my approach to investing. I am often asked whether the bubble and subsequent collapse in the equity market over the past few years have caused me to shift my view of stocks. The answer is yes, it has, but in such a way that makes me just as optimistic about the future for investors.

Irrational fluctuations in the market, instead of being a source of alarm, give investors the opportunity to do even better than the buy-and-hold returns available on indexed securities. And world economic growth will open new opportunities and new markets to globally oriented firms on an unprecedented scale.

I believe that to take full advantage of these developments, investors must expand the scope of their portfolios and avoid the common pitfalls that cause the returns of so many to lag the market. It is my goal to provide such guidance in *The Future for Investors.*

PART ONE

Uncovering the Growth Trap

CHAPTER ONE

The Growth Trap

The speculative public is incorrigible. It will buy anything, at any price, if there seems to be some "action" in progress. It will fall for any company identified with "franchising," computers, electronics, science, technology, or what have you when the particular fashion is raging. Our readers, sensible investors all, are of course above such foolishness.

—Benjamin Graham, *The Intelligent Investor*, 1973

The future for investors is bright. Our world today stands at the brink of the greatest burst of invention, discovery, and economic growth ever known. The pessimists, who proclaim that the retiring baby boomers will bankrupt Social Security, upend our private pension systems, and crash the financial markets, are wrong.

Fundamental demographic and economic forces are rapidly shifting the center of our global economy eastward. Soon the United States, Europe, and Japan will no longer hold center stage. By the middle of this century, the combined economies of China and India will be larger than the developed world's.

How should you position your portfolio to take advantage of the dramatic changes and opportunities that will appear in the world markets?

To succeed in this rapidly changing environment, investors must grasp a very important and counterintuitive aspect of growth that I call the *growth trap.*

The growth trap seduces investors into overpaying for the very firms and industries that drive innovation and spearhead economic expansion. This relentless pursuit of growth—through buying hot stocks, seeking exciting new technologies, or investing in the fastest-growing countries—dooms investors to poor returns. In fact, history shows that many of the best-performing investments are instead found in shrinking industries and in slower-growing countries.

Ironically, the faster the world changes, the more important it is for investors to heed the lessons of the past. Investors who are alert to the growth trap and learn the principles of successful investing revealed in this book will prosper during the unprecedented changes that will transform the world economy.

The Fruits of Technology

No one can deny the importance of technology. Its development has been the single greatest force in world history. Early advances in agriculture, metallurgy, and transportation spurred the growth of population and the formation of great empires. Throughout history, those who possessed technological superiority, such as steel, warships, gunpowder, airpower, and most recently nuclear weapons, have won the decisive battles that allowed them to rule over vast parts of the earth—or to stop others from doing so.

In time, the impact of technology spread far beyond the military sphere. Technology has allowed economies to produce more with less: more cloth with fewer weavers, more castings with fewer machines, and more food with less land. Technology was at the heart of the Industrial Revolution; it launched the world on a path of sustained productivity growth.

Today, the evidence of that growth is seen everywhere. In the developed world, only a small fraction of work is devoted to securing life's necessities. Advancing productivity has allowed us to achieve better health, retire earlier, live longer, and enjoy vastly more leisure time. Even in the poorer regions of our globe, advances in technology during the past century have reduced the percentage of the world's population faced with starvation and those living in extreme poverty.

Indeed, the invention of new technologies has enabled thousands of inventors and entrepreneurs—from Thomas Edison to Bill Gates—to become fabulously wealthy by forming public companies. The corporations that Edison and Gates founded—General Electric and, a century later, Microsoft Corp.—are now ranked number one and two in the world in market value, having a combined capitalization in excess of half a trillion dollars.

Because investors see the enormous wealth of innovators like Bill Gates, they assume they must seek out the new, innovative firms and avoid the older firms that will eventually be upended by advancing technologies. Many of the firms that pioneered automobiles, radio, television, and then the computer and cell phone have not only contributed to economic growth, but also become very profitable. As a result, we set our investment strategies toward acquiring these ground-breaking firms that vanquished the older technologies, naturally assuming our fortunes will increase as these firms profit.

The Growth Trap

But all the assumptions behind these investment strategies prove false. In fact, my research shows that exactly the opposite is true: not only do new firms and new industries fail to deliver good returns for investors, but their returns are often inferior to those of companies established decades earlier.

Our fixation on growth is a snare, enticing us to place our assets in what we think will be the next big thing. But the most innovative companies are rarely the best place for investors. Technological innovation, which is blindly pursued by so many seeking to "beat the market," turns out to be a double-edged sword that spurs economic growth while repeatedly disappointing investors.

Who Gains—and Who Loses?

How can this happen? How can these enormous economic gains made possible through the proper application of new technology translate into substantial investment losses? There's one simple reason: in their enthusiasm to embrace the new, investors invariably pay too high a price for a piece of the action. The concept of growth is so avidly sought after that it lures investors into overpriced stocks in fast-changing and overly competitive industries, where the few big winners cannot begin to compensate for the myriad of losers.

I am not saying there are no gains to be reaped from the creative process. Indeed, there are many who become extremely wealthy from creating the new. If this were not so, there would be no motivation for entrepreneurs to develop pathbreaking technologies nor investors to finance them.

Yet the benefits of all this growth are funneled not to individual investors but instead to the innovators and founders, the venture capitalists who fund the projects, the investment bankers who sell the shares, and ultimately to the consumer, who buys better products at lower prices. The individual investor, seeking a share of the fabulous growth that powers the world economy, inevitably loses out.

History's Best Long-term Stocks

To illustrate the growth trap, imagine for a moment that we are investors capable of time travel, so we are in the remarkable position of being able to use hindsight to make our investment decisions. Let's go back to 1950 and take a look at two companies with an eye toward buying the stock of one and holding it to the present day. Let's choose between an old-economy company, Standard Oil of New Jersey (now ExxonMobil), and a new-economy juggernaut, IBM.

After making your selection and buying the stock, you instruct the firm to reinvest all cash dividends back into its shares, and you put your investment under lock and key. This is an investment that will be opened a half century later, the shares to be sold to fund your grandchild's education, your favorite charity, or even your own retirement, if you make this choice when you are young.

Which firm should you buy? And why?

THE ECONOMY AT MIDCENTURY

The first question you might have asked back in 1950 is: which sector of the economy will grow faster over the second half of the twentieth century, technology or energy? Fortunately, a quick review of history readily provides the answer. Technology firms were poised for rapid growth.

Not unlike today, the world in 1950 stood at the edge of tremendous change. U.S. manufacturers had shifted from munitions to consumer products, with technology leading the way. In 1948 there were 148,000 television sets in American homes. By 1950 that number had risen to 4.4 million; two years later, the figure was 50 million. The speed of penetration of this new medium was phenomenal and far exceeded that of the personal computer in the 1980s or the Internet in the 1990s.

Innovation was transforming our society, and 1950 was a hallmark year of invention. Papermate developed the first mass-produced, leak-proof ballpoint pen, and Haloid (later renamed Xerox) developed the first copy machine. The financial industry, already a heavy user of technology, was about to take a great leap forward as Diner's Club introduced the first credit card in 1950. And Bell Telephone Laboratories, a branch of the largest corporation on earth, American Telephone & Telegraph, had just perfected the transistor, a critical milestone that led to the computer revolution.

The future looked so bright that the term "new economy," so often bandied about during the 1990s technology boom, was also used to describe the economy fifty years earlier. *Fortune* magazine celebrated its twenty-fifth anniversary in 1955 with a special series devoted to "The New Economy" and the remarkable growth of productivity and income that America had achieved since the Great Depression.

IBM OR STANDARD OIL OF NEW JERSEY?

Let me give you some other information to help you make your decision. Look at Table 1.1, which compares the vital growth statistics of these two firms. IBM beat Standard Oil by wide margins in *every* growth measure that Wall Street uses to pick stocks: sales, earnings, dividends, and sector growth. IBM's earnings per share, Wall Street's favorite stock-picking criterion, grew more than three percentage points *per year* above the oil giant's growth over the next *fifty* years. As information technology advanced and computers became far more important to our economy, the technology sector rose from 3 percent of the market to almost 18 percent.

TABLE 1.1: ANNUAL GROWTH RATES, 1950–2003

Growth Measures	IBM	Standard Oil of NJ	Advantage
Revenue Per Share	12.19%	8.04%	IBM
Dividends Per Share	9.19%	7.11%	IBM
Earnings Per Share	10.94%	7.47%	IBM
Sector Growth*	14.65%	-14.22%	IBM

*Change in market share of technology and energy sectors 1957–2003

In contrast, the oil industry's share of the market shrunk dramatically over this period. Oil stocks comprised about 20 percent of the market value of all U.S. stocks in 1950, but fell to less than 5 percent by year 2000. This shrinkage occurred despite the fact that nuclear power never attained the dominance expected by its advocates and the world continued to be powered by fossil fuels.

If a genie had whispered these facts in your ear in 1950, would you have placed your money in IBM or Standard Oil of New Jersey?

If you answered IBM, you have fallen victim to the growth trap.

Although both stocks did well, investors in Standard Oil earned 14.42 percent per year on their shares from 1950 through 2003, more than half a percentage point ahead of IBM's 13.83 percent annual return. Although this difference is small, when you opened your lockbox fifty-three years later, the $1,000 you invested in the oil giant would be worth over $1,260,000 today, while $1,000 invested in IBM would be worth $961,000, 24 percent less.

WHY STANDARD OIL BEAT IBM: VALUATION VERSUS GROWTH

Why did Standard Oil beat IBM when it fell far short in *every* growth category? One simple reason: *valuation,* the price you pay for the earnings and dividends you receive.

The price investors paid for IBM stock was just too high. Even though the computer giant trumped Standard Oil on growth, Standard Oil trumped IBM on valuation, and valuation determines investor returns.

As you can see in Table 1.2, the average price-to-earnings ratio of Standard Oil, Wall Street's fundamental yardstick of valuation, was less than

TABLE 1.2: AVERAGE VALUATION MEASURES, 1950–2003

Valuation Measures	IBM	Standard Oil of NJ	Advantage
Average P/E	26.76	12.97	Standard Oil of NJ
Average Dividend Yield	2.18%	5.19%	Standard Oil of NJ

half of IBM's ratio, and the oil company's average dividend yield was more than three percentage points higher.

A very important reason that valuation matters so much is the reinvestment of dividends. Dividends are a critical factor driving investor returns. Because Standard Oil's price was low and its dividend yield much higher, those who bought its stock and reinvested the oil company's dividends accumulated almost fifteen times the number of shares they started out with, while investors in IBM who reinvested their dividends accumulated only three times their original shares.

Although the price of Standard Oil's stock appreciated at a rate that was almost three percentage points a year lower than the price of IBM's stock, its higher dividend yield made the oil giant the winner for investors. You can find the source of total returns to investors in IBM and Standard Oil of New Jersey in Table 1.3.

The basic principle of investor return that I explain in Chapter 3 states that the long-term return on a stock depends *not* on the actual growth of its earnings but on how those earnings compare to what investors expected. IBM did very well, but investors expected it to do very well, and its stock price was consistently high. Investors in Standard Oil had very modest expectations for earnings growth and this kept the price of its shares low, allowing investors to accumulate more shares through the reinvestment of dividends. The extra shares proved to be Standard Oil's margin of victory.

TABLE 1.3: SOURCE OF RETURNS OF IBM AND STANDARD OIL OF NJ, 1950–2003

Return Measures	IBM	Standard Oil of NJ	Advantage
Price Appreciation	11.41%	8.77%	IBM
Dividend Return`	2.18%	5.19%	Standard Oil of NJ
Total Return	**13.83%**	**14.42%**	**Standard Oil of NJ**

Stocks and Long-term Returns

Standard Oil of New Jersey is not the only "old economy" firm that proved a winning long-term investment.

In Table 1.4 you will find a list of the fifty largest American stocks trading in 1950, ranked by market value. These stocks constituted about half of the total value of all stocks traded on U.S. exchanges, which at that time dominated the world's equity markets. If you had to pick the four *best* stocks to lock up for the next fifty years, which would you buy? Assume, as before, that you reinvest all dividends and hold all spin-offs and other stock distributions, never selling a single share. Your goal is to maximize your nest egg when you open up your lockbox half a century later.

Surprisingly, despite all our knowledge of what has transpired in the second half of the twentieth century, identifying the firms that have provided investors with the best returns is not an easy task. Most of those on that list were old-economy industrial firms that have either gone out of business or are in declining industries. In 1950 manufacturing accounted for almost 50 percent of the market value of the top fifty firms, while today it constitutes less than 10 percent.

Do you think Standard Oil of New Jersey or IBM made the top four? Or would you choose General Electric, the only firm of the original Dow Jones industrials that is still a member of this venerable index today? GE has kept abreast of the changing economy by diversifying out of manufacturing and developing the financial powerhouse GE Capital and the media giant NBC.

Or you might even choose the original American Telephone & Telegraph, recognizing that under the conditions of this exercise you would also own all of the fifteen firms that AT&T subsequently spun off. Back in 1950, Ma Bell, as the firm was affectionately called, was by far the most highly valued company on earth. Today, surprisingly, the aggregate market value of AT&T and all of its distributions—the huge Bell regional operating companies and all its wireless, broadband, and cable offshoots—would still exceed that of any other firm on earth.

But neither AT&T, GE, nor IBM makes the grade. The four firms with the best investor returns from 1950 through 2003, shown in Table 1.5, are National Dairy Products (later named Kraft Foods), followed by R.J. Reynolds Tobacco, Standard Oil of New Jersey, and Coca-Cola.

TABLE 1.4: FIFTY LARGEST AMERICAN COMPANIES, 1950

Top 50 U.S. Companies, December 31, 1950, Ranked by Stock Market Value

Rank	Company Name	Rank	Company Name
1	AT&T	26	Westinghouse Electric
2	General Motors	27	Phillips Petroleum
3	DuPont	28	International Paper
4	Standard Oil of New Jersey	29	Union Pacific Railroad
5	Union Carbide	30	Bethlehem Steel
6	General Electric	31	Continental Oil
7	Standard Oil of California	32	F. W. Woolworth
8	Sears, Roebuck	33	Montgomery Ward
9	Texas Co.	34	Sinclair Oil
10	United States Steel	35	International Harvester
11	Gulf Oil	36	Sun Oil
12	Standard Oil of Indiana	37	Commonwealth Edison
13	S.H. Kress	38	National Steel
14	Kennecott Copper	39	Atchison, Topeka & Santa Fe
15	Socony Vacuum Oil	40	Consolidated Edison
16	Eastman Kodak	41	Anaconda Copper
17	Procter & Gamble	42	Monsanto Chemical
18	Chrysler	43	Pittsburgh Plate Glass
19	IBM	44	American Tobacco
20	J.C. Penney	45	R.J. Reynolds Tobacco
21	Allied Chemical & Dye	46	Phelps Dodge
22	United Fruit	47	Pacific Gas & Electric
23	Dow Chemical	48	Texas Gulf Sulphur
24	Pacific Telephone	49	National Dairy Products
25	Coca-Cola	50	Minnesota Mining & Manufacturing

When the lockbox is opened fifty-three years later in December 2003, an investor who put $1,000 in each of these stocks would have accumulated nearly $6.3 million, almost six times the $1.1 million that would have accumulated if the same $4,000 were instead invested in a stock market index.

None of these top-returning stocks operated in a growth industry or at the cutting edge of the technological revolution. In fact, these four firms produce almost the identical goods that they turned out a half century ago. Their products include name-brand foods (Kraft, Nabisco, Post, Maxwell House), cigarettes (Camel, Salem, Winston), oil (Exxon), and soft drinks (Coca-Cola). Indeed, Coca-Cola prides itself on producing its flagship drink with the same ingredients it used more than 100 years ago, acknowledging that it failed when, in April 1985, it introduced "new Coke" and strayed from its tried-and-true formula.

Each of these firms has a management that focused on what they do well and concentrated on bringing a superior product into new markets. And these companies all went global; today each of them has international sales that exceed those in the United States.

TABLE 1.5: THE BEST-PERFORMING STOCKS
FOR INVESTORS, 1950–2003

Top-Performing Companies Since 1950			
Return Rank	1950 Company Name (Current Name)	Annual Return	Final Accumulation of $1,000
1	National Dairy Products (Kraft Foods)	15.47%	$2,042,605
2	R.J. Reynolds Tobacco	15.16%	$1,774,384
3	Standard Oil of New Jersey (ExxonMobil)	14.42%	$1,263,065
4	Coca-Cola	14.33%	$1,211,456
	Top 4 Companies	14.90%	$6,291,510
	Equivalent $4,000 in market	11.44%	$1,118,936

The Future for Investors

The more data I analyzed, the more I realized that my findings were not isolated observations but in fact representative of much deeper forces that prevail over far longer periods and over a much wider range of stocks.

In the most important and exhaustive research project I conducted for this book, I dissected the entire history of Standard & Poor's famous S&P 500 Index, an index containing the largest firms headquartered in the United States and comprising more than 80 percent of the market value of all U.S. stocks. This index is replicated by more investors worldwide than any other, with more than $1 trillion in investment funds linked to its performance.

What I discovered completely overturned much of conventional wisdom that investors use to select stocks for their portfolios.

- The more than 900 new firms that have been added to the index since it was formulated in 1957 have, on average, *underperformed* the original 500 firms in the index. Continually replenishing the index with new, fast-growing firms while removing the older, slower-growing firms has actually *lowered* the returns to investors who link their returns to the S&P 500 Index.
- Long-term investors would have been better off had they bought the original S&P 500 firms in 1957 and *never* bought any new firms added to the index. By following this buy-and-never-sell approach, investors would have outperformed almost all mutual funds and money managers over the last half century.
- Dividends matter a lot. Reinvesting dividends is *the* critical factor giving the edge to most winning stocks in the long run. In contrast to skeptics who claim that high-dividend paying firms lack "growth opportunities," the exact opposite is true. Portfolios invested in the highest-yielding stocks returned 3 percent per year more than the S&P 500 Index, while those in the lowest-yielding stocks lagged the market by almost 2 percent per year.
- The return on stocks depends not on earnings growth but solely on whether this earnings growth exceeds what investors expected, and those growth expectations are embodied in the price-to-earnings,

or P/E ratio. Portfolios invested in the lowest-P/E stocks in the S&P 500 Index returned almost 3 percent per year more than the S&P 500 Index, while those invested in high-P/E stocks fell 2 percent per year behind the index. The results were almost identical to those using dividend yields.

• The long-run performance of initial public offerings is dreadful, *even if* you are lucky enough to get the stock at the offering price. From 1968 through 2001, there were only 4 years when the long-term returns on a portfolio of IPOs bought *at their offer price* beat a comparable small stock index. Returns for investors who buy IPOs once they start trading do even worse.

• The growth trap holds for industry sectors as well as individual firms. The fastest-growing sector, the financials, has underperformed the benchmark S&P 500 Index, while the energy sector, which has shrunk almost 80 percent since 1957, beat this benchmark index. The lowly railroads, despite shrinking from 21 percent to less than 5 percent of the industrial sector, outperformed the S&P 500 Index over the last half century.

• The growth trap holds for countries as well. The fastest-growing country over the last decade has rewarded investors with the worst returns. China, the economic powerhouse of the 1990s, has painfully disappointed investors with its overpriced shares and falling stock prices.

The Upcoming Demographic Crisis

Will the important findings highlighted above hold true over the next fifty years?

Perhaps not, if the age wave that faces the United States, Europe, and Japan means that our future is bleak. And many believe that to be the case. There are 80 million baby boomers who own *trillions* of dollars in stocks and bonds that in the next several decades will have to be sold in order to fund their retirement. In Europe and Japan, the population is aging at an even more rapid rate than in the United States.

An overabundance of sellers could spell disaster for investors and retirees desperately attempting to convert their financial assets into cash that will buy goods and services. Moreover, as the baby boomers retire, the looming shortage of workers in the United States is threatening to reduce the supply of the goods that the baby boomers must have in order to enjoy a comfortable retirement.

Respected voices such as Peter Peterson, author of *Running on Empty,* and Larry Kotlikoff, professor of economics at Boston University and author of *The Coming Generational Wars,* prophesy economic doom ahead. Peterson, Kotlikoff, and others warn that the aging of the population, woefully inadequate savings rates, and a shortage of future workers will cause an economic meltdown that will destroy the retirement of millions of Americans.

I, too, believe our future will be demographically driven. But after conducting my own research into the demographic realities we face, I disagree strongly with the pessimistic conclusions cast by Peterson, Kotlikoff, and others. My own model of demographic and productivity trends has convinced me that, instead of teetering on the edge of disaster, the world is poised for accelerating economic growth.

The information and communications revolution has enabled the developing nations of the world, such as China and India, to rapidly increase their economic growth, and they are on target to produce more than enough goods and services for the aging population of the developed world. I predict that by the middle of this century, China and India combined will produce more output than the United States, Europe, and Japan put together.

The two most critical questions facing the developed world are: who will produce the goods that we need and who will buy the assets that we sell? I have found the answer to both questions: the goods will be produced and the assets will be bought by the workers and investors of the developing world. I call this the global solution.

The Global Solution

The global solution will have vast implications for investors. The center of the economic world will move eastward. Chinese and Indian investors, as well as others from the world's emerging nations, will eventually own most of the world's capital, as tens of trillions of dollars of assets will be transferred from the retirees of the United States, Japan, and Europe to the savers and producers of the emerging nations. The global solution also implies that the developed world will run large and increasing trade deficits with the developing world. The importation of foreign goods in exchange for our assets is an inevitable consequence of our demographically driven future.

Those firms that understand and take advantage of the growth of world markets will be the most successful. As the globalization of the equity markets accelerates in the years ahead, international firms will become increasingly important to investors' portfolios.

Nevertheless, investors must be very mindful of the growth trap: the fastest-growing countries, just like the fastest-growing industries and firms, will not necessarily provide the best return. If investors get overly enthusiastic about the growth prospects of global firms and pay too high a price, their returns will be disappointing. The poor showing of those who put their funds in China, the world's fastest-growing economy, attests to the power of the growth trap to sink investor returns.

A New Approach to Investing

The material contained in *The Future for Investors* is a natural extension of my last book, *Stocks for the Long Run*. That research established that over long periods of time not only do stock returns overwhelm fixed-income assets but, once inflation is taken into account, also do so with less risk.

My new research explores which stocks will outperform in the long run and shows that the traditional way that investors think about stocks, in terms of "international" firms and "domestic" firms, "value" and "growth" stocks, is outmoded. As globalization spreads, where companies are headquartered will fade in importance. Firms may be headquartered in several countries, produce in yet others, and sell their products worldwide.

Furthermore, the best long-term stocks will not fall clearly into a "value" or "growth" category. The best performers may be fast growers, but their valuations will always be reasonable relative to their growth. They will be run by managements that have built and maintained their reputations for quality products that are marketed on a worldwide basis.

Plan of the Book

This book is organized into five parts. In Parts 1 and 2 you will learn about the growth trap and come to understand which investment characteristics you should seek and which you should avoid when buying stocks. In Part 3 you will learn why dividends are crucial to your success as an investor. In Part 4 you will see my vision of the future for our economy and financial markets, while Part 5 will tell you how to structure your portfolio to prepare for the changes that we shall encounter.

In a world that stands on the brink of a radical transformation, *The Future for Investors* establishes a consistent framework for understanding world markets and offers strategies designed to protect and enhance your long-term capital.

CHAPTER TWO

Creative Destruction or Destruction of the Creative?

The fundamental impulse that sets and keeps the capitalist engine in motion comes from the new consumers' goods, the new methods of production or transportation, the new markets, the new forms of industrial organization that capitalist enterprise creates. . . . This process of Creative Destruction *is the essential fact about capitalism. It is what capitalism consists in and what every capitalist concern has got to live in.*

—Joseph Schumpeter, *Capitalism, Freedom, and Democracy*, 1942

"Which Stocks Should I Buy and Hold?"

The research presented in this book concludes that many investors have been making investment decisions based on the wrong assumptions about what drives stock returns. The journey that changed my views of investing began with a question I received after one of my presentations to a group of investors.

"Professor Siegel?" A hand in the audience popped up, "You make a convincing case in your book *Stocks for the Long Run* that stocks represent the single best asset class over long periods of time. As a quote on the jacket of your book states, you have written the 'buy-and-hold bible' for investors. But I am still not certain what to do. *Which* specific stocks are you recommending that I buy and hold? Should I buy stock in, say, twenty large companies and just hold on to those shares forever?"

"Of course not," I replied, having heard this question countless times before. "The returns that I quote in *Stocks for the Long Run* are identical to those used by academics and professionals and are derived from very broad indexes of common stocks, such as the S&P 500 Index or the Wilshire 5000. These indexes are continually replenished with new companies, and now it is easy for investors to match the returns of these broad-based market indicators with indexed mutual and exchange-traded funds.

"New companies are important to your returns. Our economy is dynamic: new firms and industries continually appear while old ones die or are absorbed by other firms. This process of creative destruction is the essential fact about capitalism.

"Let me give you an example. The financial sector is the largest sector in the S&P 500 Index today. Yet in 1957, when the S&P 500 Index was founded, there was not a single commercial bank, brokerage firm, or investment bank traded on the New York Stock Exchange. In 1957 health care, which is now the second largest sector, was only about 1 percent of the market. The technology sector was not much larger.

"Today these three sectors—financial, health care, and technology, which were virtually nonexistent in 1957—add up to more than one-half of the market capitalization of the S&P 500. If you never replenished your portfolio, it would be full of dying industrial firms, mining companies, and railroads."

Many in the auditorium nodded in agreement, and my questioner seemed very satisfied with my response. I was certain that the answer that I gave to his question would be approved by the vast majority of financial advisors and academics who studied historical stock market returns.

Before my research for this book, I recommended that a straightforward indexing strategy was the best way to accumulate wealth. Being fully indexed meant that as the new firms came to the market and were included in the popular indexes, investors would be able to capture their superior performance.

But over the last two years I have conducted significant and extensive research that has changed my thinking on this matter. The studies described in this chapter and the rest of the book, led me to realize that although indexing will still provide good returns, there is a better way to build wealth.

Creative Destruction in the Stock Markets

"Creative destruction" was the term that Joseph Schumpeter, the great Austrian-American economist, used to describe how new firms spearheaded economic progress by destroying older ones. Schumpeter claimed that innovative technologies trigger the rise of new firms and organizational structures whose fortunes increase as the established order declines. Indeed, much of our economic growth has come from the expansion of technology, financial, and health care industries amid the decline of the manufacturing sector. But is Schumpeter's concept of creative destruction applicable to the returns in the financial markets as well?

Yes, said Richard Foster and Sarah Kaplan, two partners at McKinsey & Co. In their 2001 best-seller, *Creative Destruction: Why Companies That Are Built to Last Underperform the Market, and How to Successfully Transform Them,* the authors wrote, "If today's S&P 500 were made up of only those companies that were on the list when it was formed in 1957, the overall performance of the S&P 500 would have been about 20% less *per year* [emphasis in original] than it actually has been."[1]

If their research was correct, replenishing one's portfolio with new firms was critical to achieving good returns in the market. The difference they reported was huge. When the magic of compounding is taken into account over the next half century, they claimed that $1,000 invested in the original S&P 500 firms would grow to less than 40 percent of the sum that would have accumulated in an updated, continually replenished S&P 500 Index.

But something about Foster and Kaplan's results deeply disturbed me. If the original "old" companies in the S&P 500 Index did so much worse than the overall index, then the newly added companies must have done much better. And if the difference between the returns on new and old companies was as large as Foster and Kaplan claimed, why wasn't everyone just buying the new, selling the old, and substantially beating the S&P 500 Index? The overwhelming evidence was that most investors—indeed, most investment professionals—could not beat this benchmark.

Looking Back to Find the Answer

I decided that the best way to determine whether the concept of creative destruction applied to stock returns was to follow the performance of each of the original stocks in the S&P 500 Index. This would be a massive undertaking and the most data-intensive research I'd conducted since I first collected financial asset returns for *Stocks for the Long Run*. The analysis would involve not only calculating the return on the founding 500 stocks in the index but also tracing the complex corporate histories of the hundreds of successive firms that were merged or distributed from these original firms. Nevertheless, such a project would provide definitive evidence about the returns of "old" and "new" firms in the stock market.[2]

Before we get into the details of the exhaustive study that changed my views of the best investment strategy, let us take a brief look at the history of the world's most famous benchmark, the S&P 500 Index.

The History of the S&P 500 Index

Standard & Poor's first developed industrywide stock price indexes in 1923 and three years later formulated the Composite Index, containing ninety stocks.[3] As the economy grew, these ninety stocks proved insufficient to be representative of the whole market, so S&P expanded the Composite Index to 500 stocks on March 1, 1957, and renamed it the S&P 500 Index.[4]

The index originally contained exactly 425 industrials, 25 railroads, and 50 utility firms. In 1988 Standard & Poor's eliminated the fixed number of firms in each sector with the stated goal of maintaining a representative index that includes 500 "leading companies in leading industries of the economy."[5] The S&P 500 Index is continually updated by adding new firms that meet Standard & Poor's criteria for market value, earnings, and liquidity while deleting an equal number that fall below these standards.

The total number of new firms added to the S&P 500 Index from its inception in 1957 through 2003 was 917, an average of about twenty per year. The highest number of new firms added to the index in a single year occurred in 1976, when S&P added sixty firms, fifteen of which were banks and ten were insurance carriers. Until that year, the only financial stocks in the index in 1957 were consumer finance companies. Other financials were excluded because most were trading on the over-the-counter market, where timely price data were not available until the formation of Nasdaq in 1971.

In 2000, at the peak of the technology bubble, forty-nine new firms were added to the index, the second highest total. In 2003, near the bottom of the subsequent bear market, the number of additions fell to a record-tying low of eight.[6]

These additions and deletions have profoundly changed the composition of the index over the past half century. Table 2.1 displays the twenty stocks with the greatest market capitalization in the index today and in

TABLE 2.1: LARGEST STOCKS IN S&P 500 INDEX IN
MARCH 1957 AND DECEMBER 2003

Original S&P 500: March 1, 1957			
Market Cap Rank	Company	Market Cap (Billions)	Sector
1	Amer. Tel. & Tel.	$11.2	Telecom
2	Standard Oil of New Jersey	$10.9	Energy
3	General Motors	$10.8	Consumer Discretionary
4	DuPont	$8.0	Materials
5	General Electric	$4.8	Industrials
6	Gulf Oil	$3.5	Energy
7	Union Carbide & Carbon	$3.2	Materials
8	Texas Co.	$3.2	Energy
9	United States Steel	$3.2	Materials
10	Standard Oil of California	$2.8	Energy
11	IBM	$2.7	Information Tech
12	Royal Dutch Petroleum	$2.7	Energy
13	Socony Mobil Oil	$2.5	Energy
14	Shell Oil	$2.4	Energy
15	Sears, Roebuck	$2.0	Consumer Discretionary
16	Standard Oil of Indiana	$1.9	Energy
17	Aluminum Co. of America	$1.8	Materials
18	Bethlehem Steel	$1.7	Materials
19	Eastman Kodak	$1.6	Consumer Discretionary
20	Phillips Petroleum	$1.6	Energy

1957, when the index originated. Five of the top twenty firms today—Microsoft, Wal-Mart, Intel, Cisco, and Dell—were not even in existence in 1957. Nine of the top twenty in 1957 were oil producers, while only two

TABLE 2.1: LARGEST STOCKS IN S&P 500 INDEX IN
MARCH 1957 AND DECEMBER 2003

S&P 500: December 31, 2003			
Company	Market Cap (Billions)	Sector	Joined S&P 500
1	General Electric	$311.1	Industrials	Original
2	Microsoft	$297.8	Information Tech	1994
3	ExxonMobil	$271.0	Energy	Original
4	Pfizer	$269.6	Health Care	Original
5	Citigroup	$250.4	Financial	1988
6	Wal-Mart Stores	$229.6	Consumer Staples	1982
7	Intel	$210.3	Information Tech	1976
8	American Inter. Group	$172.9	Financial	1980
9	Cisco Systems	$167.7	Information Tech	1993
10	IBM	$159.4	Information Tech	Original
11	Johnson & Johnson	$153.3	Health Care	1973
12	Procter & Gamble	$129.5	Consumer Staples	Original
13	Coca-Cola	$124.4	Consumer Staples	Original
14	Bank of America	$119.5	Financial	1976
15	Altria Group	$110.5	Consumer Staples	Original
16	Merck	$102.8	Health Care	Original
17	Wells Fargo	$99.6	Financial	1987
18	Verizon Comm.	$96.9	Telecom	Original
19	Chevron Texaco	$92.3	Energy	Original
20	Dell	$87.0	Information Tech	1996

are today. Today the top twenty contains twelve firms in the technology, financial, and health care sectors, while in 1957 only IBM was in the top twenty.

Portfolios of Original S&P 500 Firms

To calculate the performance of the original S&P 500 firms, I formed three portfolios. All three portfolios start out holding the original five hundred stocks in proportion to their market value, a standard "value-weighted portfolio." But over time these portfolios evolve differently depending on the assumptions we make about what investors would do when some of the original firms merge with other firms or distribute spin-offs.

The first portfolio is called the Survivors portfolio and assumes that when the original firms merge or go private, the shares are sold and the proceeds are reinvested in the surviving firms of the index. This portfolio ended up with 125 companies and included such winning firms as Philip Morris, Pfizer, Coca-Cola, General Electric, and IBM and losers such as Bethlehem Steel, United Airlines, and Kmart.

The second portfolio, called the Direct Descendants portfolio, included all merged firms, but it assumed, like the Survivors portfolio, that all corporate spin-offs were immediately sold and reinvested in the parent firm.[7]

The third portfolio, called the Total Descendants portfolio, assumed that investors held all the corporate spin-offs. No shares from this portfolio were ever sold, so this is the ultimate buy-and-hold, or "buy-and-forget," portfolio. By the end of 2003, the Total Descendants portfolio held shares in 341 firms; its composition is described in Figure 2.1.

Long-term Returns

I constructed these three portfolios to show that no matter how you define the returns on the portfolio of original S&P 500 stocks, you come up with the same astounding result:

The returns on the original firms in the S&P 500 beat the returns on the standard, continually updated S&P 500 Index and did so with lower risk.

FIGURE 2.1: FINAL PORTFOLIOS OF ORIGINAL S&P 500 FIRMS
MARCH 1, 1957, TO DECEMBER 31, 2003

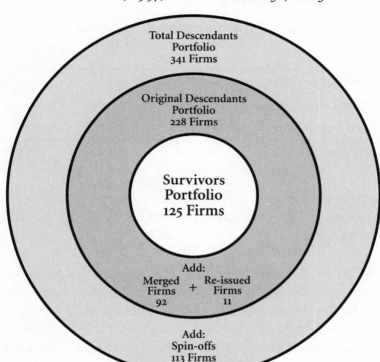

From March 1, 1957, through December 31, 2003, money put in these original S&P 500 portfolios accumulated to between 21 and 26 percent *more* than would have accumulated in a standard S&P 500 Index fund. The results are summarized in Table 2.2.

It should be stressed that all these returns could be attained by investors buying the original S&P 500 firms in 1957 and holding them to the end of 2003. No advance knowledge of which firms survived and which did not was necessary to obtain these index-beating returns.

Let us put these results another way:

TABLE 2.2: PERFORMANCE OF ORIGINAL
S&P 500 PORTFOLIOS AND INDEX

Portfolio	Accumulation Based on $1,000 Invested	Annual Return	Risk
Survivors Portfolio	$151,261	11.31%	15.72%
Direct Descendants	$153,799	11.35%	15.93%
Total Descendants	$157,029	11.40%	16.08%
S&P 500	$124,522	10.85%	17.02%

The shares of the original S&P 500 firms have, on average, outperformed the nearly 1,000 new firms that have been added to the index over the subsequent half century.

I do not deny that these new firms that have been added to the S&P 500 Index drive the creative destruction process that stimulates economic growth. But on the whole, these new firms did not serve investors well. Those who bought the original 500 firms and never sold any of them outperformed not only the world's most famous benchmark stock index but also the performance of most money managers and actively managed equity funds.

Reasons for Underperformance of the S&P 500 Index

Why did this happen? How could the new companies that fueled our economic growth and made America the preeminent economy in the world underperform the older firms?

The answer is simple. Although the earnings, sales, and even market values of the new firms grew faster than those of the older firms, the price investors paid for these stocks was simply too high to generate good returns. These higher prices meant lower dividend yields and therefore fewer shares accumulated through reinvesting dividends.

Recall my analysis of Standard Oil of New Jersey and IBM in the first chapter. IBM was one of the most innovative and fastest-growing stocks of the twentieth century, and it beat Standard Oil in every growth category imaginable. But IBM could not beat the oil company's return to its investors. IBM's share price was consistently too high to overcome the gains made by reinvesting the oil company's dividends. This was the same fate that on average impacted the 917 new firms added to the S&P 500 Index over the past half century.

The overpricing, and resultant underperformance, of the new firms in the index is not the fault of Standard & Poor's or the members of its Index Committee, which chooses the stocks in its indexes. In fact, S&P wisely resisted adding a number of Internet and technology firms to the index in the late 1990s, although some of these stocks attained market values far in excess of minimum requirement to belong to the index.

As I shall show numerous times throughout the book, overpricing of new stocks is common throughout the entire market and is indicative of the growth trap. When euphoria strikes a particular sector of the market, as it did with technology in the late 1990s or oil and gas exploration firms twenty years earlier, it is impossible for S&P to avoid including some of these stocks in its index. In order for the S&P 500 or any other index to remain representative, it must admit firms whether or not it considers them overvalued.

Yahoo!

Another reason the new firms added to the S&P 500 Index underperform involves the very success of the index. It has been estimated that more than $1 trillion of investor capital is committed to funds that are linked to the S&P 500 Index. This means that when the S&P adds a firm to its index, there will be a huge and automatic increase in the demand for that stock, pushing up its price and hence lowering the return of indexed investors.[8]

A perfect example of an overvalued stock that became even more overvalued was Yahoo!, the leading Internet portal company. On November 30, 1999, near the peak of the Internet boom, Standard & Poor's announced that Yahoo! would be added to its index on December 8. Up to that date, AOL, which had been admitted in January 1999, was the only Internet stock in the index.

The next morning, a flood of buy orders, prompted by the recognition that index funds would soon have to purchase substantial blocks of this stock, pushed Yahoo! up almost $9 at the opening of trading. The stock continued to rise until it closed at $174 per share on December 7. In just five trading days, the stock soared $68, or 64 percent above the price it was trading at before the S&P announcement. On December 7, the last day index funds had to buy the stock, volume hit 132 million shares, representing $22 billion of Yahoo! stock traded.

Now, I believed Yahoo! was grossly overvalued when it was selling at $106 a share, before Standard & Poor's added the firm to its index. As I will discuss in Chapter 5, I included Yahoo! as one of the nine most overvalued large-cap stocks in an article that I published in the *Wall Street Journal* in March 2000. At that time Yahoo!'s market value was more than $90 billion, and the stock was selling at about 500 times earnings, more than twenty times the average for the S&P 500 Index.

Holding a substantial position in an S&P 500 Index fund at the time, I was quite distressed with the surge in Yahoo!'s price. It was clear to me that Yahoo! would drag down the future returns of the index and that this would not be the last time such an incident occurred.

Subsequent events confirmed my fears. What happened to Yahoo! was also happening to other firms added to the S&P 500 Index. In the year 2000, King Pharmaceuticals jumped 21 percent from its announcement dates to its inclusion in the S&P 500, CIT Group rose 22 percent, JDS Uniphase increased by 27 percent, Medimmune jumped 31 percent, Power One rose over 35 percent, and Broadvision rocketed up 50 percent.

All these price jumps meant that the return to popular index products could be subject to a downward bias over time. Standard & Poor's is very aware of this situation, and in March 2004 it announced steps to reduce the price impact of being added to or deleted from the index.[9] Nevertheless, it is likely there will always be a premium on S&P 500 stocks as long as the index retains its popularity.[10]

The Confusion Between Market Value and Investor Return

Where did Foster and Kaplan go wrong when they concluded that it was the new firms that drove the S&P 500 returns? They incorrectly used changes in the market value of a stock as a measure of investor return. Market value, which is often called market capitalization or market cap, is the product of the number of shares outstanding for a company and the price per share. For example, in 2004 there were approximately 11 billion shares of Microsoft stock outstanding. At Microsoft's price per share of $27, Microsoft had a market capitalization of approximately $300 billion. This market cap can change if either the price of Microsoft's stock changes or the number of shares changes.

Investor return is a very different concept. It is equal to change in the price per share plus the dividend, if there is any. The return on Microsoft will change if either the price of Microsoft stock changes or the dividend changes. The only common factor in both definitions is the price of the stock. Dividends and changes in the number of shares outstanding have a very different impact on investor returns.

Confusing investor return and market capitalization is a mistake that many other investors and even professionals make. Market value and return are indeed very tightly linked in the short run. Day to day or week to week, there is nearly a perfect correlation between the two concepts. But as the period lengthens, the correlation becomes much weaker. For a long-term investor, dividends become the primary source of investor return.

THE IMPORTANCE OF REINVESTING DIVIDENDS

Recall that the price of IBM's shares increased at over 11 percent per year, almost three percentage points above that of Standard Oil of New Jersey, but Standard Oil's return surpassed that of IBM. Standard Oil's high dividend yield made a huge difference in boosting its return. The price of Standard Oil increased by a factor of about 120 from 1950 through 2003, while IBM's price increased almost 300-fold. But shareholders who bought Standard Oil (now ExxonMobil) in 1950 and reinvested their dividends would have over fifteen times the number of shares they started with, while shareholders in IBM would only have three times the number of shares.

Many investors and advisors fail to realize the impact of reinvesting dividends on long-term performance. This neglect occurs because investors focus excessively on short-term price appreciation when they should focus on long-term returns. This is yet another manifestation of the growth trap. Investors must be patient and understand that accumulating extra shares through dividend reinvestment increases their returns. A crucial lesson for long-term investors, a lesson that will be emphasized in Part 3 of this book, is that the reinvestment of dividends matters—and it matters a lot.

FALLING MARKET VALUE AND RISING RETURNS

There are other reasons for the disconnect between market value and return. Take AT&T, which was the most valuable company in the world when the S&P 500 was founded in 1957. By the end of 1983, its market capitalization had grown to almost $60 billion. When the Justice Department ordered AT&T to divest all of its Baby Bells (regional Bell operating companies), AT&T shareholders received additional shares of seven separate companies.[11]

This restructuring caused AT&T's market capitalization to plunge from $60 billion to $20 billion by the end of 1984. Yet when taking into account the divestitures, the investor return on AT&T was positive. Instead of the 66 percent decline in market value, investors who held their spin-offs saw their wealth grow by 30 percent that year.

RISING MARKET VALUE, FALLING RETURNS

But the reverse can also occur: market values can rise while returns fall. This happens when a company issues shares to finance a new project or, frequently, arranges to merge with another firm.

The largest all-stock merger in history occurred when AOL merged with Time Warner in 2000 at the peak of the technology boom. AOL issued Time Warner shareholders 1.5 shares of AOL for each Time Warner share, creating the world's largest media company. Each AOL shareholder's slice of the total pie shrank when these new shares were issued, but the entire pie grew larger because the two companies became one.

When the merger was complete, AOL had increased its market capitalization from $109 billion to $192 billion, making it one of the largest corporations in the world. Unfortunately for Time Warner shareholders, they were given AOL's stock at the very peak of the market and suffered dreadful returns in the following years. By 2003, AOL Time Warner dropped the AOL name, perhaps trying to erase the bad memory of a deal gone sour.

There is also a substantial difference between the return and market value of the original and updated firms in the S&P 500 Index. The market value of the S&P 500 Index increased from $172 billion in 1957 to $10.3 trillion by December 31, 2003, a 9.13 percent annual rate. In contrast, the market value of the original firms in the index has grown at a lower 6.44 percent annual rate, reaching only $3.2 trillion by the end of 2003.

The important point is that while the market value of the survivors grew at a far lower rate than the market value of the S&P 500 Index, the return on the portfolio of survivors exceeded the return on the index. The market value of the S&P 500 increased more rapidly because all the new companies added to the index increased its market value, but these additions did not increase its return. This is where Foster and Kaplan went wrong in their research and why the pursuit of growth is often the wrong investment strategy.

Should Investors Hold or Sell Spin-offs?

The historical analysis of the S&P 500 Index also sheds some light on whether investors should hold spin-offs and other stock distributions or sell them and redeploy the funds elsewhere. The difference between holding and not holding the spin-offs can be found by examining the returns on the Total Descendants portfolio and the Direct Descendants portfolio.

Solely on the basis of risk and return, there is not much to choose between them. Sometimes the spin-offs did better than the parent firm, sometimes they did not. For example, investors would have been much better off holding AT&T's Baby Bells, whose returns were almost three percentage points per year more than those of AT&T itself. Similarly, Morgan Stanley and Allstate outperformed their parent, Sears, Roebuck. On the other hand, Praxair, a natural gas producer, failed to match the return on its parent, Union Carbide, as did the energy and gold properties spun off by Atchison, Topeka & Santa Fe Railway.

But from a tax and transaction costs standpoint, holding the spin-offs is likely to be very advantageous. By holding the Total Descendants portfolio, no shares are ever sold in the open market, and the only shares purchased arise from the receipt of dividends and other cash distributions, so that trading costs are minimized.[12] Moreover, with very few exceptions, no capital gains are realized on this portfolio, as no shares are ever sold.[13]

Investors should not take these cost savings lightly. One of the most serious drags on investor returns comes from the transaction costs and taxes incurred by trading too much. Although the returns on these portfolios do not take these costs into account, the Total Descendants portfolio incurs lower costs than investors would in S&P 500 mutual or exchange-traded funds. The cost savings alone implies that investors would do well by holding on to all spin-offs they receive.

Lessons for Investors

Schumpeter's concept of creative destruction fittingly describes the way capitalist economies function. New firms upstage old firms, forcing change, driving growth, and overthrowing the status quo. But the process of creative destruction works very differently in the capital markets. It is investors in the firms deemed "creative" who get hammered by paying prices for their shares that are too high.

What do these findings mean for investors? Should one just buy a portfolio of stocks such as the S&P 500 and hold it forever? The short answer is no. As we will learn in subsequent chapters, there are opportunities for investors to do even better than the returns on the portfolios of original S&P 500 firms reported here.

But the research contained in this chapter destroys the myth that updating one's portfolio is essential to obtain superior returns. In fact, extremely popular indexes, such as the S&P 500, can lead to overpricing of newly admitted firms and lower future performance. Furthermore, "buy-and-hold" portfolios are very tax efficient and lower transaction costs and are an attractive way to build wealth in the long run.

The next chapter identifies the firms that have powered these original S&P portfolios ahead of the market.

CHAPTER THREE

The Tried and True:

FINDING CORPORATE EL DORADOS

But how, you will ask, does one decide what [stocks are] "attractive"?
Most analysts feel they must choose between two approaches custom-
arily thought to be in opposition: "value" and "growth."... We view
that as fuzzy thinking.... Growth is always a component of value
[and] the very term "value investing" is redundant.

—Warren Buffett, Berkshire Hathaway annual report, 1992

The last chapter summarized the long-term returns to portfolios of the original firms in the S&P 500 Index. In the appendix to this book, you will find a record of the transformation and returns of each of the original S&P 500 firms, including a detailed description of the twenty best-performing stocks from the Total Descendants portfolio and the performance of the twenty largest firms, which accounted for almost half of the market value of the index when it was founded in 1957.

These lists, including the ones described in this chapter on the best-performing surviving companies, give you an appreciation of the tremendous changes that have taken place in corporate America over the past five decades and go a long way toward answering the following questions: What firms give the best returns? What industries are they from? And most important, what characteristics make a stock a successful long-term investment?

The Corporate El Dorado: The Number-One-Performing Stock

In *Creative Destruction: Why Companies That Are Built to Last Underper-form the Market, and How to Successfully Transform Them,* Richard Foster and Sarah Kaplan commented, "[Our] long-term studies of corporate birth, survival, and death in America clearly show that the corporate equivalent of El Dorado, the golden company that continually performs better than the markets, *has never existed* [emphasis in original]. It is a myth."[1]

On the contrary, my research shows that not only does the corporate equivalent of El Dorado exist, but in fact there are many corporate El Dorados. Finding these firms can make a huge difference to your portfolio.

In the last chapter I showed that $1,000 placed in an S&P 500 Index fund on February 28, 1957, would have grown, with dividends reinvested, to almost $125,000 by December 31, 2003. But $1,000 placed in the top-performing company from the original S&P 500 firms would have grown to almost $4.6 million. What was this golden company that beat the market by 9 percent per year over the last half century and left every other firm far behind in the race to be number one?

It was Philip Morris, which in 2003 changed its name to Altria Group.[2] Philip Morris introduced the world to the Marlboro Man, one of the world's most recognized icons, two years before the formulation of the S&P 500 Index. Marlboro subsequently became the world's best-selling cigarette brand and propelled Philip Morris stock upward.

Philip Morris's outstanding performance does not just date from mid-century. Philip Morris was also the best-performing company since 1925, the date when comprehensive returns on individual stocks were first compiled. From the end of 1925 through the end of 2003, Philip Morris delivered a 17 percent compound annual return, 7.3 percent greater than the market indexes. An initial $1,000 invested in this firm in 1925, with dividends reinvested, would now be worth over a quarter of a billion dollars!

Philip Morris's bounty did not only extend to its own stockholders. As the appendix describes in detail, Philip Morris eventually became the owner of nine other original S&P 500 firms. Many investors in such little-known companies as Thatcher Glass became enormously wealthy because their shares were exchanged for successful companies such as Philip Morris and its predecessors. Riding on the coattails of such winners is an unexpected, but not uncommon gift for investors.

How Bad News for the Firm Becomes Good News for Investors

Some readers may be surprised that Philip Morris is a top performer for investors in the face of the onslaught of governmental restrictions and legal actions that have cost the firm tens of billions of dollars and threaten the cigarette manufacturer with bankruptcy.

But in the capital markets, bad news for the firm often is transformed into good news for investors. Many shun the stock in the company and fear that its legal liability for producing a dangerous product—cigarettes—will eventually crush the firm. This aversion to the firm pushes down the price of Philip Morris shares and raises the return to investors who stick with the stock.

As long as the firm survives and continues to be very profitable, paying out a good fraction of its earnings in the form of dividends, investors will continue to do extraordinarily well. With the price of its stock so low and its profits so high, Philip Morris's dividend yield is one of the highest in the market. Those reinvested dividends have turned its stock into a pile of gold for investors who have stayed with the company. The power of Philip Morris's high dividend to propel its higher returns is discussed in Chapter 10.

The superb returns in Philip Morris illustrate an extremely important principle of investing: what counts is not just the growth rate of earnings but the growth of earnings relative to the market's expectation. One reason investors had low expectations for Philip Morris's growth because of its potential liabilities. But its growth has continued apace. The low expectations combined with high growth and a high dividend yield provide the perfect environment for superb investor returns.

Later in this chapter I will state and explain the basic principle of investor return, which will enable you to find the winning stocks. But before I do so, let us take a look at the original S&P 500 firms and determine which have performed best for investors. Once we study their characteristics, we shall be able to identify the true corporate El Dorados.

The Top-Performing S&P 500 Survivor Firms

Table 3.1 indicates the twenty best-performing surviving firms of the original S&P 500 Index in 1957. These are firms whose corporate structure remained intact, as they have not been merged into any other firms. The shareholder return on each of these companies has beaten the return on the S&P 500 Index by at least two and three-quarters percentage points per year since the index was founded in 1957, and some have beaten the index by much wider margins. This means that an investment in any of these

TABLE 3.1: TOP-TWENTY PERFORMING SURVIVORS,
1957–2003

Rank	2003 Name	Accumulation of $1000	Annual Return
1	Philip Morris	$4,626,402	19.75%
2	Abbott Labs	$1,281,335	16.51%
3	Bristol-Myers Squibb	$1,209,445	16.36%
4	Tootsie Roll Industries	$1,090,955	16.11%
5	Pfizer	$1,054,823	16.03%
6	Coca-Cola	$1,051,646	16.02%
7	Merck	$1,003,410	15.90%
8	PepsiCo	$866,068	15.54%
9	Colgate-Palmolive	$761,163	15.22%
10	Crane	$736,796	15.14%
11	H.J. Heinz	$635,988	14.78%
12	Wrigley	$603,877	14.65%
13	Fortune Brands	$580,025	14.55%
14	Kroger	$546,793	14.41%
15	Schering-Plough	$537,050	14.36%
16	Procter & Gamble	$513,752	14.26%
17	Hershey Foods	$507,001	14.22%
18	Wyeth	$461,186	13.99%
19	Royal Dutch Petroleum	$398,837	13.64%
20	General Mills	$388,425	13.58%
	S&P 500	$124,486	10.85%

stocks has accumulated anywhere from three to thirty-seven times the accumulation of the S&P 500 Index.

What strikes one immediately is the dominance of two industries: well-known consumer brand companies and large, well-known pharmaceutical firms. All these firms have built wide name recognition and consumer trust. They have survived and prospered over the past half century through significant changes in the economic and political climates, and virtually all have expanded aggressively into international markets. The success of these firms is what I call the triumph of the tried and true.

THE POWER OF CONSUMER BRAND NAMES

Philip Morris is one of many firms with a strong brand name that has made it to the top of the pack. In fact, eleven of the top twenty are well-known consumer brand stocks.

As the medical, legal, and popular assault on smoking has accelerated, Philip Morris (as well as the other giant tobacco manufacturer, R.J. Reynolds) has diversified into brand-name food products. In 1985 Philip Morris purchased General Foods, and in 1988 the company purchased Kraft Foods for $13.5 billion. It completed its food acquisitions with Nabisco Holdings in 2001. Currently, Philip Morris receives more than 40 percent of its revenues and 30 percent of its profits from food products.

The tobacco manufacturers are among the few successful long-term companies that have ventured outside their original specialty—the manufacture and sale of tobacco products. We take a closer look at the corporate evolution of Philip Morris in the appendix, where we will find that the company's shares end up in the portfolios of investors in ten of the original S&P 500 firms, all of which beat the S&P 500 Index. But first let us take a look at some of the other consumer brand name firms on the best-performing list.

Number four on this list is a most unlikely winner—a small manufacturer originally named the Sweets Company of America. This company has outperformed the market by 5 percent a year since the index was formulated. The founder of this firm, an Austrian immigrant, named its product after his five-year-old daughter's nickname, Tootsie. The Sweets Company of America changed its name to Tootsie Roll Industries in 1966.[3]

In 2002, Tootsie celebrated its 100th year of listing on the New York Stock Exchange. The company produces over 60 million Tootsie Rolls and 20 million lollipops per day, making it the world's largest lollipop supplier. Remarkably, the company's Web site proudly proclaims that the price of its flagship product (the single wrapped Tootsie Roll) has remained unchanged at one penny for the past 107 years (although I'm sure that its size has shrunk).

The surviving company with the sixth highest return produces a product today with the exact same formula as it did over 100 years ago, much like Tootsie Roll. This company was highlighted in Chapter 1 as one of the four best-performing of the largest fifty firms from 1950. Although the company keeps the formula for its drinks secret, it is no secret that Coca-Cola has been one of the best companies you could have owned over the last half century.

What about Coke's well-known rival, Pepsi, which also was on the list of the original S&P 500 firms? Pepsi also delivered superb returns to its shareholders, coming in at number eight and beating the market by over 4 percent a year.

Two others of the twenty best-performing stocks also manufacture products virtually unchanged over the past 100 years: the William Wrigley Jr. Company and Hershey Foods. Wrigley came in at number twelve, beating the market by almost 4 percent a year, whereas Hershey came in at seventeen, beating the market by 3 percent a year.

Wrigley is the largest gum manufacturer in the world, commanding an almost 50 percent share in the global market and selling in approximately 100 countries. Hershey is currently the number-one U.S.-based publicly traded candy maker (Mars, a private firm, is number one, followed by Swiss-based Nestlé).

Founded by Milton Hershey in 1905, Hershey Foods did not advertise its products until 1970, maintaining that its high quality would speak for itself. For years Hershey's success showed that strong brands can be sold through word of mouth.

Heinz is another strong brand name, one that is virtually synonymous with ketchup. Each year, Heinz sells 650 million bottles of ketchup and makes 11 billion packets of ketchup and salad dressings—almost two packets for every person on earth. But Heinz is just not a ketchup producer, and it does not restrict its focus to the United States. It has the number-one or -two branded business in fifty different countries, with products such as Indonesia's ABC soy sauce (the second-largest-selling soy sauce in the world) and Honig dry soup, the best-selling soup brand in the Netherlands.[4]

Colgate-Palmolive also makes the list, coming in at number nine. Colgate's products include Colgate toothpastes, Speed Stick deodorant, Irish Spring soaps, antibacterial Softsoap, and household cleaning products such as Palmolive and Ajax.

No surprise that Colgate's rival, Procter & Gamble, makes this list as well, at number sixteen. Procter & Gamble began as a small, family-operated soap and candle company in Cincinnati, Ohio, in 1837. Today, P&G sells three hundred products, including Crest, Mr. Clean, Tide, and Tampax, to more than five billion consumers in 140 countries.

Fortune Brands started off as a tobacco giant, American Tobacco. After it gained control of almost the entire cigarette industry, it was dissolved in an antitrust suit in 1911. The major companies that emerged from it were American Tobacco, R.J. Reynolds, Liggett & Myers, Lorillard, and British American Tobacco.

Two of the most popular brands that remained with American Tobacco were Lucky Strike and Pall Mall. In the 1990s the company divested all tobacco products, selling its large tobacco brands privately to British American Tobacco and divesting its large stake in Gallaher Group, another British tobacco company that it had purchased earlier. Today, American Brands, renamed Fortune Brands in 1997, sells branded products such as Titleist golf balls and Jim Beam spirits.

Number twenty on the list is General Mills, another company with strong brands, which include Betty Crocker, introduced in 1921, Wheaties (the "Breakfast of Champions"), Cheerios, Lucky Charms, Cinnamon Toast Crunch, Hamburger Helper, and Yoplait yogurt.

What is true about all these firms is that their success came through developing strong brands not only in the United States but all over the world. A well-respected brand name gives the firm the ability to price its product above the competition and deliver more profits to investors.

THE PHARMACEUTICALS

Besides the strong consumer brands firms, the pharmaceuticals had a prominent place on the list of best-performing companies. It is noteworthy that there were only six health care companies in the original S&P 500 that survive to today in their original corporate form, and all six made it onto the list of best performers. All of these firms not only sold prescription drugs but also were very successful in marketing brand-name over-the-counter treatments to consumers, very much like the brand-name consumer staples stocks that we have reviewed.

The top-performing pharmaceutical firm for investors was Abbott Laboratories, coming in second and beating the market by more than 5.5 percent per year. Since 1957, Abbott turned each $1,000 invested into $1.2 million by the end of 2003. Abbott went public in 1929 and is a leading producer of antiviral drugs, particularly those used to treat HIV/AIDS, as well as treatments for epilepsy, high cholesterol, and arthritis. In the consumer division, the company has succeeded with such nutritional supplements as Similac and Ensure as well as the best-selling acid reflux remedy, Prevacid.

The next three successful pharmaceuticals, Bristol-Myers Squibb, Pfizer, and Merck, came in third, fifth, and seventh on the list of best-returning survivor firms. All would have turned $1,000 into roughly $1 million.

Bristol-Myers was founded more than a century ago and in 1989 purchased Squibb, a New York drug firm that dates back to the mid-1850s. Bristol-Myers Squibb has such household name over-the-counter drugs as Excedrin and Bufferin, as well as nutritional products for children through its Mead Johnson subsidiary. Its prescription blockbusters include Pravachol for cholesterol and the platelet inhibitor Plavix.

Pfizer, formed in 1900, discovered such blockbuster antibiotics as Terramycin, was the producer of the Salk and Sabin polio vaccines in the 1950s, and pioneered Viagra and the cholesterol-reducing, best-selling drug of all time, Lipitor. Its consumer division features such brand names as Listerine, Benadryl, Rolaids, Ben-Gay, and many others.

Rounding out the top twenty are Schering (later Schering-Plough) and American Home Products (renamed Wyeth in 2002), ranking number fifteen and number eighteen, respectively. Schering was a German firm seized by the U.S. government in the Second World War and then privatized in 1952. Schering pioneered antihistamines, such as Coricidin, and has had success with Tinactin, Afrin, and Coppertone, and Di-Gel from its merger with Plough in 1971.

American Home Products developed Preparation H in the 1930s, bought Anacin, and produces such well-known over-the-counter products as Advil, Centrum, Robitussin, and others. In the pharmaceutical area, its antidepressant Effexor and sleep aid Sonata have been profitable.

The prices of Bristol-Myers Squibb and Schering-Plough stock have declined nearly three-quarters by the end of 2003 from their peak three or four years earlier as a result of the loss of patents on some key pharmaceuticals (such as Claritin for Schering-Plough). Had these firms maintained their value, they would have ranked number two and three, right behind Philip Morris.

When these six pharmaceuticals are added to the eleven name-brand consumer firms, seventeen, or 85 percent, of the twenty top-performing firms from the original S&P 500 Index, feature well-known consumer brand names.[5]

Except for the cigarette manufacturers, which vigorously expanded into foods as cigarette consumption declined, each of these firms, with rare exceptions, was run by a management that stuck with the products it knew best and was committed to maintaining quality and expanding their markets abroad.

Finding Corporate El Dorados:
The Basic Principle of Investor Returns

How do you find these great firms? The first step is to understand a concept called the basic principle of investor return, or BPIR. Before I formally define this principle, consider the following question. Suppose I give you the following facts. Firm A will deliver a 10 percent earnings growth rate over the next ten years, while firm B will deliver 3 percent growth. Which firm would you choose to buy?

Many would say firm A, the one with the higher earnings growth rate. But you cannot answer the question without one more piece of critical information: what growth rate do investors *expect* from these two companies?

If investors expected firm A to grow at 15 percent over the next decade while firm B was only expected to grow at 1 percent per year, you should buy firm B, not firm A. This is because firms with high growth expectations carry a high price that drags down their future returns, while firms with low growth expectations have prices low enough so that even moderate growth can lead to very good returns.

The basic principle of investor return states:

The long-term return on a stock depends not on the actual growth of its earnings, but on the difference *between its actual earnings growth and the growth that investors expected.*

Investors will receive a superior return only when earnings grow at a rate higher than expected, no matter whether that growth rate is high or low.

Recall the case of IBM and Standard Oil of New Jersey, discussed in Chapter 1. IBM's earnings grew rapidly, but investors expected them to grow rapidly. Standard Oil's earnings did not grow nearly as fast as IBM's earnings did, but its investors had far more modest expectations, allowing Standard Oil to deliver higher returns than IBM.

To find the corporate El Dorados and earn superior returns, your ultimate goal is to find stocks whose growth will be high relative to expectations. The best way to determine those expectations is by looking at the price-to-earnings (P/E) ratio of a stock. High P/E ratios mean that investors expect above-average earnings growth, while low P/E ratios indicate below-average growth expectations.

VALUATION MATTERS—ALWAYS

Expectations are so important that without even knowing how fast a firm's earnings actually grow, the data confirm that investors are too optimistic about fast-growing companies and too pessimistic about slow-growing companies. This is just one more confirmation of the growth trap.

Since price-to-earnings ratios are the best way to measure the growth expectations already incorporated in the price of a stock, I computed the P/E ratio on all 500 firms in the S&P 500 Index on December 31 of each year by dividing the last twelve months of earnings by the end-of-year price. I then sorted these firms by P/E ratios into five groups, or quintiles, and computed the returns of each group over the next twelve months.[6]

Figure 3.1 displays the results of this research. High-P/E stocks are, on average, overvalued by the market and lead to lower returns. A $1,000 investment in 1957 in a portfolio of the highest-priced stocks accumulated to only $56,661, earning an annual return of 9.17 percent. This accumulation was less than half of the approximately $130,768 that would have accumulated in the benchmark S&P 500, which delivered an 11.18 percent annual return.

By contrast, the lowest-priced stocks accumulated to a sum that was over three and a half times greater than the wealth accumulated in the market, earning an extraordinary 14.07 percent annual return and doing so with less risk than the S&P 500 Index.

These results show that investors must always look at price relative to

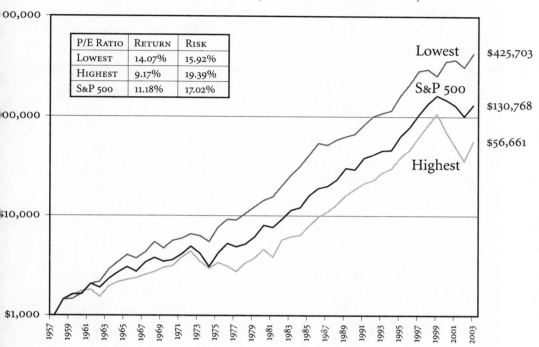

FIGURE 3.1: CUMULATIVE RETURNS TO S&P 500,
SORTED BY P/E RATIOS (SOURCE: COMPUSTAT®)

P/E Ratio	Return	Risk
Lowest	14.07%	15.92%
Highest	9.17%	19.39%
S&P 500	11.18%	17.02%

earnings when deciding what to buy. Investing by looking at growth prospects alone will trap investors into poor returns.

VITAL STATISTICS

Interestingly, most of the corporate El Dorados listed in Table 3.1 *do not* come from the lowest-P/E stocks. Table 3.2 reports the return, the average earnings per share growth and P/E ratio, and the dividend yield on the top twenty survivor companies over the period from 1957 through 2003.

There was no question that the earnings of these winning firms grew rapidly, far faster than the earnings of the S&P 500 Index. But the average valuation of these firms, measured by the price-to-earnings ratio, was only slightly above the average stock in the index. This indicates that investors expected these firms' earnings to grow only slightly faster than the earnings of the average stock in the S&P 500 index. The fact that the average earnings of these firms grew almost four percentage points per year above the average firm in the S&P 500 Index over nearly half a century explains their superior returns.

Table 3.2 shows why Philip Morris beat the competition so decidedly. Its P/E ratio was among the lowest on the list, indicating expectations of low earnings growth, while its actual earnings growth was the highest. The gap between Philip Morris's actual growth and expectations of growth was the greatest and enabled the cigarette manufacturer to produce the highest rate of return.

DIVIDENDS MAGNIFY EFFECT

So far we have ignored the dividend paid by the firm. But dividends are far from unimportant. In fact,

The power of the basic principle of investor return is magnified when the stock pays a dividend.

Consider this. If earnings are better than expected, that means that the stock is underpriced and purchasing more shares through dividend reinvestment will enhance your returns even more.[7] All the firms in Table 3.2 were underpriced, so their dividend yields further enhanced their returns.

We have now found a second reason why Philip Morris was the best-returning stock in the market. Not only was the difference between actual and expected earnings growth the highest among these twenty best-performing stocks, but the cigarette manufacturer had the fourth highest dividend yield. The high dividend yield enabled investors to purchase even more shares of Philip Morris stock. Each time Philip Morris paid its ever-rising quarterly dividend (Philip Morris has never lowered its dividend), investors were accumulating more shares of an undervalued stock.

PEG RATIOS AND GROWTH AT ANY PRICE (GARP)

One of the biggest advocates of searching for growth stocks at reasonable prices is Peter Lynch, the legendary stock picker for Fidelity's Magellan Fund from 1977 through 1990. During those years his fund outperformed the market by an incredible 13 percent per year.

In his best-seller *One Up on Wall Street* Lynch advocated a simple strategy for choosing stocks. He instructed readers to "[f]ind the long-term

TABLE 3.2: VITAL STATISTICS ON THE TOP-TWENTY SURVIVORS

Return Rank	2003 Name	Annual Return	Earnings Per Share Growth	Average P/E Ratio	Dividend Yield
1	Philip Morris	19.75%	14.75%	13.13	4.07%
2	Abbott Laboratories	16.51%	12.38%	21.37	2.25%
3	Bristol-Meyers Squibb Co	16.36%	11.59%	23.52	2.87%
4	Tootsie Roll Industries	16.11%	10.44%	16.80	2.44%
5	Pfizer	16.03%	12.16%	26.19	2.45%
6	Coca-Cola Co	16.02%	11.22%	27.42	2.81%
7	Merck	15.90%	13.15%	25.32	2.37%
8	PepsiCo	15.54%	11.23%	20.42	2.53%
9	Colgate-Palmolive	15.22%	9.03%	21.60	3.39%
10	Crane	15.14%	8.22%	13.38	3.62%
11	H.J. Heinz	14.78%	8.94%	15.40	3.27%
12	Wrigley	14.65%	8.69%	18.34	4.02%
13	Fortune Brands	14.55%	6.20%	12.88	5.31%
14	Kroger	14.41%	6.21%	14.95	5.89%
15	Schering-Plough	14.36%	7.27%	21.30	2.57%
16	Procter & Gamble	14.26%	9.82%	24.28	2.75%
17	Hershey Foods	14.22%	8.23%	15.87	3.67%
18	Wyeth	13.99%	8.88%	21.12	3.32%
19	Royal Dutch Petroleum	13.64%	6.67%	12.56	5.24%
20	General Mills	13.58%	8.89%	17.53	3.20%
	Average of Top 20	15.26%	9.70%	19.17	3.40%
	S&P 500	10.85%	6.08%	17.45	3.27%

growth rate . . . add the dividend yield . . . and divide by the p/e ratio. . . . Less than a 1 is poor, and 1.5 is okay, but what you're really looking for is a 2 or better."[8]

Others have advocated a similar strategy called GARP, or growth at a reasonable price. Advocates here compute a very similar statistic called the PEG ratio, or price-to-earnings ratio divided by the growth rate of earnings. The PEG ratio is essentially the inverse of the ratio that Peter Lynch recommended in his book, assuming you add the dividend yield to the growth rate. The lower the PEG ratio, the more attractively priced a firm is with respect to its projected earnings growth. According to Lynch's criteria, you would be looking for firms with lower PEG ratios, preferably 0.5 or less, but certainly less than 1.

But the days of getting those wonderfully low PEG ratios may be gone for good. A look at Table 3.2 shows none of these corporate El Dorados would have qualified as a buy according to Lynch's rules, and only Philip Morris had a PEG ratio less than 1. Yet all of these firms did extremely well for their shareholders. Their secret: above-average earnings growth for a long period needs only a small growth advantage to do fabulously in the long run. Persistence of good earnings growth is better than transience of superb growth.

COMMON CHARACTERISTICS OF THE CORPORATE EL DORADOS

The characteristics of these winning firms have become clear. The corporate El Dorados had earnings growth expectations that were only slightly above the market average, but they delivered considerably faster earnings growth, especially when viewed over a forty-six-year period. None of these firms had an average P/E ratio above 27, and virtually all paid consistent and rising dividends, with a dividend yield near the market average. Because of their higher-than-expected earnings growth, the reinvestment of dividends at undervalued prices magnified the returns of these companies, just as it did for Philip Morris.

The overwhelming number of these firms have developed high-quality, branded consumer products that have been marketed successfully not only in the United States but around the world. Trust in the product quality is of paramount importance to their success, allowing the firms to charge a higher price than the competition and attain higher profit margins.

Charlie Munger, Warren Buffett's long-time partner at Berkshire Hathaway, hit the nail on the head when he described why some companies are able to charge higher prices:

If I go to some remote place, I may see Wrigley chewing gum alongside Glotz's chewing gum. Well, I know that Wrigley is a satisfactory product, whereas I don't know anything about Glotz's. So if one is 40 cents and the other is 30 cents, am I going to take something I don't know and put it in my mouth, which is a pretty personal place after all, for a lousy dime?[9]

Those "lousy dimes," summed over billions of dollars of sales, can add up to a pretty penny.

Corporate El Dorados of the Past: The Nifty Fifty of the 1970s

This is not the first time I noticed these corporate El Dorados. In the early 1990s I did a study of a set of stocks that gained notoriety in the early 1970s and were referred to as the "Nifty Fifty."[10] These were a group of premier stocks, such as Philip Morris, Pfizer, Bristol-Myers, PepsiCo, Coca-Cola, General Electric, Merck, Heublein, Gillettte, Xerox, IBM, Polaroid, and Digital Equipment, that had excellent growth records over the past decade and had become widely sought by institutional investors. Some analysts called these firms "one-decision stocks," as they urged investors to buy but never sell.

These stocks hit a peak in December 1972, when their average P/E ratio exceeded a then unheard-of 40. They were crushed in the 1973–74 bear market and held up as examples of unwarranted optimism about the ability of growth stocks to continue to generate rapid and sustained earnings growth. Yet buy-and-hold proved to be a good decision for many of these stocks—as long as you were careful not to buy those with the highest growth expectations and prices.

The twenty-five Nifty Fifty stocks with the highest P/E ratios, which in 1972 averaged a stunning 54, returned more than three percentage points *less* than the twenty-five stocks with the lowest P/E ratios, which averaged a more reasonable 30. Johnson & Johnson was the *only* stock with a P/E above 50 in the original Nifty Fifty that subsequently outperformed the S&P 500 Index, and Polaroid, the stock with the highest P/E ratio and highest expectations, delivered the absolute worst returns.

It is remarkable that not a single technology or telecommunication stock in the Nifty Fifty performed well for investors: not IBM, Digital Equipment, Xerox, Burroughs, or ITT. All of these technology firms lagged the market, some by very wide margins. There is also no technology or telecommunication stock on *any* of the top-twenty lists that we generated in this chapter. This is because investors generally expect the technology firms to have very strong earnings growth, so even when these firms do prosper, these optimistic expectations were already built into their prices.

Peter Lynch summed up the seductive allure and empty promises made by the technology companies well in his 1993 best-seller *Beating the Street,*

> Finally, I note with no particular surprise that my most consistent losers were the technology stocks, including the $25 million I dropped on Digital in 1988, plus slightly lesser amounts on Tandem, Motorola, Texas Instruments, EMC (a computer peripherals supplier), National Semiconductor, Micron Technology, Unisys, and of course that perennial dud in all respectable portfolios, IBM. I never had much of a flair for technology, but that didn't stop me from occasionally being taken in by it.[11]

Lessons for Investors

This research suggests that investors should be willing to pay twenty or thirty times earnings for these corporate El Dorados. But don't be dazzled by newcomers whose long-term prospects are yet to be tested. The research of the past half century showed that the tried and true clearly triumphed over the bold and new.

What are the most important lessons that can be taken from this chapter?

- The best-performing firms for investors have been those with strong brand names in the consumer staples and pharmaceutical industries. As Warren Buffett rightly claimed, "The products or services that have wide, sustainable moats around them are the ones that deliver rewards to investors."[12] The familiar brand-name firms that have achieved such superior returns for their shareholders are what I call the triumph of the tried and true.
- The basic principle of investor return states that stockholder re-

turns are driven by the difference between actual and expected earnings growth, and the impact of this difference is magnified by dividends.

• The majority of best-performing firms have had (1) slightly higher-than-average P/E ratios, (2) average dividend yields, but (3) much higher-than-average long-term earnings growth. None of the best-performing stocks had an average P/E over 27. These are the characteristics of the corporate El Dorados.

• No technology or telecommunications firm made the list of best-performing stocks.

• Portfolios invested in the lowest-P/E stocks—in other words, those with modest expectations for growth—far outperformed those with higher valuations and expectations.

• Be ready to pay up for good stocks (as you would for good wine), but there is no such thing as a "buy at any price."

Now that I have specified the principles of choosing superior individual stocks, I will shift to one of the hottest trends in the investment business: investment by industry or sector. In the next chapter I will explore how sector investing impacts your portfolio.

CHAPTER FOUR

Growth Is Not Return:

THE TRAP OF INVESTING IN HIGH-GROWTH SECTORS

Obvious prospects for physical growth in a business do not translate into obvious profits for investors.

—Benjamin Graham, *The Intelligent Investor*, 1973

Sector-based investment strategies that are based on industries rather than geographical location or valuation are rapidly gaining popularity. In June 2004, Morgan Stanley's quantitative analytics team concluded that there was "no basis for the traditional methodology of global asset allocation, namely 'regional first, then sector.' " Instead, Morgan Stanley believes investors ought to focus their asset allocation strategies more prominently on industry groups.[1] Industry-based strategies are becoming so important that global investment banking firm Goldman Sachs recently created a new equity research group that focuses only on sector strategies.[2]

Investors frequently ask me, "What are the next fast-growing industries that I should invest in?" There is the near-universal belief that the fastest-growing industries will yield the best returns.

But the reality differs from this perception.

Of the ten major industries, the financial sector has gained the largest share of market value since the S&P 500 Index was founded in 1957. Financial firms went from less than 1 percent of the index to over 20 percent in 2003, while the energy sector has shrunk from over 21 percent to less than 6 percent over the same period. Had you been looking for the fastest-growing sector, you would have sunk your money in financial stocks and sold your oil stocks.

But if you did so, you would have fallen into the growth trap. Since 1957, the returns on financial stocks have actually fallen behind the S&P

500 Index, while energy stocks have outperformed over the same period. For the long-term investor, the strategy of seeking out the fastest-growing sector is misguided.

What is going on here is identical to what we have already learned: growth in market value and investor returns, especially in the long run, can move in very different directions. This chapter shows that the same holds true for entire industries as well as individual firms.

The Global Industrial Classification Standard (GICS)

Our current sector classification system was reformulated in 1999 when Standard & Poor's joined Morgan Stanley to create the Global Industrial Classification Standard, or GICS. This system arose from earlier classification standards, devised by the U.S. government, that had grown less suited to our service-based economy.[3] GICS breaks the U.S. and world economy down into ten sectors: materials, industrials, energy, utilities, telecommunication services, consumer discretionary, consumer staples, health care, financial, and information technology.

We have gone back and classified each of the original S&P 500 firms and their successors into the current GICS system. Table 4.1 summarizes the returns of these sectors as well as the change in market share of each industry since the S&P 500 was first formulated in 1957.

You can see that there is no strong correspondence between the expansion or shrinkage of the sector and the returns to investors. The two sectors that expanded the most, financial and information technology, experienced only mediocre returns. Furthermore, the original 1957 firms in each sector except one outperformed the new firms that were added to that sector.

These data confirm my basic thesis: the underperformance of new firms is not confined to one industry, such as technology, but extends to the entire market. New firms are overvalued by investors in virtually every sector of the market.

The change in market share of some of the sectors has been dramatic. The materials and energy sectors, which in 1957 were the largest sectors, have by 2003 become among the smallest sectors, making up less than 10 percent of the index. In contrast, the three smallest sectors in 1957, the

TABLE 4.1: MARKET SHARE AND RETURNS, 1957–2003

Sector	Market Share 2003	Market Share 1957	Market Share Expansion (Shrinkage)	Actual Sector Return	Return on Original Firms
Financial	20.64%	0.77%	19.87%	10.58%	12.44%
Information Technology	17.74%	3.03%	14.71%	11.39%	11.42%
Health Care	13.31%	1.17%	12.14%	14.19%	15.01%
Consumer Discretionary	11.30%	14.58%	-3.28%	11.09%	9.80%
Consumer Staples	10.98%	5.75%	5.23%	13.36%	14.43%
Industrials	10.90%	12.03%	-1.13%	10.22%	11.17%
Energy	5.80%	21.57%	-15.68%	11.32%	12.32%
Telecommunication Services	3.45%	7.45%	-4.00%	9.63%	10.47%
Materials	3.04%	26.10%	-23.06%	8.18%	9.41%
Utilities	2.84%	7.56%	-4.81%	9.52%	9.97%
S&P 500	100%	100%	0%	10.85%	11.40%

financial, health care, and technology sectors, today account for more than half of the market value of the index.

Figure 4.1 shows the change in market weights over time. One can see the jump in financial market share in 1976 when, as noted in Chapter 2, Standard and Poor's added twenty-five banks and insurance companies to the index. The surges in the energy share in the late 1970s and the technology share in the late 1990s are also visible.

It is important to remember that the rising or falling market weights are not the same as rising or falling investor returns, especially in the long run. As noted earlier, even though the financial and technology sectors show pronounced market value expansion over the past half century, their returns were no better than average.

In the rest of the chapter, I will go through each of the ten sectors, describing its transformation, why new firms underperformed the older firms, and what this means for investors.

FIGURE 4.1

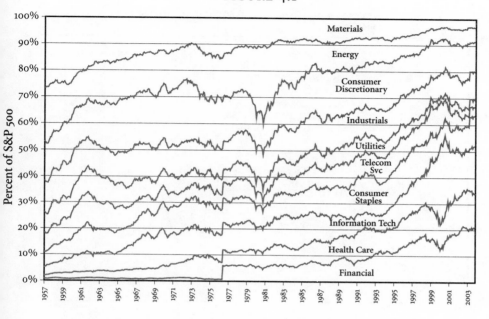

Bubble Sectors: Oil and Technology

Figure 4.2 shows how the share of the market value of the energy and technology sectors has changed from 1957 through 2003. What jumps out is that both sectors experienced sharp surges in market value that quickly subsided.

These spikes—or bubbles, as I will call them—are strikingly similar and separated by almost exactly twenty years. The oil sector was driven by fear in the late 1970s that the world would soon run out of oil and the price of oil stocks, especially those connected with oil and gas exploration, surged. In the technology sector, a rush of spending on Y2K and excitement about the Internet sent technology stocks sharply higher in the late 1990s. Both of these sectors hit their peak at just over 30 percent of the total value of the S&P 500.

The behavior of energy and technology suggests that investors should sell if a sector becomes this large. But that is not necessarily the case. There is a difference between sectors whose weights are rising on a long-term basis, such as financial or health care, and those, like energy and technology,

FIGURE 4.2: THE ENERGY AND
INFORMATION TECHNOLOGY BUBBLES

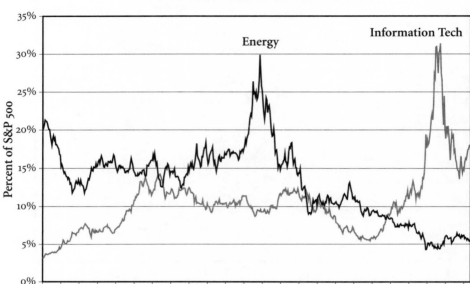

that suddenly surge to a higher level. It is the latter that should worry investors.

One clear indication of a bubble is the rapidity of the price rise. Although there are occasions when sharp increases in the price of individual stocks are justified, this has never been true of market sectors. Fundamentals do not change rapidly enough to justify the sudden increase in the market share of major sectors, such as oil and technology experienced. The causes of the oil and technology bubbles will be described in great detail in Part 2.

While both the energy and technology sectors experienced bubbles, their market shares have been moving in opposite directions—technology upward and energy downward.

Nevertheless, investors would have far preferred to link their fortunes to the falling share of energy stocks rather than to the rising share of technology stocks. The return on the original firms of the shrinking energy sector far surpassed that of the expanding tech sector, just as the return on Standard Oil of New Jersey surpassed that of IBM. The fast-paced technology sector, clearly responsible for much of our economic growth, could not keep up with the slow-growing but high-returning oil companies.

ENERGY

Why did the energy sector perform so well? The oil firms concentrated on what they did best: extracting oil at the cheapest possible price and returning profits to the shareholders in the form of dividends. Furthermore investors had low expectations for the growth of energy firms, so these stocks were priced modestly. The low valuations combined with high dividends contributed to superior investor returns.

Nevertheless, even in the shrinking energy sector, the growth trap ensnared many investors. The sharp rise in energy prices during the 1970s caused investors to rush to buy many new oil and gas exploration firms, sending their price upward.

In August 1980, right at the peak of the oil bubble, Standard & Poor's put out an oil industry survey entitled "Shares Have Long-term Appeal," in which they predicted that profits would continue to grow. They singled out five firms, Baker International, Global Marine, Hughes Tool, Schlumberger, and Western Co. of North America, noting:

> These very favorable incentives [high oil prices] have not been lost to the investor, and most of the stocks in the oil well equipment and services and offshore drilling sectors are selling at hefty P-E premiums to the general market. But it is hard to argue with the favorable prospects for the group, and we recommend the issues on a long-range basis.[4]

Unfortunately, these analysts violated a fundamental rule of investing: never buy stocks, especially large-cap stocks, selling at "hefty P-E premiums to the general market," particularly for the long run. These oil services and oil exploration stocks flamed out in the 1982 worldwide recession. Oil prices plummeted, and drilling activity abruptly came to a halt. Global Marine and Western Co. of North America went bankrupt, and the other three firms seriously underperformed the market. In fact, twelve of the thirteen energy stocks that were added to the S&P 500 during the late 1970s and early 1980s did not subsequently match the performance of either the energy sector or the S&P 500 Index.

TECHNOLOGY

Many investors assume that firms that have developed path-breaking technologies rank among the best long-term investments. But the spectacular gains in Microsoft, Cisco, Intel, Dell, and others are overshadowed by the dreadful losses in innovative firms such as Digital Equipment (minicomputers), Sperry Rand (Univac, first computer), Xerox (first copier), and Burroughs (first electronic calculating machines). As a result, the technology sector barely managed to match the S&P 500 Index and would have dropped below the index if not for the superior performance of IBM from 1957 through the early 1960s when it monopolized the computer market.

The technology companies consistently commanded high valuations. In the early 1960s the tech sector, fueled by expectations of rapid growth of computers, sported a P/E ratio of 56, more than two and a half times that of the market. From 1957 through 2003, the average P/E of the technology sector was 26, a full ten points higher than the overall market. There was only one stretch in the last forty-five years when expectations for earnings growth in the technology sector were below that for the overall market, and that was in the early 1990s, after three consecutive years of large losses by IBM. Although many technology firms experienced rapid earnings growth, investors typically had even *higher* growth expectations built into share prices, resulting in poor investment returns.

About 30 percent of the 125 firms that have been added to the technology sector of the S&P 500 since 1957 were done so in 1999 and 2000. Those added in 1999 subsequently underperformed the technology sector by 4 percent per year, while those admitted in 2000 underperformed by a whopping 12 percent per year. Furthermore the technology sector itself greatly underperformed the market from 1999 onward. Many newly added S&P technology stocks, such as Broadvision, Vitesse Semiconductor, Palm, and JDS Uniphase, fell by 95 percent or more.

Despite their similarities, the energy and technology bubbles displayed some important differences. In the technology bubble, the P/E ratios rocketed to extreme levels because of overly optimistic expectations of future earnings growth. In the oil sector, valuations never reached such extreme levels because the price of oil stocks rose along with earnings. In fact, the large integrated oil producers that dominated the sector sold at lower P/E ratios than the rest of the market at the peak of the bubble. The oil bubble centered on the oil drillers and explorers that sold at large premiums to the market.

Financial and Health Care: Expanding Industries

Health care and financial are the two sectors with the most pronounced expansion in market share. In 1957 they were the two smallest sectors, responsible for a total of 1.9 percent of the market value. By the end of 2003, they were the largest sectors, together accounting for 34 percent of the value of the S&P 500 Index.

But these two sectors experienced very different returns. At 14.19 percent per year, health care had the best return of all ten sectors of the S&P 500 Index, averaging more than three percentage points per year above the S&P 500 Index. But the financial sector, which expanded more than any other sector in the economy, had returns that fell behind the index.

FINANCIAL

The financial sector experienced mediocre returns, despite the rapid expansion of its share, because much of its growth has come from the addition of new firms to the index. I noted in Chapter 2 that Standard & Poor's put a large number of banks in the index in 1976, and this explains the jump in the sector weight in Figure 4.1. Currently the financial sector is now dominated by such giant firms as Citigroup, AIG, Bank of America, Wells Fargo, and J.P. Morgan Chase that were not in the Index in 1957.

Some of the financial sector's growth is attributable to the privatization of the government-sponsored enterprises Fannie Mae and Freddie Mac, which were added to the S&P 500 Index in 1988 and 1992. These two firms together accounted for 5 percent of the market value of this sector at the end of 2003.

Further fueling growth in market share was the addition of brokerage houses and investment banks. Virtually all brokerage firms were private partnerships until 1970, when Donaldson, Lufkin, and Jenrette (DLJ) went public. Later Merrill Lynch, Dean Witter, Schwab, Lehman Brothers, Bear Sterns, T. Rowe Price, and others subsequently went public and were admitted to the S&P 500 Index. Finally, real estate investment trusts, or REITs, were added to the sector in 2001. I shall speak more of REITs and other dividend-rich companies in Chapter 9.

The tremendous growth in financial products has spurred the growth of many new firms. This has caused a steady increase in the market share of the financial sector, but competition has kept the returns on financial stocks close to average over the whole period.

HEALTH CARE

The health care sector, like the financial sector, has steadily increased its share over the past half century. The increase in market value has gone hand in hand with the dramatic increase in health care expenditures. In 1950, 4.5 percent of our GDP was devoted to health care. Today the percentage is 15 percent and growing rapidly.

Many of the firms that dominate the health care sector today, such as Pfizer, Johnson and Johnson, and Merck, have long and distinguished histories. These firms have been joined by biotechnology firms such as Amgen and Genentech, health care providers such as UnitedHealth and Cardinal Health, and medical equipment companies such as Guidant.

Although on the whole investors in the health care sector were richly rewarded, they would have done even better without the newcomers. In an industry where research leads to continuous, well-publicized breakthroughs, investor excitement had led to higher prices and disappointing returns.

Of the eleven health services companies added to the health care sector since 1957, nine of them subsequently underperformed the sector, and some, such as Beverly Enterprises, Community Psychiatric Centers, and HealthSouth, have lagged dramatically. American Hospital Supply, Baxter Travenol (now Baxter International), and Becton Dickinson, three medical equipment providers that were added to the index in 1972, have also underperformed the sector. Bausch & Lomb, added to the S&P 500 in 1986, underperformed the health care sector by 9 percent per year. The tried and true trumped the new in this sector as it did in others.

The Consumer Sectors: Discretionary and Staples

Both the consumer staples and consumer discretionary sectors target the consumer, but that is where the similarity between these sectors ends. The firms in the discretionary sector have gone through much turmoil while the staples sector has nurtured the best tried-and-true companies. *Staples* refers to products described as necessities, whose sales are less prone to economic cycles, and include food, beverages, tobacco, soap, toiletries, and groceries. The consumer discretionary sector, which includes goods and services not viewed as necessities, are purchased relatively infrequently and are more dependent on consumers' discretionary income. This includes automobiles, restaurants, department stores, and entertainment.

To some extent, this division is arbitrary—what is one man's necessity is another's indulgence. The arbitrariness was illustrated when Standard & Poor's switched Wal-Mart from the consumer discretionary sector to the consumer staples sector in April 2003 as the retailing giant successfully entered the food market.

However defined, there has been a world of difference between the performance of firms in these two sectors. The consumer staples sector has been marked by unusual stability. Most of the largest firms in this sector (excepting the recent addition of Wal-Mart) have been around for fifty years or more and provided investors with superb returns. We have already noted the superior long-term performance of such companies as Coca-Cola, Philip Morris, Procter & Gamble, PepsiCo, and others. Twelve of the top twenty surviving stocks of the original S&P 500 firms came from the consumer staples sector.

In contrast, the consumer discretionary sector has been marked by tumult. The sector was once dominated by the auto manufacturers (GM, Chrysler, and then Ford), their suppliers (Firestone and Goodyear), and large retailers (Sears, J.C. Penney, and Woolworth). All these companies fared very poorly.

The old-line retailers were pushed aside by Wal-Mart and Home Depot, and the auto manufacturers were shellacked by foreign imports and high labor costs. Today, four out of the five largest firms in the sector are in entertainment: Time Warner, Comcast, Viacom, and Disney. It is amazing that one has to go down to the *eleventh* largest firm in the current S&P consumer discretionary sector to find a firm (Ford Motor) that was a member of the original S&P 500 Index.

The consumer discretionary sector is the only one of the ten sectors where the original firms in the S&P 500 Index did not outperform the new ones that were added. The dreadful performance of GM, an original S&P

500 firm, and the superior performance of newcomer Wal-Mart is the prime reason for this difference.

The fate of the autos and retailers in the consumer discretionary sector and the rise of Home Depot, Wal-Mart, and the new entertainment companies is consistent with the creative destruction theory of stock selection: old, dying companies eclipsed by young, vigorous firms. What is noteworthy is that this is the *only* sector where the principle of creative destruction actually worked for investors, as the new firms did outperform the old.

Two questions come to mind: why did the discretionary sector experience so much upheaval, and why did the returns of the consumer staples sector far outstrip returns of the consumer discretionary sector?

This was a most unexpected outcome on the basis of economic trends. Over the past half century, one would have never expected the staples sector to outperform the discretionary sector. The last fifty years have witnessed a dramatic rise in discretionary income (after which the sector is named), as prosperity enabled millions of Americans to expand their purchases beyond basic necessities.

But the discretionary sector did not prosper. The firms in this sector were unable to maintain quality and foster consumer loyalty. And they ignored the growing threat of foreign competition, particularly from the Japanese, whose emphasis on quality quickly won over consumers.

In contrast, firms in the staples sector marketed their products internationally, maintaining and capitalizing on their reputation for high quality. They fully understood that trust and reliability were their most sought-after products and rewarded investors accordingly. In Chapter 17 I shall explain why I think the consumer staples sector will continue to give investors superior returns.

INDUSTRIAL SECTOR

The industrial sector includes industrial conglomerates, transportation, and defense firms. The heavyweight in this sector, General Electric, was the largest firm in the industrial sector when the S&P 500 Index was founded, and it remains so today.

But GE's dominating size is about the only aspect of this sector that remains unchanged. Although 3M (formerly Minnesota Mining and Manufacturing), United Technologies (formerly United Aircraft), and Boeing were members of the original S&P 500 Index, none of the five airlines (American, Eastern, United, Pan Am, and TWA) that was in the 1957 index is still there today.[5]

As of this writing, General Electric had the highest market capitalization of any firm in the United States. Its legendry former chairman, Jack Welch, took over the reins of the company in 1981 and transformed GE into one of the most dynamic and well-respected companies in the world. The "GE Way," promoted by Welch, demanded excellence in every business the firm entered and has contributed much to the company's success. Welch's strategy concentrated on the core competencies of the firm; if a division was not profitable, GE sold it.

Although General Electric has recently moved into the entertainment industry (with NBC and now Universal), its prize division is financial, which includes consumer and commercial financing as well as insurance, and provides almost half of the company's revenues and profits. GE Capital, would be, if divested from the parent, one of the largest financial institutions in the world.

The iconic status of GE and Jack Welch encouraged investors to push the price of GE stock to unsustainable levels during the great bull market of the 1990s. In 2000, GE reached a price-to-earnings ratio of 50—an unheard-of and, unfortunately, unsustainable level for an industrial firm.

GE's stock price subsequently declined by two-thirds, and its return from 1957 has since been eclipsed by 3M, one of the few industrial firms that has not been buffeted by the economic, financial, and legal storms that have rocked such companies as Boeing, Honeywell, Caterpillar, and more recently Tyco.

The railroad firms in this sector shrunk dramatically in size relative to the rest of the market, declining from 21 percent of the market value of the industrial sector to less than 5 percent today. The railroad industry is a good illustration of how creative destruction gets turned on its head when applied to investors. The industry was already in decline in the mid-1950s when it was hit with a one-two punch. First, the completion of the interstate highway system created severe competition from the trucking industry and reduced rail passenger travel. Many railroads, such as Penn Central, Reading, and Erie Lackawanna, were forced into bankruptcy. Second, the airlines took almost all long-haul passengers away from the railroads.

Nevertheless, since 1957 railroad stocks have surprisingly outperformed not only the airlines and trucking industries but even the S&P 500 Index itself.

How did this happen? How could the lowly railroad industry outperform one of the world's hardest to beat market indexes? Again, it's all about expectations. The bankruptcies and other problems the rail companies faced dramatically lowered investor expectations. Only a small improvement was necessary for these companies to subsequently beat this dim outlook.

And better times were coming. In 1980 there was a major deregulation of the railroads that spurred consolidation and greatly increased their efficiency. Despite falling revenues, rail productivity has tripled since 1980, generating healthy profits for the carriers. Burlington Northern Santa Fe, the star performer of the four major surviving railroads, has achieved an astounding 17 percent annual return since 1980, more than 4 percentage points higher than the S&P 500 Index.

The railways offer an important lesson for investors: an industry that has been in a long decline can provide stockholders with excellent returns. This is because investor expectations are so low. If the firm halts its decline and becomes profitable—particularly if management can pay dividends—then these shares can provide excellent forward-looking returns. Who would have thought thirty years ago that investors would do so well in the dying railroad industry and do so badly with soaring airlines?

MATERIALS SECTOR

The materials sector consists of manufacturing firms producing basic commodities, such as chemicals, steel, and paper. This sector has experienced the greatest erosion in market share and the lowest returns.

In 1957, when the S&P 500 Index was formulated, materials was the largest sector in the index, responsible for over 25 percent of the market value of all S&P 500 firms. Chemical and steel companies led this sector, which included such behemoths as United States Steel and Bethlehem Steel and large chemical companies such as DuPont, Union Carbide, and Dow Chemical. These five firms dominated the U.S. industrial landscape in the late nineteenth century and the first half of the twentieth century and were 10 percent of the S&P 500's market value when the index was formulated.

But in the last fifty years, these great firms witnessed a rapid decline, and the materials sector's share fell by almost 90 percent. The combined market valuation of those five big steel and chemical firms declined to less than 1 percent of the index today.

The decline can be traced to international competition and the economic shift from manufacturing to services. Through the 1970s and 1980s production from Japan and then the rest of Asia made these industries vulnerable to lower-cost producers. These old-line manufacturing firms, saddled with high labor costs and crushing pension benefits that were negotiated when profits were high, have seen their shares decimated. Some, such as Dow Chemical, the best performer of the lot, were almost brought down by litigation, in Dow's case over silicone implants.

THE TELECOMMUNICATIONS SECTOR

The telecommunications sector, which includes AT&T, once the world's largest firm, has seen its share of the index cut in half, falling from 7.5 to 3.5 percent over the past half century. Telecom experienced a brief surge in the late 1990s when it soared to over 11 percent of the index as the excitement of the Internet fueled expectations of vastly increased profits. But oversupply, plunging prices, and expanding debt incurred to build huge fiber-optic networks caused telecom stocks to collapse.

The telecommunications industry sadly illustrates how rapid productivity growth can be devastating to both firms and investors; its story will be featured in Chapter 8. This industry, which laid the foundation for the productivity revolution that will sweep the world in the coming decades, is a prime example of how firms operating at the forefront of Schumpeter's creative destruction process can themselves be destroyed by their own inventiveness.

Like energy in the 1980s and tech in the late 1990s, telecommunications demonstrates how outsized expectations during a boom increase the number of firms in the sector and how these new firms subsequently underperform. The telecom sector added virtually no new firms from 1957 through the early 1990s. But in the late 1990s, new firms, such as WorldCom, Global Crossing, and Qwest Communications, entered the index with great fanfare, only to collapse afterward.

In June 1999 WorldCom constituted over 16 percent of the telecom sector's market value, but the firm subsequently lost 97.9 percent of its value by the time it was deleted from the index in May 2002. Global Crossing fell more than 98 percent before it was deleted from the index in October 2001, and Qwest lost over 90 percent of its value since its admission in July 2000. These overpriced new firms significantly underperformed the original firms in the telecom sector.

THE UTILITY SECTOR

The utility sector also experienced a sharply declining market share. One source of the decline is the fall in the real price of energy as the generation and consumption of electricity became more efficient.[6] The U.S. economy can produce almost twice as much GDP per unit of fossil fuel now as it did in the early 1970s.

But a more important source of utilities' troubles was the deregulation of the energy industry, which has removed these firms from the protected monopolist status that they enjoyed during most of their history. Until the mid-1980s regulators would routinely allow utilities to pass on any increase in costs directly to the consumers, who had no choice but to buy energy from these monopoly producers and distributors. But consumers balked at accepting the mammoth cost overruns of nuclear power generation, and when communities were able to obtain cheaper power from more distant sources, utility profits plummeted. Only recently have some of these firms begun to learn to deal with a deregulated environment, raising hopes for better returns.

Utility firms do have high dividend yields, which, as I noted, is an important factor in generating good long-term returns. However, there is not enough history to be certain how these firms will continue to perform in a deregulated environment.

Sector Shifts and Sector Returns

The returns of these ten great sectors tell an important story. In Chapter 2 I explained why market value does not necessarily correlate with investor returns. This chapter shows that it holds true for the returns to market sectors as well as individual firms. Figure 4.3 summarizes the data. It plots the return on each sector in the S&P 500 Index against the change in the sector's weight over the entire period from 1957 through 2003.

Both the financial and health care sectors experienced strong growth. The health care sector delivered, by a wide margin, the highest returns of all the sectors, but the financial sector had below-average returns. The reason is that the growth in market capitalization of the financial sector was mostly fueled by the entrance of new firms, a factor far less important in the health care sector.

Information technology had the second highest gain in market share but only slightly above-average returns. The single reason why the sector outperformed the S&P 500 Index was IBM's performance from 1957 to 1962. On average, the other technology firms gave investors below-average returns despite their critical importance to the economy.

On the opposite side of the ledger, the materials sector had the greatest loss in market value share, as well as the lowest return. But not all contracting sectors experienced poor returns. The energy sector had the second largest contraction but, as we noted earlier, experienced above-average returns.

The overall relation between the change in sector weights and returns is only weakly positive. A statistical regression shows that less than one-third

FIGURE 4.3: RELATION BETWEEN CHANGE IN GICS SECTOR
SHARE AND RETURN FOR EACH SECTOR

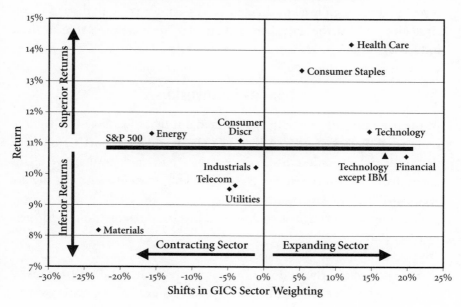

of each sector's return can be attributed to changes in the sector's share of the market, while two-thirds is attributed to other factors, such as valuation, the reinvestment of dividends, and the entry of new firms.

The fact that less than one-third of a sector's returns comes from the expansion or shrinkage of the sector shows why so many investors fall into the growth trap. They fail to realize that the addition of new firms causes industry expansion, while often leading to poor returns.

Sector Strategies

The data show that three sectors emerge as long-term winners. They are health care, consumer staples, and energy. Health care and consumer staples comprise 90 percent of the twenty best-performing surviving firms of the S&P 500 Index. These two sectors have the highest proportion of firms where management is focused on bringing quality products to the market and expanding brand-name recognition on a global basis.

The energy sector has delivered above-average returns despite experiencing a significant contraction of its market share. The excellent returns in this sector are a result of two factors: the relatively low growth expectations of investors (excepting the oil and gas extractors during the late 1970s) and the high level of dividends. In Chapter 17 I will discuss sector strategies and list the global firms that play an increasing role in these industries.

Lessons for Investors

At the beginning of this chapter I pointed out that most investors want to know what the next hot sector is going to be. If you are a short-term trader, that is the right question to ask, since returns and market values are highly correlated in the short run. But if you are a long-term investor, chasing hot sectors will lead to very cold returns.

The important conclusions from the historical research on sector performance are:

• Rapid sector growth does not necessarily mean good investor returns. The financial and technology sectors expanded greatly over the past years yet gave mediocre to poor returns. The energy sector contracted sharply yet outperformed the S&P 500 Index.

• Over the long run, less than one-third of sector returns can be attributed to expansion or contraction of that sector. This means that over two-thirds of the return can be attributed to other factors, such as new firms and dividends.

• Two sectors, energy and information technology, experienced almost identical bubbles separated by twenty years. Both bubbles popped when their sector weighting reached 30 percent of the value of the S&P 500 Index. The rapid increase in the weighting of a particular sector is a warning signal to investors to reduce their allocations to that sector.

• New firms that were added to the S&P 500 Index generated lower returns than the original firms in nine of the ten economic sectors. New firms that are added when the sector is expanding rapidly generate particularly poor returns for investors.

PART TWO

Overvaluing the Very New

CHAPTER FIVE

The Bubble Trap:

HOW TO SPOT AND AVOID MARKET EUPHORIA

The meaning of life is creative love, loving creativity. And loving creativity may explain why tech stocks are high and going higher. The Internet revolution is allowing for creativity like never before, perhaps putting more of us in touch with the meaning of life.

—Merrill Lynch, Global Fundamental Equity Research Department,
February 14, 2000

In the last chapter I described the oil and technology bubbles. Investors lose more money during bubbles and their nasty aftermath than during any other period of the market cycle. For many, losses are so severe that they forsake stocks forever and cling tightly to their remaining savings in low-yielding money funds and bank CDs.

Is there a way to avoid these episodes of market euphoria? Can investors identify bubbles and avoid being trapped by their enticing promises?

Alan Greenspan, chairman of the Federal Reserve, who received much heat for not popping the Internet bubble, is skeptical. In a speech in August 2002 he commented, "It was very difficult to definitely identify a bubble until after the fact—that is, when its bursting confirmed its existence."[1]

But I respectfully disagree. Read the quotation at the head of this chapter. It was written by one of the best research departments on Wall Street at the top of the market. When "new age" thinking grips even these sophisticated analysts, you know you are in a bubble.

This chapter will teach you how to look for the telltale symptoms of a bubble. But once you have identified one, it does not mean that you've found a road to easy profits. Bubbles last much longer than anyone expects, defying the skeptics and boosting the believers. Once the bubble starts expanding, no one knows when it will pop.

When you have identified a bubble, step back and stop investing in the companies or sectors involved. If you should be so lucky as to hold some of the stocks that are caught in the frenzy, cash in your profits and don't look back. The stocks you sold will probably rise further before they collapse, but in the long run, you will come out way ahead.

The Internet and Technology Bubble

Bubbles usually form after long periods of financial prosperity. This was exactly the setting at the end of the twentieth century, as the United States was well into the longest and strongest bull market in its history. The Internet enabled online trading, which made buying and selling stocks easy and inexpensive. A casino-like atmosphere attracted thousands who would not otherwise have invested in financial markets. Fear of Y2K—the anticipated breakdown of computer systems when we entered the year 2000—pumped capital spending and led to a surge of profits for technology firms.

Investor excitement centered on the belief that the Internet would change the way the world did business. This excitement caused a sharp increase in media coverage of Internet firms and the stock market. There was a sense, amply reported in the media, that there was about to be a significant shift in the paradigm governing buying, selling, and marketing of all goods and services.

As my good friend Bob Shiller of Yale University reported in his book *Irrational Exuberance,* "Although the news media . . . present themselves as detached observers of market events, they are themselves an integral part of these events. [Speculative bubbles] generally occur only if there is similar thinking among large groups of people, and the news media are essential vehicles for the spread of ideas."[2]

Since the Internet allowed huge markets to be accessed at minimal cost, the prevailing opinion was that the convenience afforded by online shopping would likely dominate all other forms of marketing. "Clicks over bricks" was the rallying cry of the Internet enthusiasts, who foresaw the new medium threatening the very existence of retail firms.

As the media spread the word, more and more investors, many of whom had never before invested in individual stocks, began to play the market. Prices skyrocketed. In April 1999, after an astonishing 4,800 percent price increase in less than two years, Amazon.com, the online book retailer, had a market value over $30 billion. This was almost ten times the combined market value of its two greatest bricks-and-mortar competitors, Barnes and Noble and Borders, which operated over 1,000 bookstores worldwide apiece. Ironically, Amazon had never up to that point made a profit; in fact, it had losses that year of over $600 million.

In October 1999 the market value of eToys, an online toy retailer, was more than double the value of Toys "R" Us, the world's largest bricks-and-mortar toy retailer, which owned more than 1,600 stores worldwide. In that same month Priceline.com, a company that sells cheap airline tickets over the Web, had a peak market value that was more than half the equity of the entire U.S. airline industry. It was only a matter of time before the bubble burst.

Have Investors Learned Their Lesson?

I used to think it would take many years before investors' appetites for such speculation returned. But recent evidence suggests otherwise.

Fast-forward just a few years to 2003. The biggest gains in the stock market are coming from companies specializing in nanotechnology, the supposed next great innovation that will lead to dramatic changes in our world. Nanotechnology promises "to make supercomputers that fit on the head of a pin and fleets of medical nanorobots smaller than a human cell able to eliminate cancer, infections, clogged arteries, and even old age."[3]

As a *Wall Street Journal* article reported, nanotech firms such as Nanogen, Nanophase Technologies, and Veeco Instruments all at least doubled or tripled in the prior year. Not one of them had any earnings and Nanogen and Nanophase had little to no revenue.[4] Nanogen, a company with a sparse $1.7 million in revenue per quarter and losses of over $7 million per quarter, was trading at $1 per share in March of 2003. But the company's scant vital statistics did not deter speculators from climbing on board. By early 2004, the company shot up to a high of $14.95, giving it a market value of almost $400 million.

Just as companies rushed to associate the term *dot-com* with their names in the late 1990s, companies raced to capitalize on the nanotech craze. One company, U.S. Global Aerospace, changed its name to US Global Nanospace. The company's stock, which a year earlier was selling at a nickel, shot up to $1.66 after its name change.

To be sure, the nanotech boomlet was a shadow of the huge Internet bubble that occurred a few years earlier. What is so surprising is that this type of speculation occurred with memories of the last debacle still so fresh.

But the excitement of the new can obliterate the memories of the old. It is likely that new technologies will be appearing with increasing frequency in the coming decades. As I will detail in Chapter 15, the Internet revolution is likely to accelerate the rate of discovery all across the globe. There will be profound advances in all types of new products and new companies that will have tremendous growth opportunities. But buyers beware. Most of these new companies and new technologies will be overhyped and overpriced.

Lesson One: Valuations Are Critical

AMERICA ONLINE

Before the Internet mania hit its peak in 1999, I warned in a *Wall Street Journal* article entitled "Are Internet Stocks Overvalued? Are They Ever" about the unprecedented developments taking place in the markets.[5] Using AOL as an example, I showed that the Internet stocks could not possibly be worth the price that investors were paying for them.

The day my piece appeared, April 19, 1999, the prices of Internet stocks collapsed. AOL fell from $139.75 on the previous Friday to close at $115.88, slicing about $22 billion from its market value. Other Internet stocks were also hit: Yahoo! slid from $189 to $165, and the dot-com index fell from 670 to 560, a drop of almost 17 percent.

I was shocked at the responses this article received. I traveled from Philadelphia to Chicago that morning, and I was thankful I wasn't traveling to Silicon Valley. I was sure my article was not the only factor causing the price decline, but all the major television networks, CNBC, CNN, National Public Radio, and the print media wanted to discuss my views.[6]

That evening I found myself face-to-face with Henry Blodget, Merrill Lynch's Internet cheerleader, on Lou Dobbs's *Moneyline*. Lou started the interview bluntly: "What in the world—Jeremy, if I may ask, you write one article in the *Wall Street Journal,* and see what you did! Why did you do that?"

I explained my reasoning, and Lou then turned to Blodget, who responded that my arguments had been made many times before. In a show of rare candor, he claimed, "These stocks have always been expensive by classical measures; there's no question about that. Really, our argument has always been that nobody knows what they're worth."

Do not be fooled by Blodget's response. A firm pioneering a new technology can be priced with the same valuation tools that had priced IBM and other technology giants in the past, and I did so that day in my article.

I chose to look at AOL, the "blue chip" Internet stock—the only Internet firm in the S&P 500 at the time—and a firm that was making a profit. When I wrote the article, AOL's market value of $200 billion placed it among the ten largest companies in the United States.

Yet in the prior year, AOL's sales ranked only 415th in the country, and its profits ranked 311th. If AOL's market value ranking was in line with its sales or profits rankings, its market cap would have been closer to $4.5 billion.

Moreover, AOL's price-to-earnings ratio, the critical measure of valuation that I discussed in Chapter 3, was over 700 based on its prior twelve months' earnings and 450 based on projected current-year earnings. For large firms, these valuations were absolutely unprecedented.

The average P/E ratio of the stock market has been only 17 over the last forty-five years. Chapter 3 showed that the best-performing stocks over the past fifty years had much higher earnings growth than the average stock, but their valuation ratios were only slightly higher than the market's. Certainly those stocks could have stood a higher valuation than they received, but AOL's price was out of the ballpark. A subsequent fall in AOL stock was inevitable.

Lesson Number Two: Never Fall in Love with Your Stocks

There is another sign that tells investors when stocks are in a bubble. One of the cardinal rules in investing is to never fall in love with your stocks. You must at all times be objective: if the fundamentals do not justify the price, you should sell, notwithstanding how optimistic you are or how much money you've made or lost on the stock.

I soon realized that thousands of investors had fallen in love with "their" AOL. After my article appeared in the *Wall Street Journal* questioning AOL's valuation, I received scores of angry e-mails from people claiming that AOL was in fact undervalued and that I was completely out of touch with reality. Quite a number forwarded me a response article, published by Kevin Prigel of StreetAdvisor.com, who claimed my piece "was the most flawed piece of literature the *Journal* has ever run."

Many e-mails were sent to the dean's office of the Wharton School recommending that I should not be teaching at Wharton—or at any other business school, for that matter. One wrote, "Not only is this guy a dinosaur, but he knows absolutely nothing about Y2K and forward business models. . . . I hope that he may soon retire from dear old Wharton . . . or to the funny farm—whichever comes first. He is nuts, period, and should have a muzzle." Another wrote, "My regard for your school has lessened. Siegel needs to retire. Ultimately it is the school that suffers when it harbors this sort of individual. Check out the article from StreetAdvisor.com."

But the cake goes to the following e-mail, forwarded to me by Kirsten Speckman, a spokesperson for Wharton Public Affairs, who told me they had been getting a number of messages similar to this one at their general public affairs e-mail address.

> Good morning, Mr. Siegel. I hope you're happy. You cost me $14,000.00 for no reason! What do you have against this mammoth company? Are you jealous because you didn't get in on the run-up? Did you want to buy in cheaper? You have no business making decisions like this. After all, you're still a child when it comes to Internet knowledge. You're a preschooler in diapers when it comes to recognizing opportunities. By the way, when was the last time you got laid? You're a party pooper. Thanks a lot, jerk. I suggest you go to the StreetAdvisor.com to read about why you're so wrong, idiot. Do you even know how to get to a Web site, you child?

I recently checked out StreetAdvisor.com. It is now an inactive Web site up for sale to the highest bidder. In February 2003, Sanford C. Bernstein & Co. estimated that if AOL Time Warner were broken up, the America Online unit would be worth $5.78 billion, 97 percent *less* than the value when I wrote the article. Other analysts called that estimate far too optimistic.

The emotions and passion for Internet stocks displayed by the Internet enthusiasts proved that these investors were not judging their investments rationally. Most Internet investors were convinced that "this time was different" and were in no mood to hear otherwise. They had made the fatal error of falling in love with their stock.

Lesson Number Three:
Beware of Large, Little-Known Companies

Another sign of a bubble is the enormous valuations placed on little-known companies. On February 11, 2000, I saw a headline scrolling on my Bloomberg Terminal, "Cisco May Be Headed for $1 Trillion Market Value." David Wilson, author of the article, quoted Paul Weinstein, an analyst at Credit Suisse First Boston, who said that Cisco's market value could reach $1 trillion dollars in two years. At that time its market value was just over $400 billion, the highest in the world. Five years earlier the market value of *all* stocks listed on Nasdaq had not been worth $1 trillion, yet Weinstein was predicting Cisco alone might reach that level in two years.

There is no doubt that Cisco did well for its investors. The company was founded in 1984 and went public on February 16, 1990, when it sold $50.4 million of stock. By February 2000 those who invested $1,000 into its IPO would have made $1 million—a return that doubled the initial investment on average each year.

Cisco vaulted into the position of being the world's most valuable stock just two days before the Weinstein prediction was released. Cisco overtook General Electric, a company that had been around for more than a century and had one of the highest name recognitions in the world. But Cisco was different. It was astounding that the vast majority of Americans, including many (if not most) shareholders, had absolutely no idea what Cisco did. When I asked some of my friends what Cisco Systems made, many shook their head and recalled Crisco, a popular shortening produced by Procter & Gamble that was heavily advertised in the 1950s. When I said that 70 percent of Cisco's sales are for switches and routers for the Internet, most had no idea what switches and routers did.

That the world's most valuable company would be virtually unknown is unprecedented. In the late nineteenth and early twentieth centuries, Rockefeller's Standard Oil and Carnegie's U.S. Steel vied for top honors, and both firms were household names.

At the peak of the 1929 bull market, General Electric and General Motors joined U.S. Steel to take top honors (the Standard Oil empire had been broken up by then), and both firms were extremely well known. In the mid-1960s American Telephone & Telegraph again dominated the field: Ma Bell, as the firm was affectionately called by stockholders, was the most widely held stock, and most of the U.S. population was a customer of AT&T or one of its subsidiaries.

IBM dethroned AT&T in 1967. Although most individuals had no idea (and still don't) how a computer works, everyone had heard of IBM and knew what the computer did. In fact, the term "IBM machine" became synonymous with the computer, as the firm dominated more than 80 percent of the computer market in the 1950s and 1960s.

General Electric, under the leadership of Jack Welch, reemerged in late 1993 and held the top post until late 1998, when Microsoft, the enormously successful software company, took over. Almost all who had operated a computer used Microsoft's operating system, if not its word processing, spreadsheet, and graphics programs. When Cisco, a virtually unknown firm, took the lead from Microsoft, it further confirmed that dramatic changes had taken place in the markets. Two and one-half years after Weinstein's trillion-dollar prediction, Cisco's market value fell to $50 billion, less than one-tenth its peak value.

Lesson Number Four: Avoid Triple Digit P/E Ratios

After my article "Are Internet Stocks Overvalued? Are They Ever" appeared, Internet stocks fell about 40 percent over the next four months. But the fall did little to discourage Internet enthusiasts. As reports of strong online sales growth continued to surface, the Internet stocks recovered and blew past their April highs. In fact, the Street.com Internet Index, after falling from 800 in April to below 500 in August, nearly *tripled* to 1,300 in early March 2000.

As the Internet mania raged on, a popular opinion emerged that the equipment providers to the Internet firms would surely make a lot of money even if many of the Internet start-ups failed. As a result, the big-cap technology companies that supplied the Internet and the burgeoning personal computer market also surged to new highs.

Most investors and analysts who had taken a bearish position on stocks such as Cisco, Sun Microsystems, EMC, Nortel, and others did so because they did not believe that earnings could grow as rapidly as analysts were projecting. But there was another, more fundamental question: did these firms deserve their lofty valuations *even if* their rosy earnings forecasts were actually met?

In late February 2000, I researched this question for a presentation that I was to give to the Securities Industry Association, which holds a week-long educational conference every March at the Wharton School. I analyzed the nine large-capitalization stocks with P/E ratios over 100 in March 2000: Cisco, AOL, Oracle, Nortel Networks, Sun Microsystems, EMC, JDS Uniphase, Qualcomm, and Yahoo! What I found was not comforting to the technology bulls. Even if these optimistic earnings forecasts, which ranged from 21 percent to 56 percent per year, were maintained for five years (long-term earnings projections are usually three to five years in the future), the average price-to-earnings ratio of these nine stocks would have been an eye-popping 95. And three of them (AOL, JDS Uniphase, and Yahoo!) would still have price-earnings ratios over 100.

If these optimistic estimates for earnings growth could be maintained for ten years (and virtually no one believed these firms could maintain those growth rates for so long), the price-to-earnings ratios on these stocks would fall only to the mid-40s, still extraordinarily high. Investors were projecting that tech stocks would totally dominate the market over the next decade and would be valued at two to three times the historical valuation of the S&P 500. This was just not possible. A substantial decline in these stocks was certain.

Big-Cap Tech Stocks

On March 8, 2000, I received a call from Max Boot, editor of the *Wall Street Journal,* asking me if I wished to write another op-ed piece on what was going on in Nasdaq.

Given the research I'd just completed, I quickly consented and gave my article the innocuous title "The Lessons of History." It is a standing practice in the newspaper industry for the editors to pick the titles of op-ed pieces, yet I was shocked when I picked up the *Journal* and saw at the top of the op-ed page "Big-Cap Tech Stocks Are a Sucker Bet." I always avoid name-calling, and some of my best friends owned these stocks! I thought those who had purchased them might be misguided, but calling them suckers was not right. I prepared apologies to those who might call, explaining that I had nothing to do with picking the word "sucker," but I received surprisingly little flak about the title.

On Friday, March 10, two days after I was contacted by the *Wall Street Journal*, I received a call from Stuart Varney, who had replaced Lou Dobbs on CNN's *Moneyline* and wanted me to appear on his show at six that evening to discuss what was going on in the markets.

Varney started the interview this way: "Let's hit the nail on the head, shall we. Are you full-out forecasting a huge decline in tech stocks in the very near future?"

I wanted to talk of Cisco and the other overpriced tech stocks, but I didn't want viewers to think I was just slamming these companies. With memories of the reactions I received from AOL shareowners fresh in my mind, I overstated my admiration for Cisco. I said, "Cisco is a wonderful company. It's a great company. It's a super company. I would probably buy it at 80 times earnings, but at 150 times earnings? We have six stocks in the top twenty [market value] over 100. We have had no history of this. Never have stocks been worth over a hundred times earnings once they've gotten to the size of these companies."

I noted that the valuations of these big-cap tech stocks had increased dramatically in just the last five months, and I didn't see where the price increases came from, saying, "It can disappear as easily as it came." I then said that "momentum players," short-term speculators who ride a trend in price, "are saying that they are going to get off the train before it crashes." When everyone thinks that way, there can be some very nasty declines.

Wanting to sum up, Varney asked, "It's a bubble and the air will come out of it soon and come out of it fast, bottom line?" I answered definitively, "It will come out. . . . I think we are going to see some very big declines in the sector this year."

The day of this CNN interview, Friday, March 10, 2000, the Nasdaq Composite Index closed at 5,048.62. This marked the index's all-time high and coincided with the absolute top of the technology market. Two years later, Nasdaq was down more than 75 percent.

During the week of April 10, 2000, Nasdaq experienced a meltdown, falling more than 1,100 points, or almost 25 percent. *Moneyline* interviewed me again, replaying large parts of my interview from a month earlier. For the next year, Varney showed clippings of that March 10 tape frequently, claiming I was the man who had called the market top.

It soon became clear that my article "Big-Cap Stocks Are a Sucker Bet" had become my most well-known piece of journalism. When I lecture across the country, investors come up to me holding copies of that article and saying that my opinion convinced them to cash out of the tech stocks, saving their fortunes. Many more approached and commended me on the article, noting wryly that they wished they'd followed my advice.

Being feted by the news media and investors as a "guru" of the market was a very uncomfortable position for me. The short-run direction of the market is so unpredictable that anyone who calls it right should attribute it to pure luck. The bubble in technology stocks could have lasted another month or another year. But I (along with many others, even those with long positions in these stocks) knew that it had to burst at some point.

There was another important conclusion that I pointed out in my article that received much less attention: the fifteen largest *non*-technology-related stocks in March 2000 were not overvalued. This was a technology bubble, pure and simple—a bubble that exempted most of the rest of the market. Non-technology-related stocks did not really decline until 2002, when the earnings scandals spurred by Enron and others hit the headlines. The non-tech-related stock averages fully recovered by the end of 2003, whereas the tech sector was still down over 60 percent.

The Follies of Predicting Technology Earnings Growth

A year after the "sucker bet" article appeared, Max called me again and wanted to know if I wanted to pen an anniversary follow-up. I did so reluctantly, knowing full well that it was extremely unlikely that I would be able to predict the market as accurately as I had happened to do at the market peak.

I stated that although the tech stocks had declined markedly over the previous year, the earnings growth forecasts for three to five years out were hardly changed. Given the collapse in earnings over the prior twelve months, I believed it was totally unreasonable to maintain the same outlandishly optimistic forecasts.

I started my piece this way: "You'd think the plummeting Nasdaq would have wised up Wall Street to the fact that its analysts blew it on the tech sector. But in fact the Street's long-run earnings forecasts for the big tech companies are still grossly out of line with reality. Even at today's deflated prices, many of these stocks are still overvalued." The article was entitled "Not-Quite-So-Big-Cap Tech Stocks Are Still a Bad Bet." (I had convinced Max to change the word *sucker* to *bad*.)

I indicated how bad Wall Street's earnings forecasts were. I noted that on January 9, 2001, nine days after the quarter ended, analysts were forecasting operating earnings of the technology sector to come in at $10 in the fourth quarter of 2000. Six weeks later, when all the profits were tallied, operating earnings for tech stocks came in at $7.69.

If analysts can be off by nearly 25 percent in forecasting earnings of a quarter that has just ended, what confidence can investors have in their prediction for the coming year—or, for that matter, for the next three to five years? The truth is, very little. Earnings estimates in the rapidly shifting tech sector had become a crap shoot. But premium P/E ratios should belong only to stocks that have a reasonable certainty of superior long-term growth. And these certainly were not technology firms.

Lesson Number Five: Never Short Sell in a Bubble

After all these warnings, many assumed that I had made a killing shorting those Internet and technology stocks.[7] But the truth is that I had no interest in shorting the Internet stocks, and I do not advise the average investor to pursue this practice. Even if the investor is right in the long run, she may be very wrong in the short run.

As every investor who has studied the market knows, taking a short position in a stock exposes you to unlimited losses, while the maximum gain is the value of the shares sold. The payoffs for a short seller are the mirror image of those for someone who buys or "longs" the stock. The gains for buyers of stock are unlimited, while the maximum loss is the amount invested. This means that a trader who shorts a stock is treated as a margin account, so the brokerage firm constantly monitors the value of the short position and demands additional funds if the price of the shorted stock rises. If the investor is unable to put up extra money, his position is liquidated at the market price.

It is very possible to be 100 percent correct that a stock is overpriced. But being right in the long run doesn't guarantee being right in the short run, and if you are short on a stock, you might be unable to continue to feed sufficient money to the account if the price continues to rise. In fact, there is evidence that short sellers get squeezed in all bubbles. Some investors begin shorting the stock as it goes above its "justified" price, and if the correction occurs quickly, they make money. But bubbles usually last much longer and go to much greater extremes than most short sellers expect. Most shorts cannot hold out as the price continues to rise and eventually cover their position at a loss.

Covering the short position, which involves buying back the borrowed stock, provides more buying pressure on the shares that are already being forced higher by momentum investors who long ago jumped on the bandwagon. This adds fuel to the fire, often causing an explosive upward movement in the price of the stock.

It is often said that bubbles peak when all the bears have thrown in the towel and covered their short position. In the meantime, bears with plenty of excess liquidity and nerves of steel who can hold through the euphoria will eventually be rewarded. For the rest of us, the best advice is just to stand back, enjoy the show, and refuse to play.

Recommendations for Investors

Just as a doctor uses symptoms and lab tests to diagnose a disease, investors can watch for telltale symptoms of a bubble. These include wide and increasing media coverage, extraordinarily high valuations based on concepts and names instead of earnings or even revenues, and an unwavering belief that the world has fundamentally changed and that these firms cannot be measured by traditional means. If you diagnose a bubble, the best advice is to stay away!

Remember, valuations *always* matter, bubble or no bubble. Markets will ultimately deal a severe blow to those who believe that growth is worth any price.

CHAPTER SIX

Investing in the Newest of the New:

INITIAL PUBLIC OFFERINGS

Most new issues are sold under "favorable market conditions"—which means favorable for the seller and less favorable for the buyer.

—Benjamin Graham, *The Intelligent Investor,* 1973

In January 1999, Alan Greenspan, responding to a question from Senator Ron Wyden of Oregon, said, "Investing in Internet stocks is like playing the lotteries; some may succeed, but the vast majority will fail."

In a lottery, the odds are clearly stacked against you. Yes, there will occasionally be a $100 million winner who will receive huge publicity and whet the appetites of others. But the overwhelming majority of those who regularly play their lucky numbers are guaranteed to be throwing away their hard-earned money.

Yet when Greenspan made this statement, buying newly issued Internet stocks was far better than playing the lottery. In 1999 virtually none of these initial public offerings (IPOs) was a loser, and many investors had made tidy fortunes buying these stocks, which soared after they hit the public markets.

It was widely believed that the old "bricks and mortar" companies were going to be destroyed by these up-and-coming start-ups. Excitement was high and money was being thrown at any new company with a dotcom in its name.

Others realized that most of these new ventures would fail, yet they eagerly bought these new stocks, claiming that anyone who owned just one big winner could suffer dozens if not hundreds of losers and still come out ahead. These investors were certain that one or two of these new firms would inevitably become the next Microsoft, Intel, or Dell Computer.

There is an element of truth in this observation. Big winners can indeed compensate for many losers. One thousand dollars invested in Microsoft when it went public in 1986 was worth $289,365 by the end of 2003. Intel, which went public in October 1971, is an even better example. One thousand dollars invested in what is now the world's largest chip maker would have turned into almost $1.9 million by the end of 2003. You could survive many failed startups if you had invested in one of these successes.

What Does This Mean for Investors?

Does the prospect of finding these few diamonds in the rough justify investments in initial public offerings in general? Should buying these newly issued companies be part of a sound wealth-building strategy?

The extensive research conducted for this chapter indicates that investing in IPOs is much akin to playing the lottery. There will be a few huge winners, such as Microsoft and Intel, but those who regularly invest in all IPOs will fall significantly behind those who invest in stocks that are already trading in the public markets.

I examined the buy-and-hold returns for almost 9,000 initial public offerings that have occurred since 1968. I assumed that investors purchased the IPOs either at the end of the first month of trading or at the IPO offer price and held these stocks until December 31, 2003.[1]

Although there were a few big winners, there were far too many losers. IPO investors generally lagged the market by two to three percentage points per year. Here again, we find an illustration of the paradox of creative destruction. While all the new products and services these IPO firms create are vital for the economy, buying them when they are issued is not a good way to build your wealth.

Long-term IPO Returns

There is no question that the losing IPOs far outnumber the winners. Figure 6.1 shows that nearly four out of five newly issued firms have subsequently underperformed a representative small stock index measured from the IPO date through December 31, 2003.[2] Of these, almost half have underperformed by more than 10 percent per year; more than one-third have underperformed by more than 20 percent per year, and 1,417, or almost 17 percent, have underperformed by an astounding 30 percent per year or more.

FIGURE 6.1. PERFORMANCE OF 8,606 IPOS FLOATED 1968–2000

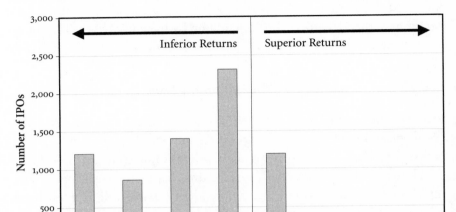

Annualized Return Minus Small Stock Index

In contrast, only one-fifth of the IPOs have outperformed the market. Less than 5 percent have done so by more than 10 percent per year, and only forty-nine, or one-half of 1 percent have outperformed by more than 30 percent per year.

Who are these rare winners, and are there enough of them to compensate for the losers?

Best Long-term IPOs

There are indeed some striking winners among newly issued companies. Table 6.1 lists the best-performing IPOs ranked by total cumulative return from the end of the first month of trading through December 31, 2003.

Intel, which went public in October 1971, is at the top of the list. Next comes Wal-Mart, the world's largest corporation by total sales, and then Home Depot. All three of these firms enabled investors to turn a $1,000 initial investment into more than $1 million. These firms are followed by St. Jude Medical, Mylan Labs, Sysco (the food corporation), Affiliated Pub-

TABLE 6.1: IPOS WITH HIGHEST CUMULATIVE RETURNS
PER DOLLAR INVESTED, 1968–2000

Rank	Year	Company	Accumulation of $1,000	Annual Return
1	1971	Intel	$1,887,288	27.55%
2	1970	Wal-Mart Stores	$1,521,036	26.58%
3	1981	Home Depot	$1,066,691	36.80%
4	1977	St. Jude Medical	$867,695	28.68%
5	1973	Mylan Labs	$816,436	24.29%
6	1970	Sysco	$691,204	22.04%
7	1973	Affiliated Publications	$673,348	23.95%
8	1971	Southwest Airlines	$627,284	23.10%
9	1979	Stryker	$576,885	29.51%
10	1971	Limited Stores	$562,546	22.80%

lications (purchased by the *New York Times* in 1993), Southwest Airlines, Stryker, and Limited Stores.

Table 6.2 ranks the ten IPOs with the highest annual returns of all those floated on or before 1990. By going back more than a decade, we eliminate those that have been recently issued that may have excellent returns for a few years but do not become long-term winners. Cisco Systems, issued in 1990, heads this list and has racked up an astounding 51 percent annual return, beating the benchmark small stock index by 38.6 percent per year. Cisco is followed by Dell Computer, issued in 1988, American Power Conversion, and Electronic Arts, the wildly successful video game manufacturer. Microsoft, which ranks twenty-second by cumulative return, ranks fifth with an annual rate of return of 37.6 percent.

Returns on IPO Portfolios

Now we return to the question of whether these huge winners, found in Tables 6.1 and 6.2, can compensate for the thousands of losing IPOs. The

TABLE 6.2: IPOS WITH HIGHEST ANNUAL RETURNS,
1968–2000

Rank	Year	Name	Annual Return	Accumulation of $1,000
1	1990	Cisco Systems	51.04%	$300,139
2	1988	Dell Computer	45.87%	$347,955
3	1988	American Power Conversion	39.50%	$169,365
4	1989	Electronic Arts	38.48%	$103,441
5	1986	Microsoft	37.62%	$289,367
6	1981	Home Depot	36.80%	$1,066,691
7	1988	Maxim Integrated	36.18%	$132,927
8	1986	Oracle Systems	34.98%	$205,342
9	1984	Concord Computing	33.15%	$266,025
10	1987	Fastenal	31.93%	$92,414

answer is found in Figure 6.2. It shows the differences in the returns between a portfolio that buys an equal dollar amount of *all* the IPOs issued in a given year and a portfolio that puts an equivalent dollar amount into a small stock index. Returns are computed from two starting points: (1) from the end of the month when the IPO was first issued, and (2) at the IPO offer price. All portfolios are held until December 31, 2003.

The results are clear. For twenty-nine out of the thirty-three years, IPO portfolios underperformed a small stock index when measured either from the last day of trading in the month they were issued or from the IPO issue price.

Even the portfolio of IPOs issued in 1971, when Southwest Airlines, Intel, and Limited Stores all went public, trailed the returns on a comparable small stock index. This outcome also occurred in 1981, when the enormously successful Home Depot went public.

Even in the banner year 1986, when Microsoft, Oracle, Adobe, EMC, and Sun Microsystems all went public and delivered 30-plus percent annual returns, a portfolio of IPOs from that year just barely managed to beat the small stock index.

FIGURE 6.2: ANNUALIZED RETURNS ON YEARLY IPO
PORTFOLIOS MINUS RETURNS ON SMALL STOCK INDEX,
RETURNS MEASURED THROUGH DECEMBER 31, 2003

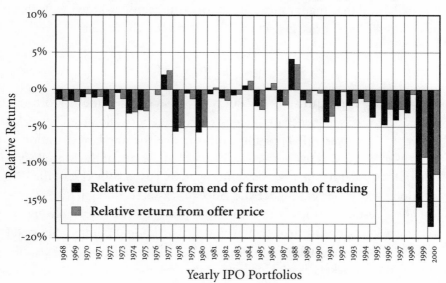

Yearly IPO Portfolios

The only other years when the IPO portfolios managed to outperform the small stock index were 1977 (when St. Jude Medical was issued), 1984 (when Concord Computing went public), and 1988 (when Dell Computer was floated). Before the late 1990s, 1980 was the single worst year for all our IPO portfolios. In 1980 there were thirty-seven IPOs classified as oil and gas extractors. Not one of them managed to keep pace with the market, and twenty-four were eventually delisted through either liquidation or bankruptcy. Even though the oil bubble burst in that year, in 1981 there were fifty-four oil and gas IPOs, and their fate was no different. Again, not a single oil and gas IPO kept pace with the market, and thirty-five firms were liquidated or bankrupted.

The disastrous performance of the IPOs issued in the late 1990s during the technology bubble is readily apparent in the data. In 1999 and 2000, IPOs underperformed the small stock index by 8 and 12 percent per year, respectively, if measured from the IPO price, and 17 percent and 19 percent per year if measured from the end of the first month of trading.

During the late 1990s it was almost impossible for the average investor to buy technology IPOs at their offer price, and the prices jumped significantly when the stock opened for trading. The distribution of these coveted IPOs to favored clients meant billions of dollars of extra revenues to Wall Street. It is sobering that many "lucky" investors who were rewarded with these IPOs at their offer price lost all their gains in a few short years.

Risk in IPOs

Not only are the returns of the IPO portfolios poor, but the risk of these IPO portfolios is higher than that of a diversified portfolio of small stocks. The risk of the yearly IPO portfolio, measured as the standard deviation of returns over the next five years, was higher than the risk of the Russell 2000 small stock portfolio in *every* year since 1975. Since 1968, the risk of the IPO portfolio was 17 percent higher and since 1975 35 percent higher.

These results mean that investors who purchase IPOs not only are receiving a lower return than they would if they bought comparable small stocks but are also incurring more risk. It is clear that buying IPOs, like buying lottery tickets, is a losing long-term strategy.

The Hot IPO Markets

The absolute worst time to buy a newly issued firm occurs during hot IPO markets, when investors clamor to buy any new firms in the "must-have" industries. Hot IPO markets occur during bubbles, such as the technology bubble of the 1990s and the oil bubble of the late 1970s. In fact, a telltale sign of a bubble is a flood of initial public offerings, with prices jumping to hefty premiums when trading begins. These IPOs invariably give investors the worst long-term returns.

In a paper called "The 'Hot Issue' Market of 1980," Professor Jay Ritter, the foremost academic authority on initial public offerings, documented that out of the initial public offerings from January 1980 through March 1981, the average first-day return of the seventy natural resource firms with sales under $500,000 was 140 percent.[3] Virtually all these companies proved disastrous to investors.

Ritter also notes that following the oil boom, it was extremely rare for an IPO to double in price from its offering price in its first day of trading.[4]

Genentech doubled from its offer price of $35 to $71.25 in 1980, but for the next fourteen years there were only ten other IPOs that did so.

But 1995 changed all of that. Eleven companies doubled in value on their first trading day, more than the total in the prior two decades. The floodgates were opened on August 9, 1995, when Netscape, the first widely used Internet portal, sold 5 million shares through Morgan Stanley at a price of $28 per share. Netscape shares opened at $71 and traded as high as $74.75 before closing at $58.25 on a trading volume of almost 28 million shares. Although other stocks had increased more on the first day of trading, none drew the media coverage of Netscape.

In 1996 and 1997 there was a slight slowdown in the number of companies doubling on the first trading day, as only six companies accomplished the feat, including Yahoo!. But in 1998 the pace picked up yet again, with twelve companies more than doubling in price. Some of the more well-known (and well-hyped) included Broadcom, Inktomi, GeoCities, and eBay.

But doubling was no longer unusual. Owners of these Internet firms had greater heights to scale. On November 13, 1998, TheGlobe.com, which helped users personalize their online experience, went public at an IPO price of $9 a share and closed after the first day of trading at $63.50, an increase of 606 percent in one day.

But TheGlobe.com's record wouldn't last long. The next year, on December 9, 1999, VA Linux, a software developer (now VA Systems), went public at $30, raced ahead to $320 on the first day, and settled at $239.25, up almost 700 percent in its first day, an all-time record.[5]

In total, in 1999 there were 117 IPOs that doubled on their first day of trading. This was almost three times the *total* of the previous twenty-four years. In the first nine months of 2000, seventy-seven more companies doubled on their first day of trading, before the bottom fell out of the tech bubble.

The next time you see these large first-day price increases in the IPO market, be sure to stand clear. The higher the pop, the further the drop.

The Old, the New, and Creative Destruction

In Chapter 2 I showed that the new stocks added to the S&P 500 Index underperformed the older, original stocks in the index. In this chapter I've shown that the newest of the new stocks, the initial public offerings, also underperform a portfolio of seasoned small stocks.

These results raise an important question: if the old consistently outperforms the new, how does the new get created in the first place?

The answer is simple. The new firms *are* enormously profitable to entrepreneurs, venture capitalists, and investment bankers, but not to the investors who buy them. The public, in its enthusiasm to grasp the new, overpays for the very firms that drive our economy forward.

Burton Malkiel, the author of *A Random Walk Down Wall Street*, notes that "the major sellers of stock of IPOs are the managers of the companies themselves. They try to time their sales to coincide with a peak in the prosperity of their companies or with the height of investor enthusiasm for some current fad."[6] These entrepreneurs and venture capitalists dump a good part of their shares to the public soon after trading begins. Investors who think they are getting in on the ground floor of a great opportunity are instead about to fall through the basement.

The Founders, Venture Capitalists, and Investment Bankers
TELECOM MISADVENTURES

The Internet has been called the single greatest legal creation of wealth in the history of the planet. For the insiders—the founders who create, the venture capitalists who fund, and the investment bankers who sell—this statement certainly rings true. But just as Main Street investors were pouring their savings into the high-flying technology issues, insiders in many of the newly issued companies were selling their stakes. For the ordinary investor, the Internet is perhaps the single greatest legal (or not so legal) *transfer* of wealth from their savings to the pockets of others.

Examples abound of how the founders and the venture capitalists benefit while the investors crash and burn. Take Global Crossing, a telecommunications company that went public in August 1998 at a price of $9.50 and proceeded to rise to over $64 per share in the next seven months. At its peak in February 2000, the company was worth over $47 billion. Unfortunately for the stockholders who held on, all this value evaporated in the next two years as the company filed for bankruptcy in January 2002.

But many insiders didn't hold on. Chairman and founder Gary Winnick and other directors made out quite nicely. Winnick sold approximately $750 million worth of stock before the company took its plunge—enough for Winnick to buy the country's most expensive home (at that time) from billionaire and real estate mogul David Murdock in Beverly Hills, for $40 million. Winnick built up a reputation as being a big spender, with his philosophy that "money is no fun unless you spread it around."[7]

Winnick didn't spread it around to the outside shareholders, however. Six other members of Global Crossing's board of directors, from the CFO to senior vice presidents, sold another $580 million in stock. But these gains were small change compared to early-stage venture capital investors. The Canadian investment bank CIBC World Markets turned a $41 million investment into a whopping $1.7 billion. CIBC, fortuitously enough, sold its shares and jumped ship before the company sank. Loews/CNA Financial, owned by well-known real estate and hotel mogul Larry Tisch, also raked in $1.6 billion in profits from its early funding of Global Crossing and subsequent well-timed cash-out of 40 million shares.

And Global Crossing is just one example. At JDS Uniphase, insiders cashed out $1.2 billion; at Foundry Network, $700 million; at now-defunct wireless data provider Metricom, where yearly revenues never exceeded $18.5 million, more than $35 million in stock.[8] According to a *Wall Street Journal*/Thomson Financial survey, telecom insiders directly cashed out over $14.2 billion in shares during the bubble, and venture capitalists sold another $4 billion.[9]

THE VENTURE CAPITALISTS

Venture capitalists have helped launch thousands of companies, such as America Online, Sun Microsystems, and Genentech, that are household names.

The VCs had grandiose objectives for many of them, such as the goal of connecting every home in the country with high-speed cable Internet when At Home was launched in 1995. The firm went public in July 1997 at $5.25 and attracted over 300,000 subscribers. But the directors and venture capitalists thought the company was not growing as fast as it could and needed to align itself with a content provider. At Home found a partner in Internet portal Excite, and At Home acquired Excite in a $6.7 billion merger in June 1999, the largest-ever Internet merger up to that time, just after the firm hit its high of $99 a share.

At Home ranks as one the largest home runs ever hit by a venture capital firm.[10] Public investors who held on to their shares were not as lucky, as the company went out of business in February 2002, rendering their shares, which were once worth $20 billion, worthless.[11]

Although the venture capital firms did far better than the investors in the Internet stocks, it would be wrong to blame them for the speculative bubble. They brought many fine and extraordinarily successful firms public. The venture capital firms never claimed that the shares of the companies that they had helped create were worth anything near as much as investors finally paid for them in the subsequent buying frenzy.

THE INVESTMENT BANKS

There is another group that makes a killing during the IPO mania, and that is the investment banks. The investment banks are usually paid a fee of up to 7 percent of the value of the IPOs they bring to the market.

From 1997 through 2000, over 1,500 companies were floated to the public markets. These IPOs raised over $300 billion in fresh capital for these companies. Given Wall Street's commissions, we can estimate that the investment bankers pocketed up to a cool $21 billion for their efforts in bringing these companies public. Very few I-banks risk their own capital for these huge fees, as most IPOs are pre-sold long before they are released to the public.

But commissions are only the visible part of the pie that the investment banks receive. The bankers are able to allocate these sought-after shares to their favorite customers and friends and family. Since the offer price is often far below the price at which the shares start trading, the pop in price is pure profit to whomever they choose to give the shares.

From the difference between the offer price and the first-day trading price, I estimated that from 1997 through 2000 almost $200 billion of profits was spread to the investment bankers' friends, family, and favorite (commission-paying) customers. Had you been lucky enough to be a preferred client of the investment banks leading TheGlobe.com's IPO at its offer price of $9, you could have sold it as high as $63.50 on its very first day of trading. Many of the clients who received the shares cashed out their enormous gains quickly. If you are lucky enough to get a sought-after IPO at the offer price, the best advice is to sell it quickly.

IPOs with No Earnings and No Assets

The demand for the "new" reached such extremes during the Internet bubble that investors were reaching beyond the new to the unborn. Until the mid 1990s, firms that went public had several quarters of profitable operations behind them. This mold was broken when Netscape went public in 1995. Although the Internet portal lost money that year, its revenues were $85 million and rising rapidly. But as the Internet mania raged, there was increasing disregard for not only earnings but also revenues. This was a recipe for disaster. Professor Jay Ritter's research has shown that the performance of IPOs with sales below $50 million has been horrendous.[12]

Consider the following examples. Sycamore Networks, which developed and marketed software-based optical networking products, went public on October 22, 1999. The firm attained a market value of $14.4 billion at the end of the first trading day. Sycamore had had sales of only $11.3 million in the previous twelve months and had an operating loss of $19 million. Akamai Technologies, which provided delivery services for Internet content, went public a week later with a market value of $13.3 billion on sales of only $1.3 million while losing a whopping $57 million.

But the prize for the most highly valued—and overvalued—IPO goes to Corvis Corporation. Corvis, which designs products for the management of Internet traffic, went public on July 28, 2000. At the time of the offering, the firm had never sold a dollar's worth of goods and had $72 million in operating losses. Nevertheless, Corvis had a market value of $28.7 billion at the end of the first trading day, a capitalization that would place it in the top 100 most valuable firms in the United States.

It is sobering to compare Corvis Corporation with Cisco Systems, which went public ten years earlier. At the time of its IPO in February 1990, Cisco was already a profitable company, earning a healthy $13.9 million on annual sales of $69.7 million. The market value of Cisco's IPO at the end of the first trading day was $287 *million,* exactly one hundredth of the market value of Corvis, which had no sales, not to mention no profits.

To illustrate how absurd the valuation of Corvis was, if Cisco had been valued at the same $28.7 billion that Corvis was, its annual return, instead of being a record 51 percent per year over the next thirteen years, would have been below 8 percent, lagging almost four percentage points behind the overall market. This means even if Corvis had been as successful as Cisco in the next ten years (and earlier we saw that Cisco was *the* most successful IPO in the last thirty years in terms of its annualized return), it would still have been grossly overvalued.

It is no surprise that these stocks collapsed when the bubble burst. Sycamore Networks, which traded as high as $199.50 shortly after it was issued, subsequently fell to $2.20; Akamai, which hit $345.50 a share, fell to a low of 56 cents, while Corvis, which a few weeks after it was issued reached $114.75, giving the firm an even larger market value of $38 billion, subsequently fell as low as 47 cents a share, a decline of 99.6 percent.

As Benjamin Graham has written, "Some of these new issues may prove excellent buys—a few years later, when nobody wants them and they can be had at a small fraction of their true worth."[13]

Extraordinary Popular Delusions and the Madness of Crowds

During speculative manias, the degree of investor gullibility is astounding. Two strikingly similar IPOs, separated by almost three centuries, caught my eye. One occurred during the South Sea bubble that struck England in the early eighteenth century, and the second occurred during the latest Internet bubble that overran the markets in 1999 and 2000. One would think that the level of financial sophistication has risen dramatically over the past three hundred years. I will let the reader judge which set of investors showed the most financial savvy—or lack of it.

THE SOUTH SEA BUBBLE

The South Sea bubble that struck Britain in the eighteenth century has taken its place in history as one of the most extraordinary examples of collective mania. No better description of this craze is provided than by Charles Mackay, who penned an investment classic, *Memoirs of Extraordinary Popular Delusions and the Madness of Crowds*, in 1841.[14]

Mackay depicts how men and women who are normally quite prudent with their affairs and investments can be deluded into throwing substantial sums into the market, bolstered not only by glowing reports of the profitability of the enterprise behind these shares but also (and primarily) by seeing others, quite like themselves, profiting handsomely from similar investments.

The South Sea Company, started in 1711 by the earl of Oxford, was given monopoly rights by the British Parliament to trade in South America. The west coast of South America was known to be rich in gold and silver mines, and investors envisioned South Sea Company ships, loaded with gold and silver, sailing back to England and enriching shareholders of this new venture.

British mining technology was considered the best in the world, so it was plausible this company could purchase large veins of precious metals for nominal sums from those who had no way to access its riches. These fantasies fueled the increases in the demand for the shares of the South Sea Company.

As the public was drawn into this bull market in South Sea shares, other joint stock companies were formed to take advantage of the public's new-found excitement with stocks. These other new ventures were particularly attractive to those who didn't get in on the ground floor of the South Sea shares. This behavior was not dissimilar to what occurred when Netscape went public in 1995 and primed investors' interest in Internet and technology companies.

Mackay noted that all manner of projects were proposed, and most were quickly funded and sold for a profit in the open market. This behavior, too, was identical to the act of "flipping" or "spinning" IPOs during the Internet bubble when shares acquired at the issue price were quickly sold to the public for a profit.

It is of interest that the term *bubble*, which is now almost universally used to denote a period of intense speculative activity, actually originated during the South Sea fiasco. Although this word strongly implied an ephemeral and insubstantial existence, the designation did little to deter speculators.

During the South Sea bubble, some of the schemes proposed were plausible, but most were devised to take advantage of the public's willingness to buy shares in any newly formulated companies. One bubble company was formed for the construction of a perpetual-motion machine. But Mackay regarded the most absurd scheme of all an enterprise that went under the name "A Company for carrying on an undertaking of great advantage, but nobody to know what it is." This company's business, if it had any, would be kept secret, even from the investors in the company. As Mackay put it, "Were not the fact stated by scores of credible witnesses, it would be impossible to believe that any person could have been duped by such a project."[15] But the next morning, when the founder of this firm opened his office, crowds of people besieged his door. When he closed for the day, he had sold no less than 1,000 shares, and he collected cash deposits of £2,000 for the shares.[16] After accumulating the cash, the perpetrator set off that same evening for the Continent and was never heard from again.[17]

NETJ.COM, A PERFECT BUBBLE COMPANY

Could this happen today? Short of outright fraud, one would think not. New shares must be registered, and a prospectus filed with the Securities and Exchange Commission must reveal all financial information and give a realistic assessment of the risks of the enterprise. Certainly nothing quite like the secretive bubble company Mackay referred to could be floated today.

But fast-forward 280 years from Georgian England to the United States at the turn of the millennium. A new form of communication, the Internet, has burst upon the scene. Investors see this communication revolution as enabling virtually costless access to not just hundreds of millions of Americans but *billions* of potential consumers throughout the world.

The shares of all Internet companies are flying high. But one stock stands out among the others. A company called NetJ.com is actively traded, and in early March 2000 its nearly 12 million shares are selling for about $2 per share, making its market capitalization $24 million.[18]

And what did NetJ.com do? I quote from its filing with the Securities and Exchange Commission on December 30, 1999: "The company is not currently engaged in any material operations or had any revenues from operations since inception." Note that this statement is much stronger than the warnings that appeared on many prospectuses during previous bubbles. Burton Malkiel noted that during the electronics boom of the early 1960s, investors routinely ignored the words printed on the cover of many a prospectus: "Warning: This company has no assets or earnings and will be unable to pay dividends in the foreseeable future. The shares are highly risky."[19]

But NetJ.com's filing went much further. The company had *never* collected a dime of revenue, and its original business plan had long since been abandoned. The company's balance sheet registered an accumulated loss of $132,671, and the firm had no prospects of any revenues, not to speak of earnings or dividends.

Then what could give NetJ.com a market value of almost $25 million? Its value, so investors believed, lay in the fact that it was already a going concern and was listed for trading. It takes time for private companies to complete the process of floating shares to the public. And in the heady days of late 1999, time was money.

To bypass the lengthy process of going public, a company could conduct a "reverse acquisition" and effectively merge with NetJ.com. In other words, NetJ.com was a shell in which other new companies could live. With Internet mania raging, dot-com companies rushed to sell shares quickly to a more-than-willing public, and a merger was much faster than the lengthy process of issuing an IPO.

But could NetJ.com's potential as a "reverse acquisition" candidate be worth $25 million? A quick reading of the company's filing with the SEC suggests not. The company's own paperwork states, "Other better capitalized firms are engaged in the search for acquisitions or business combinations which firms may be able to offer more and be more attractive acquisition candidates." Furthermore, "There is no compelling reason why this Registrant should be preferred over other reverse-acquisition public corporation candidates. It has no significant pool of cash it can offer and no capital formation incentive for its selection. It has a limited shareholder base insufficient for acquisition target wishing to proceed for application to NASDAQ." And the next sentence of its SEC filing should disturb any potential investor: "In comparison to other 'public shell companies,' this Registrant is unimpressive, *in the judgment of management* [emphasis added], and totally lacking in unique features which would make it more attractive or competitive than other public shell companies." The only source of value for NetJ.com will be "entirely dependent" upon its management in locating a "suitable acquisition or merger candidate."

But in the very next paragraph, the firm states, "Management will devote *insignificant* [emphasis added] time to the activities of the company." Furthermore, management "is not desperate or overly eager to find a business partner." And if all the above was not enough to discourage investors, NetJ.com was also under an SEC investigation for hyping its prospective mergers, none of which materialized.

It seems incredible that any investor would pay good money for such a venture. But wait! A couple of months after this filing, on March 9, 2000, one day before the absolute peak of the Nasdaq stock market, NetJ.com claimed it had found a merger candidate. It was going to merge with Global Tote Limited, a firm based in the United Kingdom that developed interactive horse racing via satellite and the Internet. On this announcement, its shares surged upward, reaching a high of $7.44 on March 24. This valued the company at over $80 million.

But this merger quickly fell through, as had previous ones. The announcement only temporarily discouraged investors, who sent the price of NetJ.com back to the $2 to $3 range, still valuing the company at tens of millions of dollars and anxiously waiting for the next "merger" to be announced.

A few months later NetJ.com announced a merger with BJK Investments, but that also was abandoned, as was a proposed merger with Genosys Corporation a month after that. Eventually NetJ.com sank in price to a penny per share, engineered a 100-to-1 reverse split, and transformed itself into Zoolink, an Internet service provider with a market value in April 2004 of $98,000, a loss of 99.8 percent from its market peak.

POSTMORTEM

NetJ.com had revealed all its faults in gory detail, and the public didn't care. As long as speculators thought they could unload NetJ.com's shares at a higher price, they were more than eager to buy. All the information, transparency, and full disclosure in the world will not prevent people from throwing money at an investment that captures their imagination or convinces them there is someone out there that will buy the stock at an even higher price.

Who was more foolish, the eighteenth-century speculators who lost £2,000 in 1720 buying a company that claimed it had a profitable "secret" that it would not yet reveal, or the twenty-first-century speculators who lost tens of millions of dollars buying a company that had no operations and no revenue and was under government investigation for hyping nonexistent mergers? You be the judge.

A Recap

"Those who cannot remember the past are condemned to repeat it." This saying by George Santayana is quoted by those who believe disaster can be avoided by heeding the lessons of history. Yet when it comes to the financial markets, no matter how often the lessons are told and retold, the public seems forever condemned to repeat the past.

If investors want to find someone to blame for the Internet bubble, they should look in the mirror and say mea culpa. The bubble was fueled by the investors themselves, motivated by talk of easy stock profits at company breaks and social gatherings and a speculative craze so intense that CNBC often replaced ESPN as the channel of choice at the local bar. Bubbles are perpetuated by the "greater fool's theory," a belief that no matter how ridiculous the price is today, there is always going to be someone who will pay more. But when that "someone" doesn't show up, the last buyer is left holding the bag.

Although a disaster for investors, there is a silver lining to these euphoric episodes. They have marked, and perhaps encouraged, many of the advancements that have occurred in the last three hundred years, from the canals and railways to the automobile, the radio, the airplane, the computer, and of course the Internet. The railroad boom in Victorian England became an investment bust, but England's rail system enabled the country to advance economically and politically.

Each of these innovations changed our lives profoundly. Their development was made possible by the huge quantities of capital that were thrown at them by overexcited investors.

But history proves that it is best to let others fund these innovations. Originality in no way guarantees profits. In fashion, you may want to buy what everybody else is buying. In the market, such impulses are a road to ruin.

CHAPTER SEVEN

Capital Pigs:

TECHNOLOGY AS PRODUCTIVITY CREATOR
AND VALUE DESTROYER

"The great lesson in microeconomics is to discriminate between when technology is going to help *you* and when it's going to kill you. And most people do not get this straight in their heads."*

—Charles Munger

Conventional investment wisdom has it that getting in on the ground floor of new products and technologies is the way to wealth. Living in an age of rapid technological change, we seek out new companies with new inventions that will capture both the public's imagination and consumers' dollars. These are the companies that drive and create economic growth. Investors assume that by buying their stock, their fortunes will grow along with these great corporations.

But these assumptions are wrong. Economic growth is not the same as profit growth. In fact, productivity growth can destroy profits and with it stock values.

A striking example is embodied in three of today's most popular technology gadgets, the TiVo video recorder, the iPod music player, and the Xbox game machine. All of these products sprung from remarkable advances in data storage technology. In 1976, it cost roughly $560,000 to store one billion bytes of data. Today, it costs less than $1.[1]

While technological advances in the storage industry went well above expectations, the data storage firms struggled to make profits. In the run up to the new millennium, when all other technology companies' profits were reaching record highs, the storage drive companies were still losing money. Seagate Technology, Maxtor Corporation, and Western Digital, leaders in this industry, have consistently disappointed investors.

The travails of these firms capture one important theme of this book:

technological change does not guarantee good returns or good profits. Storage technology is only one example. Nowhere was technology more destructive to investors than in the telecommunications industry.

"You Have to Stop Inventing Things"

As Internet mania mounted in the 1990s, there was near-universal agreement: the Internet was the wave of the future, and profits were guaranteed for those who could provide the pipeline for this communications revolution.

Growth in demand for bandwidth—the pipeline that connects users to Web sites—seemed insatiable. "Internet traffic," the Commerce Department said in a 1998 report, "doubles every 100 days."[2] If that were so, demand would increase twelvefold every year—resulting in an increase in demand of nearly 100 billion over the next decade.

Many predicted there could never be enough capacity. In April 1998, Salomon Smith Barney analyst Jack Grubman prepared a research report saying, "Like the attic of a house gets filled, no matter how much bandwidth is available, it will get used."[3]

Technology guru George Gilder echoed these sentiments. In 2001 he wrote, "Today, there is no economy but the global economy, no Internet but the global Internet, and no network but the global network." Gilder predicted that two telecom companies, Global Crossing and 360networks, "will battle for worldwide supremacy, but in a trillion-dollar market, there will be no loser."[4]

At first, bandwidth enthusiasts were dead on. Supply struggled to keep up with demand. Prior to 1995, telecom carriers were restricted to piping only one beam of data-carrying light through the fiber-optic lines, which was the equivalent of 25,000 one-page e-mails per second.[5] But a new technology, called dense-wave division multiplexing, or DWDM, essentially split that light beam into many colors, thereby multiplying the available wavelengths and capacity by up to 320. In 2002, one could send 25 million e-mails over the same strand of fiber, a thousandfold increase of capacity in just seven years. This increase far exceeded the pace cited in Gordon Moore's famous law, which states the number of transistors that could be placed on an integrated circuit would double every two years.

Compounding these technological breakthroughs was one of the largest building sprees in history. The *Wall Street Journal* estimates that 40 million miles of fiber were laid during the technology bubble, enough to make more than eighty round-trips to the moon.[6]

Unfortunately for all of the telecoms, demand did not keep pace with this gargantuan increase in supply. From 1999 through 2001, demand only quadrupled, far less than had been predicted.[7] It turned out that one of the most widely quoted statistics of the Internet age was false: Internet traffic was at best doubling every *year,* not every 100 days or less.[8]

As the glut of capacity became apparent, the telecom firms had no choice but to discount their prices. In 2000 it cost over $1.6 million to lease a telecom line that could send 150 megabytes per second of data between Los Angeles and New York. Just two years later, the same line could be leased for $150,000, and in 2004 it could be leased for close to $100,000. There was no way that the industry that raised over three-quarters of a trillion dollars since 1996 to lay the cable and make the connections could begin to cover their mammoth building costs.

In March 2000, at the height of telecom optimism, the aggregate market value of the telecommunications sector in the United States was about $1.8 trillion, representing 15 percent of all stock market value. By 2002, this sector had fallen 80 percent to about $400 billion. *The Economist* speculated that "the rise and fall of telecoms may indeed qualify as the largest bubble in history."[9]

Dr. David Payne of England's Southampton University, who is regarded by many as the grandfather of the capacity-multiplying technology, said he could never forget how one leading industrialist admonished him at an industry conference a few years ago. "He said, 'You guys have to stop inventing things!' and he was deadly serious."[10]

"You have to stop inventing things!" captures the essence of why technology can destroy value. All of the telecommunication innovations that fueled productivity and greatly enhanced our ability to transmit data also devastated profits, equity values, and many investors' portfolios. It is yet another example of the growth trap, where a technology spurs productivity while it spurns profitability.

The aftermath of the telecom bust was ugly: 360networks and Global Crossing, the firms touted by George Gilder, as well as Worldcom and 113 other telecom firms, filed for bankruptcy from 1999 through 2003.[11] 360networks, which spent $850 million to create one of the fastest fiber-optic lines across the globe, sold its fiber route for nearly 2 cents on the dollar.[12] Jack Grubman, Salomon Smith Barney's telecom analyst and the linchpin of their investment banking efforts, was ordered to pay a $15 million fine and banned from ever again working in an investment advisory firm.

And the buzz about the future growth of Internet traffic that caused much of the overinvestment? It is a fascinating tale of how a single statistic—that Internet traffic would double every 100 days—became the Holy Grail for the industry, although it had no grounding in fact and virtually all the data contradicted it.[13] In a bubble, hype becomes the truth, and hard facts that don't fit the new paradigm are discarded as "irrelevant."

The Fallacy of Composition

Investors and analysts alike who believed that productivity increases would lead to higher profits ignored a classic principle in economics called the fallacy of composition. Simply stated, this principle says that what is true for the parts is not necessarily true for the whole.

Any individual or firm through its own effort can rise above the average, but *every* individual and firm, by definition, cannot. Similarly, if a single firm implements a productivity-improving strategy that is unavailable to its competition, its profits will rise. But if all firms have access to the same technology and implement it, then costs and prices will fall and the gains of productivity will go to the consumer.

Warren Buffett, the world's greatest investor, understood the fallacy of composition. When he purchased Berkshire Hathaway, a textile manufacturer, in 1964, the firm was losing money. But Berkshire was generating a lot of cash, and Buffett had high hopes that his managers could stop the bleeding. Most of the problems plaguing Berkshire, as well as all other textile manufacturers, stemmed from high labor costs and foreign competition.

To combat these problems, Berkshire's management continuously presented Buffett with plans that would improve its workers' productivity and lower the company's costs. As Buffett noted:

> Each proposal to do so looked like an immediate winner. Measured by standard return-on-investment tests, in fact, these proposals usually promised

greater economic benefits than would have resulted from comparable investments in our highly profitable candy and newspaper businesses.

But Buffett never accepted a single investment proposal because he understood the fallacy of composition. Buffett knew that these improvements were available to all textiles companies and that the benefits would ultimately flow to his customers in cheaper prices, not to Berkshire in higher profits. As Buffett remarked in his 1985 annual report:

> [T]he promised benefits from these textile investments were illusory. Many of our competitors, both domestic and foreign, were stepping up to the same kind of expenditures and, once enough companies did so, their reduced costs became the baseline for reduced prices industrywide. Viewed individually, each company's investment decision appeared cost-effective and rational; viewed collectively, the decisions neutralized each other and were irrational (just as happens when each person watching a parade decides he can see a little better if he stands on tiptoes). After each round of investment, all the players had more money in the game and returns remained anemic.[14]

Buffett would have liked to have sold this textile business to someone else, but unfortunately, most other investors came to the same conclusion. He had no choice but to close Berkshire's doors and liquidate his textile operations, retaining only the name of what was to become the world's best-known and best-performing closed-end investment firm.

Buffett contrasts his decision to close up shop with that of another textile company that opted to take a different path, Burlington Industries. Burlington Industries spent approximately $3 billion on capital expenditures to modernize its plants and equipment and improve its productivity in the twenty years following Buffett's purchase of Berkshire. Nevertheless, Burlington's stock returns badly trailed the market. As Buffett states, "This devastating outcome for the shareholders indicates what can happen when much brain power and energy are applied to a faulty premise."[15]

This "faulty premise" is not limited to the textile industry. There is strong evidence that firms with the highest level of capital expenditures suffer the worst performance across the entire stock market. Five portfolios are formed, ranging from the firms with the lowest to the firms with the highest capex to sales ratios. The portfolios are rebalanced each December 31 using the last twelve months' sales and capital expenditures. Figure 7.1 shows the cumulative returns of the firms with the highest and lowest capital expenditures (capex) to sales ratios relative to the S&P 500.[16]

The results are a blow to those who believe that capital expenditures drive profits. Those firms that engaged in the most capital expenditures provided investors with the worst returns, while those that had the lowest expenditures had overwhelmingly better returns—more than 3.5 percent per year higher than the S&P 500 Index over almost half a century.

Many on Wall Street believe that capital expenditures are the lifeblood of the productivity revolution. But the truth is that most capital expenditures provide investors with poor returns. It is so easy for management to be talked into expenditures because "everyone else is doing it." But as consumer demands and technology shift, today's grand projects become tomorrow's dinosaurs. Firms are left with a legacy of debt and, finding themselves strapped for funds, discover that they have less rather than more flexibility to meet future needs.

FIGURE 7.1: RETURNS TO S&P 500 FIRMS SORTED
BY CAPITAL EXPENDITURE/SALES RATIOS, 1957–2003
(SOURCE: COMPUSTAT®)

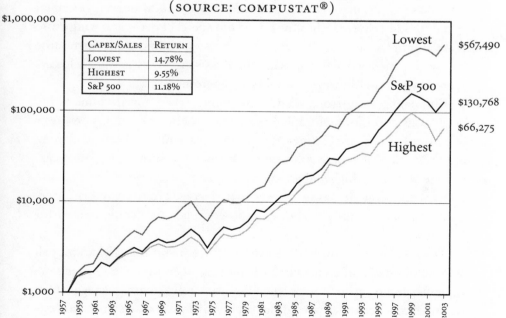

CAPEX/SALES	RETURN
LOWEST	14.78%
HIGHEST	9.55%
S&P 500	11.18%

Capital Austerity and Profligacy

Of all ten market sectors, the two with the highest ratios of capital spending to sales are the telecommunication and utilities sectors; and, save for the materials sector, they also had the poorest returns. From 1957 through 2003, the telecoms had a capex-to-sales ratio of almost .28 and the utilities had a ratio of .25, as compared to under .10 for all the firms in the S&P 500 Index. In contrast, the best-performing sector, health care, had an average capex to sales ratio of only .07, and the second-best sector, consumer staples, had the lowest ratio, .044.

I wrote about the telecommunications boom and bust at the beginning of this chapter. The capital spending spree on fiber-optic cable bankrupted much of the industry. The utilities suffered a similar fate in the 1970s and 1980s when a capital spending spree on nuclear power plants sent a number of firms into or near insolvency.

These results hold for individual firms as well as industries. Returns to investors when a firm is in the highest group of capital spenders is often far lower than when it restrains capital expenditures.

AT&T had average returns of 9.11 percent when it was in the highest-spending group but a return of over 16 percent when it was not. Procter & Gamble spent twenty-eight of the last forty-six years with average capital spending and delivered a healthy return of 17 percent per year during those years. But in the six years it was in the highest-spending group, its returns averaged a measly 2 percent, while in the twelve years it was in lower-spending groups, its returns averaged 19.8 percent per year.

Companies with strong brand-name products are not immune to the deleterious effects of high capital spending. Gillette, the famous producer of razor blades, had middling capex ratios for twenty-five years and averaged returns of 16.6 percent during this time. But during the seven years Gillette was in the higher-than-average expenditure group it had negative returns, and when it was in a lower-than-average group its returns averaged an amazing 26.4 percent per year. A similar story could be told for Hershey.

The retail giants Kmart, CVS, Woolworth, Kroger, and Allied Stores all showed dramatic differences in their returns when they were in the low-capital-spending group versus when they were not. Kmart's average return was over 25 percent per year in the twenty-five years it was in the lowest-capital-expenditure quintile. In sharp contrast, in the nineteen years when the retailer was not in the lowest quintile, it had average returns of -3.8 percent per year.

The negative impact of capital expenditures on stock returns extends to many subindustries. Since 1984, the energy sector has had fairly high expenditure ratios and overall good returns. But when you go beneath the surface you find that the oil and gas extractors, which had very poor returns, had a huge .225 capex-to-sales ratio, while the integrated "big oil" firms, which performed very well, had a more modest .10 ratio.

Technological Growth

Historical economic data indicate that the fruits of technological change, no matter how great, have ultimately benefited consumers, not the owners of firms. Productivity lowers the price of goods and raises the real wages of workers. That is, productivity allows us to buy more with less.

Certainly, technological change has transitory effects on profits. There is usually a "first mover" advantage. When one firm incorporates a new technology that has not yet been implemented by others, profits will increase. But as others avail themselves of this technology, competition ensures that prices fall and profits will revert to normal.

This is exactly what happened with the introduction of the Internet. At first, many analysts figured the Internet would boost profit margins since firms would be able to lower their costs of procurement, inventory, and data retrieval because of the Internet's ability to facilitate business communications. But the Internet did not increase profit margins substantially, and in many cases it actually decreased them. Why? Because the Internet has made all our markets more competitive.

A More Competitive Economy

In order to understand the Internet's impact on corporate profits, one must recognize how search costs—the time and dollars spent by consumers (or businesses) to find a cheaper price for the goods or services they are buying—enter the profits equation.

In years past, sellers knew that if they could draw the customer to their stores, they had won most of the battle. The corner drugstore could mark up goods that were in demand because it knew that it was unlikely that consumers would spend costly time to shop for cheaper alternatives. Convenience and location became critical factors in marketing goods.

But the Internet sharply reduced the costs of searching alternatives and changed the game dramatically. Many of the advantages of location and convenience enjoyed by firms disappeared. Suddenly the consumer had available a full array of prices from many different providers. Price transparency vaulted price competition into the spotlight.

I vividly recall an episode a few years ago when my son, then in high school, needed a calculator for school. We priced it on the Internet, using one of the many price search engines available. The price at Staples, the store closest to our home, was by no means the cheapest. Yet we printed out the prices found over the Net and brought them to the store. When I showed the clerk that a competitor had the same item for a cheaper price, he immediately offered to match it. Considering that the margins on retail sales are already paper-thin, it was likely that the price we received was at or below Staples' cost.

The Airline Industry

The airline industry provides another example of how technological advances such as the Internet reduced profits.

The Internet enabled online travel companies, such as Orbitz and Expedia, to sell cheap seats on the Web that formerly had been sold to consolidators who would resell the tickets through toll-free numbers. But the airlines believed they could also engage this technology. They saw the Web as a way to squeeze both these consolidators and travel agents, to whom they paid commissions.

Jeffrey Katz, the CEO of Orbitz, said in July 2000 that selling and marketing tickets was one of the airlines' biggest costs, and "most of the airlines that looked at the Internet [saw] potential distribution cost savings of around 50 percent."[17]

By the fall of 2002, airlines were well on their way to replacing agents with online bookings, which surpassed 20 percent of all sales. The Internet allowed the airline industry to shed about $2 billion from its cost structure from 1998 through 2002.

But instead of celebrating these remarkable cost savings, the airlines were plagued by unsettling developments. The Internet provided travelers with tools to search out the cheapest fares.

This was an entirely different ball game. In the past, the computer software that airlines' ticket agents utilized did not use price as the primary criterion. Convenience of schedule and minimizing time en route were the most important factors for business. But as travelers became more cost conscious, they searched for cheaper alternatives, which often can be attained with just minor shifts in the schedule. The result has been a steady reduction in the average price of the tickets and an erosion of airline profits.

Airline analyst Jamie Baker of J.P. Morgan Securities summarized the situation:

> The Internet and its inherent pricing transparency may ultimately cost carriers more in lost yield than it saves in distribution expense. Combined with a growing discount sector, the Internet is expected to significantly retard any improvement in industry pricing that would otherwise accompany a strong economy or a gradual relaxation of corporate travel restraint. For anyone anticipating a return to the yield levels of 1999 and 2000, we would suggest you've underestimated the role of the Internet.[18]

It is striking how easily the Internet can cannibalize profits. Instead of boosting earnings, the Internet levels the playing field and increases the ability of consumers to find the best prices. Certainly firms can and will compete on the basis of service, immediate availability, return policy, and so on. Yet no one can deny that price transparency makes retail distribution much more competitive.

Technology from a Manager's Perspective

To many, technology seems to be the key to success. The ability to produce goods more efficiently seems like the answer to sagging profits. But this is not the case.

Rigorously questioning expenditures is something not enough companies do well. Jim Collins, in his best-selling book *Good to Great,* asked, "Do you have a 'to do' list? Do you also have a '*stop* doing' list? . . . Those who built the good-to-great companies, however, made as much use of 'stop doing' lists as 'to do' lists. They displayed a remarkable discipline to unplug all sorts of extraneous junk."

Collins interviewed the CEOs who turned their companies around into winning investments. "Across eighty-four interviews with good-to-great executives, fully 80 percent didn't even mention technology as one of the top five factors in the transformation."[19] And when executives did mention technology, its median ranking in importance was fourth, with only 2 percent of the executives listing it at number one.

For the best firms, technology plays a supporting role, enhancing the company's core competencies. Capital is the source of productivity, but it must be applied in moderation. Too much capital spells the death of profits and the destruction of value.

CHAPTER EIGHT

Productivity and Profits:

WINNING MANAGEMENTS IN LOSING INDUSTRIES

As a place to invest, I'll take a lousy industry over a great industry anytime. In a lousy industry, one that's growing slowly if at all, the weak drop out and the survivors get a bigger share of the market. A company that can capture an ever-increasing share of a stagnant market is a lot better off than one that has to struggle to protect a dwindling share of an exciting market.

—Peter Lynch, *Beating the Street*, 1993

One traditional investment approach begins by examining an industry expected to have a bright future, and then selecting a company that stands to prosper from this growth. But this type of investment approach eliminates some very prosperous firms in stagnant or declining industries. In fact, some of the most successful investments of the last thirty years have come from industries whose performances have been utterly horrendous.

These companies have bucked the trend. They all rose above their competitors by following a simple approach: maximize productivity and keep costs as low as possible.

These successful firms employed very disciplined and focused capital expenditure and investment policies. They judiciously selected the capital expenditures that matched their unique competitive strategies. Unlike "capital pigs," which spend their money unproductively, these companies find investments that complement and enhance their core competencies.

Past success does not guarantee the companies discussed in this chapter will perform well in the future. In fact, each of these firms has encountered headwinds in its pursuit of expanding profits. Nevertheless, it was superior management—not technology—that produced superior investor returns.

The Airline Industry: Southwest

Investors have lost more money in the airline industry than in almost any other. When Warren Buffett was asked why he invested $358 million in USAir in 1989, he snapped back: "Well, I think probably the best answer is temporary insanity. . . . So I now have this 800 number, and if I ever get the urge to buy an airline stock I dial this number. And I say my name is Warren, and I'm an 'air-o-holic,' and then this guy talks me down on the other end."[1]

Buffett is clearly right. The airline industry has been a disaster for investors. Richard Branson, founder of Virgin Atlantic Airways, wisecracked that the best way to become a millionaire was to start out as a billionaire and buy an airline.[2]

Certainly Buffett knows good investments. Over the thirty-year period from 1972 through 2002 his investment vehicle, Berkshire Hathaway, achieved an astounding 25.5 percent annual return, making thousands of his investors millionaires. There is only one firm that beats Buffett's return over that thirty-year period: Southwest Airlines.

While air travel has undoubtedly improved the productivity of our economy—to be no more than a few hours from major population centers or vacation destinations frees time for both business and leisure travelers—the airlines are a prime example of an industry caught in a cycle of cost cutting, overcapacity, difficult unions, and high fixed costs that have ravaged their profits and led many airlines to bankruptcy. How did Southwest buck this trend? How could the single best investment of the last thirty years conduct business in an industry plagued by failure and bankruptcies?

Southwest's triumph is marked by intense management focus on lowering costs and maintaining a competitive edge. In its 1995 annual report, the airline revealed its "six secrets of success." Number one on its list was "Stick to what you're good at."

It is hard to put it much better than this. Don't try to be what you're not, and don't try to do what you cannot. Economists call this activity "pursuing your comparative advantage" or "sticking to your core competency." By focusing only on providing low-cost, reliable airline transportation to the masses, Southwest has become one of the few winners in an industry full of losers.

Southwest's strategy is to be "*the* low-fare airline" every day in every market it serves. In order to accomplish this, Southwest knows it also has to be the low-cost airline as well. And the only way to attain the lowest costs is to obtain the most production out of its resources and its employees. Every aspect of Southwest's operating strategy follows from this very basic tenet.

Southwest's 1995 annual report lays it out: "[We] honor some simple no-nos: No assigned seats. No meals. No hassles. No problems." This no-frills approach keeps costs down and allows the employees to focus on providing the service its customers expect.

Southwest offers only single-class service (no first class or business class) on a large number of flights to convenient airports. It does not try to expand into as many markets as possible or operate on a hub-and-spoke system like most other major carriers. Rather, it finds city-to-city pairs where demand is great enough to support a large number of flights.

Another productivity-enhancing operating strategy following the "keeping it simple" approach is its use of only one type of aircraft, the Boeing 737. Instead of having to store replacement parts and train its pilots and maintenance crew on a variety of aircraft, using only one airliner delivers significant cost savings.

Southwest's approach paid extra dividends after the September 11, 2001, terrorist attacks. The airline industry faced a 20 percent drop in airline passengers following the attacks, the subsequent recession, and the start of the war in Iraq. The major carriers, burdened by billions of dollars of debt, overly generous labor contracts, and a structure that allowed little flexibility, found the downturn devastating. US Airways and then United Airlines were forced into bankruptcy, and others, such as American and Delta, have come perilously close.

But Southwest kept the profits coming, albeit at a much reduced level. In April 2003 the market value of Southwest stock *exceeded* the combined equity market value of all the other air carriers in the United States, despite carrying only 8 percent of the industry's passengers.[3]

Certainly productivity was a key aspect of Southwest's success. But more important was the focus on its comparative advantage: being a no-frills, low-cost air carrier. As I indicated in the first chapter, this has been the strategy of the world's most successful firms. It is noteworthy that the world's most successful investor, Warren Buffett, also attributes his achievement to knowing when he is "operating well within [his] circle of competence and when [he is] approaching the perimeter."[4]

Retailing: Wal-Mart

Southwest is certainly not the only company that has turned high productivity and management focus into an investment success. In 1962 Sam Walton opened a variety store in the small town of Bentonville, Arkansas, population 3,000. By the end of the century Wal-Mart would become the largest company in the world measured by sales. Its 2003 sales of $259 billion were larger than the GDP of all but twenty-three countries on this planet.

Wal-Mart's success did not come overnight. Sam Walton was never satisfied with his early stores and continually improved Wal-Mart's operations and strategies. He incessantly studied his competition in search of new ideas. One retailing chain fascinated him more than any of the others, and he conceded in the early 1970s that it was a better retail outfit than Wal-Mart. "I spent a heck of a lot of my time wandering through their stores talking to the people and trying to figure out how they did things," Walton admitted. Walton's wife, Helen, recalled, "Sam never went by one of their stores that he didn't stop and look at it. We would go through a good town, and he knew about some store there. I would sit in the car with the kids, who of course, would say, 'Oh no, Daddy, not another store.' "[5]

What was that department store chain that so enthralled the founder of the world's greatest retailing firm? Kmart. In fact, Kmart so fascinated Walton that he named his own stores Wal-Mart.

In one of the greatest ironies in business history, thirty years after Wal-Mart went public, Kmart, the inspiration for the greatest retailer in history, went bankrupt. A $1,000 investment in Wal-Mart would have been the third-best-performing investment over those three decades, falling just behind Southwest Airlines and Warren Buffett's Berkshire Hathaway, while an investment in Kmart would have yielded nothing.

Wal-Mart, like Southwest, proves that a firm need not operate in an expanding sector or be at the forefront of technology to find success. But that is not to say that technology played no role in Wal-Mart's success. Indeed, Wal-Mart pioneered the use of technology and communications equipment in managing and networking its stores to monitor sales. In 1969 Wal-Mart was one of the first retailers to use computers; in 1980 it began using bar codes at its counters for easier checkout, and in the late 1980s it was using wireless scanning guns to track inventory. And many who visited its high-technology distribution hubs exclaim that they have never seen a more impressive state-of-the-art system.

But, Wal-Mart's productivity, which ranks as much as 50 percent above that of its competitors, has less to do with technology than the company's strategic expansion strategy and management practices. A McKinsey & Co. report entitled, "The Wal-Mart Effect" concludes that:

> The Wal-Mart story is a clear refutation of new-economy hype. At least half of Wal-Mart's productivity edge stems from managerial innovations that improve the efficiency of stores and have nothing to do with Information Technology.[6]

Wal-Mart's Strategy for Success

Wal-Mart's competitive advantage was not that it discovered the power of discounting, which lured consumers away from department stores. That strategy was discovered in the early 1960s by Harry Cunningham, president of Kresge, the forerunner of Kmart. Cunningham aimed to take advantage of the shifting industry trends by closing 10 percent of Kresge's existing variety store operations per year and rapidly expanding its discount operations. He opened the doors of the first Kmart discount store in Garden City, Michigan, in 1962.

In those early years Kmart expanded rapidly. By 1977 Kmart had nearly 1,800 stores, while Wal-Mart had only 195. Kmart's success broke Sears, Roebuck's stranglehold on retailing, and its stock was riding high.

Kmarts were located in large urban markets and used the same distribution network that supplied its variety store operations. But Wal-Mart was operating from Bentonville, Arkansas—in the middle of nowhere. In these small towns, there were no big distributors to supply Walton's stores. So Walton had big deliveries shipped to an old garage in Bentonville, repacked them into smaller packages, and then contacted another distributor to deliver these smaller packages to his stores. In Walton's words, this procedure was "expensive and inefficient."

But Sam Walton finally found the competitive advantage that he used to unseat Cunningham with devastating effectiveness. Instead of opening stores all across the country, as Kmart did, Wal-Mart expanded in clusters to minimize its transportation costs. It opened a few stores in an area that could be supplied by a distribution center nearby and then copied the same format in nearby areas where demand was sufficient to support as many stores as possible. Wal-Mart called this a "saturation strategy," and it minimized transportation costs from the distribution centers to the stores. It worked beautifully. Kmart's explosive growth, in contrast, planted the seeds for the company's own destruction. Expanding with no regard for the cost of distributing its products, Kmart never fully committed to the discounting mentality.

Joe Hardin, a former executive vice president of logistics and personnel at Wal-Mart, once said, "A lot of companies don't want to spend any money on distribution unless they have to. We spend because we continually demonstrate that it lowers our costs. This is a very important strategic point in understanding Wal-Mart."[7] Wal-Mart's low cost structure is primarily a function of its distribution network and the deliberate manner in which Wal-Mart expanded.

Wal-Mart, like Southwest, initially succeeded by focusing on the small regional markets it serves. Similarly, both firms committed to low prices: Southwest's motto is "The low-fare airline, every day in every market," and Wal-Mart's is "Always low prices." Commitment to always being competitive in price is critical to their success.

Steel Industry: Nucor

After railroads and oil, the steel industry dominated the industrial landscape of the late nineteenth and early twentieth centuries. United States Steel Corporation was the single largest company ever to reach the public markets. Its market value in 1901, when it was issued, was $1.4 billion, making it the first public company in America to have a capitalization greater than $1 billion.

Bethlehem Steel has roots as far back as 1857. The Bethlehem Steel plant in Bethlehem, Pennsylvania, supplied the steel used in such landmarks as the Golden Gate and George Washington Bridges, Rockefeller Plaza, the Waldorf-Astoria, the Chicago Merchandise Mart, and the U.S. Supreme Court. During the Second World War, the company built 1,121 ships. U.S. Steel and Bethlehem were economic powerhouses that together supplied about half of this country's steel.

But by the early 1970s U.S. steel manufacturers were already suffering from foreign competition. The number of steelworkers in the United States fell from 1 million during the Second World War to 140,000 in 2002. In that year Bethlehem Steel, one of the greatest companies in the United States, filed for bankruptcy, closing operations that had once employed 300,000 people. U.S. Steel limped on, but it was only a shadow of its former self.

Certainly the environment could not be worse for steel investors. Yet one company bucked the trend and delivered superior returns. Nucor, which has pioneered the use of "minimill" technology and the recycling of scrap steel, has provided investors with superior returns over the last thirty years. While other major steel companies were laying off workers and filing for bankruptcy, Nucor's sales were growing at 17 percent per year en route to its becoming the second largest steel producer in the United States. And this paid off for Nucor's investors. While the steel industry as a whole underperformed the market by close to 4 percent a year for the last thirty years, Nucor outperformed the market by over 5 percent a year over the same span.

Many attribute Nucor's success to its use of "disruptive technologies" that overthrow old powerhouses such as the "Big Steel" companies. But Jim Collins, author of *Good to Great*, writes:

> [W]hen we asked Ken Iverson, CEO of Nucor. . . . to name the top five factors in the shift from good to great, where on the list do you think he put technology? First? No. Second? No. Third? Nope. Fourth? Not even. Fifth? Sorry, but no. "The primary factors," said Ken Iverson, "were the consistency of the company, and our ability to project its philosophies throughout the whole organization, enabled by our lack of layers and bureaucracy."[8]

Another Nucor executive said, "Twenty percent of our success is the technology we embrace [but] eighty percent is in the culture of our company."[9]

Collins concludes, "You could have given the exact same technology at the exact same time to any number of companies with the exact same resources as Nucor—and even still, they would have failed to deliver Nucor's results. Like the Daytona 500, the primary variable in winning is not the car, but the driver and the team."[10]

Although Nucor's minimill technology eventually displaced the outdated technology of the integrated steel producers, such as U.S. Steel and Bethlehem Steel, its real comparative advantage lies in its relations with its own workers.

Ken Iverson described what he considers to be the problems of most corporations in his book, *Plain Talk:*

> Inequality still runs rampant in most business corporations. . . . The people at the top of the corporate hierarchy grant themselves privilege after privilege, flaunt those privileges before the men and women who do the real work, then wonder why employees are unmoved by management's invocations to cut costs and boost profitability. . . . When I think of the millions of dollars spent by the people at the top of the management hierarchy on efforts to motivate people who are continually put down by the hierarchy, I can only shake my head and wonder.[11]

Executives at Nucor had no lavish corporate dining room to host visitors; rather, they would take special guests to Phil's Diner, a small sandwich shop across the street. At Nucor, executives received no more extra benefits than the factory workers. In fact, the exact opposite was true: executives had fewer benefits. Some of the extraordinary steps that Nucor takes to minimize class distinctions between executives and the others include:

• All workers were eligible to receive $2,000 per year for each child for up to four years of postsecondary education, while the executives received no such benefit.
• Nucor lists all of its employees—more than 9,800—in its annual report, sorted alphabetically with no distinctions for officer titles.

• There are no assigned parking spots and no company cars, boats, or planes.
• All employees of the company receive the same insurance coverage and amount of vacation time.
• Everybody wears the same green spark-proof jackets and hard hats on the floor (in most integrated mills, different colors designate authority).[12]

As Warren Buffett observed: "It is the classic example of an incentive program that works. If I were a blue-collar worker, I would like to work for Nucor."[13]

Jim Strohmeyer, in his book *Crisis in Bethlehem,* depicts a corporate culture fraught with unequal treatment for executives and workers. Strohmeyer details Bethlehem's executives using its corporate fleet for personal reasons, such as taking children to college or weekend vacations. Bethlehem renovated a country club with corporate funds, at which shower priority was determined by executive rank. Need more be said?[14]

Success amid Failure

Southwest Airlines, Wal-Mart, and Nucor. These three firms thrived despite being in industries that ravaged investors. What did they have in common and how did they buck the trend?

All these firms relentlessly pursued the goal of reducing costs and giving customers *guaranteed products and services at the lowest possible price.* These companies were pioneers in maximizing the productivity of their employees. These companies developed unique strategies that enabled them to become the low-cost producer in their respective industries.

Perhaps most important, these companies recognized that to achieve their goals, management must avoid corporate excesses and develop a model working environment where employees feel part of a team that shares in both the customer respect for and financial success of their firms.

The success of these firms must make investors stop and think. The best-performing stocks are not in industries that are at the cutting edge of the technological revolution; rather, they are often in industries that are stagnant or in decline. These firms are headed by managements that find and pursue efficiencies and develop competitive niches that enable them to reach commanding positions no matter what industry they are in. Firms with these characteristics, which are often undervalued by the market, are the ones that investors should want to buy.

PART THREE

Sources of Shareholder Value

CHAPTER NINE

Show Me the Money:

DIVIDENDS, STOCK RETURNS, AND CORPORATE GOVERNANCE

"A cow for her milk, / A hen for her eggs,
And a stock, by heck, / For her dividends.
An orchard for fruit, / Bees for their honey,
And stocks, besides, / For their dividends."

John Burr Williams, *The Theory of Investment Value*, 1938

On Tuesday, July 20, 2004, Microsoft announced an enormous one-time dividend payment of $3 per share, or a total of $32 billion for its almost 11 billion shares outstanding. In addition, the firm announced that it would double its quarterly dividend and buy back over $40 billion of stock during the next four years. Microsoft, which was founded in 1975, has given its investors an astounding 37.6 percent annual rate of return since it became public in 1986. For the first sixteen years of Microsoft's public existence, 100 percent of that return came from the rising price of its shares—not a penny from dividends. But no longer. The size of Microsoft's $32 billion special dividend was greater in value than all but about seventy companies trading in the United States, and it exceeded the entire market value of such firms as General Motors and Ford.

The day after Microsoft's announcement, 202 million shares traded hands, as opinions on Microsoft's action differed sharply. Some analysts concluded that Microsoft had finally recognized that it had few growth prospects and would not need to keep its huge horde of over $56 billion in cash. But bulls said that returning profits to shareholders is one of the primary functions of a corporation and that Microsoft's action was good for investors.

Who is right? Those who bought because Microsoft was returning its profits to the shareholders, or those who sold because paying a dividend represented poor growth prospects? History has provided an unambiguous answer to this question: dividends have been the overwhelming source of stockholder returns throughout time, and firms that have higher dividend yields have given better returns to investors.

The Big Picture

Consider the following crucial fact about historical stock market returns:

From 1871 through 2003, 97 percent of the total after-inflation accumulation from stocks comes from reinvesting dividends. Only 3 percent comes from capital gains.

Take a look at Figure 9.1. The sum of $1,000 invested in stocks in 1871 would have accumulated to almost $8 million after inflation by the end of 2003.[1] Without reinvesting dividends, the accumulation would be less than $250,000.

During these 122 years investors did collect about $90,000 in dividends. If these dividends are simply added to the price appreciation, the total

FIGURE 9.1: CAPITAL GAINS AND REINVESTED DIVIDENDS

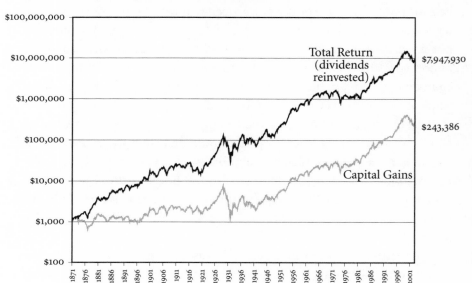

would be about a third of a million dollars. But this total is still tiny compared to the wealth accumulated when dividends are reinvested. In terms of annual returns, the numbers are equally striking. Without reinvesting dividends, the average annual after-inflation return on stocks falls from 7 percent to 4.5 percent, a drop of over a third.

Dividends are not just good for the whole market. They are also good for individual stocks.

I examined the record of firms in the S&P 500 Index from its beginning in 1957 to the present. On December 31 of each year I sorted the firms in the S&P 500 Index into five groups (or quintiles) ranked by dividend yield, and then calculated the return over the next calendar year. The first group comprises those firms in the lowest 20 percent of the dividend yields (many paid no dividends, especially in more recent years). The second group comprises the next 20 percent ranked by dividend yield, and so on up to the fifth group, which includes firms with the highest yield. I then calculated the return on each of these portfolios over the next year before I re-sorted the firms again, based on the same criteria.

Figure 9.2 shows how striking the results are. In strictly increasing order, the portfolios with higher dividend yields offered investors higher returns. If an investor started with $1,000 at the end of December of 1957, she would have accumulated $130,768 in an S&P 500 Index fund by the end of 2003, for an annual return of 11.19 percent. If instead she purchased only the highest 20 percent of dividend yielders in each year, she would have accumulated $462,750, more than three times the indexed accumulation. Although the risk of these high yielders was slightly higher than that of the S&P 500, its annual return of 14.27 percent was more than worth the extra risk. If instead, she bought the lowest-dividend-yielding stocks, she would have accumulated only about one-half the sum placed in an indexed fund—a return under 10 percent a year. Even worse for investors, the risk of the lowest-yielding group containing many no-dividend stocks was also the highest of all the portfolios.

Note that the technology bubble of the 1990s caused the return on the lowest-dividend payers, which at that time were almost exclusively firms that paid no dividend at all, to surge and almost equal that of the S&P 500 Index.

But history snapped back and punctured these high-flying tech stocks, sending their prices down to earth. The low-dividend stocks went back to the bottom rung of the ladder, as they had been before the bubble began.

FIGURE 9.2: CUMULATIVE RETURNS TO S&P 500
SORTED BY DIVIDEND YIELD (SOURCE: COMPUSTAT®)

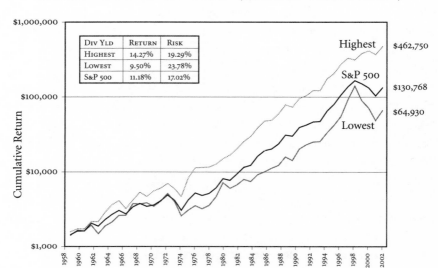

Declining Dividend Yields

The importance of dividends in generating stock returns is not just historical happenstance. Dividends are the crucial link between corporate profits and stock values. Finance theory states that the price of any asset is the present value of all its future cash flows. For stocks, cash flows are identified as dividends, not earnings. Earnings are only a means to an end— and that end is to maximize the cash returns received by investors.

In spite of the overwhelming historical and theoretical support for dividends, the dividend yield on stocks has fallen to record low levels over the past two decades. Figure 9.3 shows the trend. From 1871 through 1980, the average dividend yield on stocks averaged 5 percent. This was 76 percent of the annual real return on stocks over that period.

But the 1980s started the steady downward drift of dividend yields, a drift that became a freefall in the 1990s. At the top of the technology bubble in 2000, the dividend yield on the S&P 500 fell to just over 1 percent and has only modestly recovered since then.

FIGURE 9.3: DIVIDEND YIELDS, 1871–2003

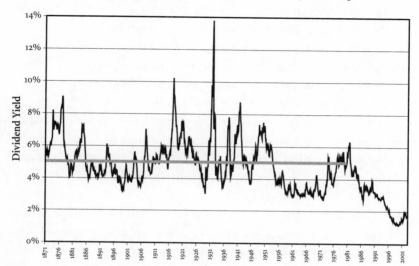

Why has this decline occurred? How could the most important source of stock returns through history suddenly become so unimportant?

There were three reasons. The first was the misguided belief that by paying dividends firms were forgoing valuable growth options that could be financed with earnings not paid out as dividends. The second was the U.S. tax system, which double-taxed the payment of dividends. And the third was the proliferation of management stock options, which shifted management's attention from paying dividends to pumping up the price of the stock.

Growth Options and Dividends

Those who scoff at the idea of firms paying out their earnings as dividends argue that money used to pay dividends would deprive fast-growing firms of their principal source of capital.

Andy Kessler, a former hedge fund manager and co-founder of a money management firm that invests in technology companies, wrote in a *Wall Street Journal* article entitled "I Hate Dividends":

Scan the list of companies worth over $10 billion that pay a high dividend and you don't exactly come away with the future of America, more like old home week. Duke Energy (5.6%), Eastman Kodak (5%), Ford (4.1%), GM (5.4%), JP Morgan Chase (5.6%), SBC Communications (3.9%), and Verizon (3.9%). Dividends entice investors into debt-laden, slow- or no-growth companies, more likely to cut their dividend, burning investors worse than conflicted research analysts. Run away. They are wearing a scarlet dollar sign. You want yield? Buy a bond . . .

[D]ividends don't create economic growth. Failing companies just bribe investors with dividends. Encourage companies with a future to invest in their operations, seeking high returns. If all that mattered were dividends, we . . . would still be investing in railroad stocks.[2]

As persuasive as Kessler's arguments may sound, the hard evidence proves otherwise. I showed in Chapter 2 that on average the returns on older firms surpassed the returns on the newer firms. In Chapter 4 I showed that in nine of the ten industry sectors studied, the firms that were added to the venerable S&P 500 Index underperformed the original firms that were in the index when it was founded in 1957.

Even though Kessler pokes fun at those who invest in the railroads, over the last forty-five years the railroad industry outperformed the industrial sector and the S&P 500 Index. And technology stocks, which pay the lowest dividends, have scarcely been market beaters.

Unfortunately, the growth options that firms sank their money into often turned into money pits. I showed in Chapter 7 that the "capital pigs," those firms that undertook high levels of capital expenditures, underperformed those that spent sparingly on such capital.

And what of those firms that carry huge hoards of cash waiting to buy other companies to boost their earnings? Not good for investors. A study by researchers from Ohio State University, the University of Pittsburgh, and Southern Methodist University entitled "Wealth Destruction on a Massive Scale" concludes that the shareholders of acquiring firms lost a total of $240 billion in the four years from 1998 through 2001: "The large losses are consistent with the existence of negative synergies from the acquisitions."[3] This research is supported by that of Jarrad Harford at the University of Washington, who published an article in the prestigious

Journal of Finance concluding, "cash-rich firms destroy seven cents in value for every excess dollar of cash reserves held."[4]

Having a large cash hoard in the corporate till is akin to a having pocket full of money—it encourages you to spend. Very often I am asked if a particular company is attractive because it is selling below the value of cash on its balance sheets. I reply, "Watch out!" The stock is only a buy if you can take control of the company and disgorge the cash to shareholders. That used to be a favorite technique of Warren Buffett's mentor, Benjamin Graham, who went after companies that were not employing their cash in the interest of shareholders. If you cannot take control quickly, I would stay away. Management may squander much of that cash in the next few years.

Warren Buffett and Berkshire Hathaway

I can visualize the Warren Buffett fans shaking their heads at all this emphasis on dividends. As a great admirer of the man, I feel it is important to explain why his no-dividend, cash-hoarding policy works so well for his firm.

Buffett's investment vehicle, Berkshire Hathaway, paid a single ten-cent dividend in 1967 and has never paid one since. Buffett, who has always opposed paying dividends on his stock, maintains that the directors of the firm voted the dividend in Berkshire's early years while he took a bathroom break during a board meeting.[5] Despite the lack of dividends, Berkshire Hathaway has been one of the best-performing stocks over the last four decades.

Taxes are a major reason why Berkshire doesn't pay a dividend. In an interview with Ted Koppel on *Nightline* in 2003, Buffett said, "If we could pay dividends out tax-free, it would be good for [our shareholders]."[6] Buffett rightly claims that even with the recent reform of the U.S. tax code, which I will discuss below, there is a tax incentive for firms to create capital gains, which are taxed only if and when investors sell their shares.

Dividends, by contrast, are taxed automatically upon receipt. As a result, if a firm can profitably reinvest its earnings, by either expanding its own operations, buying other firms, or repurchasing its own shares, then the tax that an investor would have to pay is deferred to the future.

But it is far from certain that most firms can profitably reinvest all their earnings. As noted above, all too often management spends the earnings in a way that reduces instead of increases the return to investors.

Managements that are flush with cash often lose control over costs, spend money on perquisites, or engage in empire building. Economists call these wasteful expenditures "agency costs," and they exist to some extent in all organizations where the owners are not the managers.

Admirably, Warren Buffett is one of those very rare managers who has the discipline, will, and incentive to avoid all these pitfalls. By aligning himself so closely with shareholders (virtually all of his own enormous wealth is invested in Berkshire), he acts directly in his and his shareholders' best interest.

Buffett is extraordinarily forthright with the public, revealing to all exactly what is going right, what is going wrong, and how his earnings and capital are spent. He makes no attempt to sugarcoat bad news or pump the price of his stock. If Buffett thinks there are no attractive investment opportunities, he will refrain from investing even as substantial cash flows into his company. He regards holding cash as a valuable option that enables him to pursue special opportunities if and when they appear in the market.

Holding cash in lieu of paying dividends to shareholders makes sense with Buffett's strategy. During periods when financing is hard to come by, some of the best deals can be made by those who have the cash to lend or to buy with. Buffett is particularly good at spotting those opportunities. In addition, if he thinks that his own shares are underpriced, he will buy them in the open market through share repurchases, as he considered doing in 2000 when Berkshire A shares were trading below \$45,000.[7]

Furthermore, Buffett's investment strategy focuses on buying stocks or businesses that generate healthy cash flows, the prerequisite of dividends. "Our acquisition preferences run toward businesses that generate cash, not those that consume it," he stated in the company's 1980 annual report. And in his 1991 report he reiterated that he searches for businesses with "demonstrated, consistent earnings power (future projections are of little interest to us, nor are 'turnaround' situations)." In other words, Buffett's own investment objective of buying companies with consistent cash flows at reasonable prices mimics investors who reinvest their dividends.

If the management of other companies had the same close relationship with their shareholders that Buffett has, the importance of paying dividends would be significantly reduced. But often, the difference between the goals of the shareholder and those of management can be substantial. The commitment to pay earnings back to shareholders in the form of dividends reduces the potential for management to squander shareholders' wealth.

Dividends and Corporate Governance

If management always acted completely in the interests of shareholders, dividends would not be important. But for the rest of the corporate world, dividends are a critical ingredient in generating trust between shareholders and management and confirming management's statements about earnings. I realized how crucial this trust is when the Enron crisis rocked the confidence of the stock markets in the fall of 2001.

The story of Enron is fascinating. The firm rose from an obscure Houston-based natural gas pipeline operator to become the world's largest energy trader. At its market peak in August 2000, Enron was one of the fifty largest firms in the United States, with a total market value of almost $70 billion, ahead of such giants as General Motors, Ford, and Chevron.

Enron was praised as an example of how old-line firms could adapt to the new market-based world of energy distribution. For six years in a row, *Fortune* ranked Enron near the top of its "Most Innovative Companies" and named it one of the five most admired firms in America. It was the prototype new-economy firm.

But this new-economy darling was also cooking its books, portraying steadily rising earnings while hiding its debts in off-balance-sheet entities. And investors were soon to learn that Enron was not an isolated example of earnings deception and manipulation. Other firms that had won the plaudits of investors, such as Tyco, WorldCom, Adelphia, and Health-South, also falsified their earnings. Even some of the earnings of the bluest of the blue chips, General Electric, were being called into question.

Despite the proliferation of earnings scandals, the vast majority of corporate management was not losing its moral bearings. I realized that the real problem was that the most basic source of stock values, dividends, had fallen victim to investors' undue focus on short-run performance, the U.S. tax system, and excessive issuance of management stock options. These were the true culprits for the crisis in investor confidence.

The Dividend Deficit

I put my concerns in an article published in the *Wall Street Journal* in February 2002, entitled "The Dividend Deficit." I pointed out that history provides us with important lessons about the sources of shareholder value.[8] In the nineteenth century there was no Securities and Exchange Commission, Financial Accounting Standards Board, or any of the other numerous agencies that oversee and regulate our securities markets today. A firm released whatever information it liked whenever it wanted, and management didn't fret that it would be taken to task for reporting a dubious number.

Given the total lack of standards back then, how did a firm signal that its earnings were real? The old-fashioned way, by paying dividends—an action that gave tangible evidence of the firm's profitability and proof that the firm's earnings were authentic. If there were no dividends, then the stock's value depended on trusting management's earnings reports. If there was no trust, there was no reason to buy stocks.

In the article I fingered the U.S. tax system and the excessive issuance of stock options, particularly to top-level management, as the principal causes of the decline in dividends.

Taxes on Dividends

The role of our tax system in discouraging dividends is clear. At the time I wrote the article, dividends were fully taxable to the individual and not tax deductible to the corporation. In contrast, almost all foreign countries exempted some or all dividends from personal taxation, since they were already taxed as part of corporate profits.

I called on legislators to eliminate the double taxation on dividends, and I set forward my proposals for dividend tax relief in my article entitled "This Tax Cut Will Pay Dividends," that appeared in the *Wall Street Journal* on August 13, 2002. Because of my previous advocacy of tax relief for dividends, I had been invited to President Bush's Economic Summit held on that very same day to discuss my proposal with other economists inside and outside the administration.

I proposed allowing dividends paid to stockholders to be tax-deductible to corporations, just as all interest paid to bondholders is tax-deductible. This would put all corporations on the same footing currently enjoyed by real estate investment trusts (REITs), mutual funds, and Subchapter S corporations.

On May 27, 2003, President Bush signed into law his "Jobs and Growth Reconciliation Act of 2003," central to which was a decrease in the dividend tax rate and capital gains tax rate to 15 percent. Although I preferred the deductibility at the corporate level instead of the personal level, the dividend tax relief was much needed and welcomed.

Responding in kind, many companies increased their dividends substantially, and dividend growth surged to levels not seen in more than forty years. Clearly, the dividend tax cut worked its magic.[9]

Stock Options and Dividends

Taxation was not the only factor restraining dividends. The role of employee stock options in discouraging dividends is more indirect than taxes, but just as important.

Microsoft provides the perfect illustration.

On January 16, 2003, a week after President Bush announced his plans to reduce the tax rate on dividends, Microsoft announced its first ever dividend: 8 cents a share. While the yield was small (less than one third of 1 percent), it was a giant step forward.

But an equally important decision was made at that time. No longer was Microsoft going to issue its employees options; the firm announced that its incentive compensation would consist of common stock instead of stock options.

Dropping stock options at Microsoft was a dramatic change, since the technology giant pioneered using stock options to attract its employees. Some claim that Microsoft created as many as 10,000 millionaires from generously doling out these options.[10] Everybody from programmers to "gofers" who fetched laundry was rewarded with stock options. Stories of staffers and secretaries who retired in their thirties from their millions cashed in on Microsoft options created a culture where stock options were the primary vehicle that technology firms used to recruit and motivate the best talent.

Now, instead of motivating its employees with options, Microsoft issues its employees shares that receive dividends. You can be certain that had Microsoft not canceled its stock option plan a year earlier, it would have never paid a one-time dividend of $3 per share as it did in 2004, since option holders do not benefit from dividends. This is because options pay off on the price of the stock, not the dividend. Paying dividends, although enhancing the returns of *shareholders*, does nothing for option holders.

Option Reform

To understand what must be done to curtail stock-option compensation, it's instructive to understand why it blossomed in the first place. Management stock options surged in the mid 1990s after Congress passed a law in 1993 that prohibited firms from deducting a manager's compensation above $1 million from taxes. This law, which is now part of Section 162 (m) of the Internal Revenue Code, was enacted in response to the public uproar over the ever-rising compensation paid to top executives.

But businesses argued that top managers needed incentive-based pay to boost firm profits. So at the same time this law was passed, Congress exempted incentive-based forms of compensation from the salary cap. Shortly thereafter, the IRS ruled that option grants qualified as incentive-based compensation. This opened the floodgates.

This legislation is a perfect example of the Law of Unintended Consequences. The proliferation of option grants gave CEOs strong incentives to cut dividends and do everything they could to hype the price of their stocks. What started out as well-intended legislation designed to curb excessive management pay instead contributed to massive executive option packages built around the short-term price performance of the stock and not the long-term interests of the shareholders. To reduce the incentives to issue options, I advocated that firms be required to expense these options, and I recommended that Congress repeal the 1993 law that restricted the tax deductions for cash compensation.[11]

In contrast to the taxation of dividends, we have made less progress when it comes to option reform. Although an increasing number of firms are expensing options, there is still fierce political opposition to proposals recommended by the Financial Accounting Standard Board that would make expensing options mandatory. These issues will be more thoroughly discussed in Chapter 11.

Wrapping It Up

The fundamental importance of dividends in delivering superior stock returns rests on credibility. Dividends are the way investors know that the earnings are real. If management says that the firm has a profit, stockholders have the perfect right to say: "Show me the money!" Those firms that do have delivered the best returns.

After two decades of decline, dividends and dividend-paying stocks are coming back. President Bush's dividend tax cut was effective at mitigating the double taxation of dividends. Further reform should be aimed at exempting reinvested dividends from the income tax.

In the next chapter, I shall show that not only do dividends enhance returns but they also protect investors in bear markets.

CHAPTER TEN

Reinvested Dividends:

THE BEAR MARKET PROTECTOR AND RETURN ACCELERATOR

The importance of dividends for providing wealth to investors is self-evident. Dividends not only dwarf inflation, growth, and changing valuation levels individually, but they also dwarf the combined importance of inflation, growth, and changing valuation levels.

—Robert Arnott, "Dividends and the Three Dwarfs," 2003

Chapter 9 showed us that dividend-paying stocks provide superior returns for investors. But there is another quality of dividend-paying stocks that makes them very attractive. Long-term investors who reinvest their dividends will find that bear markets not only are easier on their portfolio but also can enhance their wealth. If the price of the stock falls more than its dividend—and this almost always happens during market declines—then the dividend yield will rise. And a higher dividend yield is a ticket to higher returns. Let's see how these phenomena worked during the single worst period in U.S. stock market history.

The Great Bear Market

It took more than a quarter of a century, but on November 24, 1954, the Dow Jones Industrial Average finally closed above the level it had reached at the bull market peak on September 3, 1929. This twenty-five-year stretch is the longest time between stock market peaks in the more than one-hundred-year history of the Dow.

For many, the market had been an unmitigated disaster since 1929. The Great Depression that followed was the greatest economic contraction in U.S. history. Many stocks fell 90 percent and more, and a vast majority of those who invested on margin or with borrowed money were wiped out. Millions vowed never to invest in equities again.

But for long-term stock investors who declined to buy stocks with bor-rowed money, those twenty-five years had been far from a disaster. Take a look at Figure 10.1, which shows the total wealth of stock and bondholders during this period.

Instead of just getting back to even in November 1954, stockholders who reinvested their dividends (indicated as "total return") realized an an-nual rate of return of over 6 percent per year, far outstripping those who invested in either long- or short-term government bonds. In fact, $1,000 invested in stocks at the market peak turned into $4,440 when the Dow fi-nally recovered to its old high on that November day a quarter century later. Although the price appreciation was zero, the $4,400 that resulted solely from reinvesting dividends was almost twice the accumulation in bonds and four times the accumulation in short-term treasury bills.

Stock Returns Without a Great Depression

The impact of bear markets on long-term investors is far different from what most investors believe. Consider the following hypothetical history.

Imagine that the Great Depression had never occurred and, in fact, there never was an economic downturn. As a consequence, assume that stock dividends, instead of dropping sharply, made a smooth ascent from 1929 to 1954, and stock prices, instead of plummeting, remained stable.[1] Obviously this scenario would have been far better for the country, as the massive unemployment, bankruptcies, and economic hardships that had occurred during the 1930s never would have existed.

Yet this rosy economic scenario would have been far worse for long-term stock investors. Although the market would have reached the same level by November 1954 in either scenario, the returns to shareholders would have been far different. As Figure 10.1 shows, $1,000 invested at the market peak would have turned into only $2,720 in November 1954 had the Great Depression never occurred. This is 60 percent *less* than what in-vestors actually accumulated as a result of this economic catastrophe.

How could this happen? Although dividends declined a whopping 55 percent from their peak in 1929 to their trough in 1933, stock prices fell even more. As a result, the dividend yield on stocks, which is critical to an investor's total return, actually rose. It is true that shorter-term investors were indeed worse off between 1929 and 1949 because of the Depression,

FIGURE 10.1: ASSET RETURNS BETWEEN
SEPTEMBER 1929 AND NOVEMBER 1954

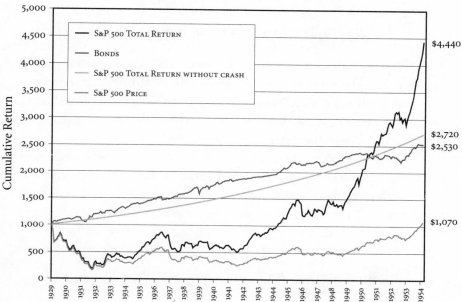

and twenty years is not an insignificant period of time. But for those who persevered, the extra shares purchased during the bear market caused their returns to rocket ahead when stock prices finally recovered.

During the Depression, long-term investors gained at the expense of all those who were forced to sell their stock, either because they had purchased their stocks with borrowed money or, more commonly, because they dumped their shares in a panic, figuring that getting some money from their investment was better than nothing. These sellers turned out to be the big losers.

There is an important lesson to be taken from this analysis. Market cycles, although difficult on investors' psyches, generate wealth for long-term stockholders. These gains come not through timing the market but through the reinvestment of dividends.

Bear markets are not only painful episodes that investors must endure; they are also an integral reason why investors who reinvest dividends experience sharply higher returns. Stock returns are generated not by earnings and dividends alone but by the *prices* that investors pay for these cash flows. When pessimism grips shareholders, those who stay with dividend-paying stocks are the big winners.

The Bear Market Protector and Return Accelerator

There are two important ways that dividends help investors in bear markets. The greater number of shares accumulated through reinvested dividends cushions the decline in the value of the investor's portfolio. It is because of the additional shares repurchased in down markets that I call reinvested dividends the "bear market protector."

But these extra shares do even more than cushion the decline when the market recovers. Those extra shares will greatly enhance future returns. So in addition to being a bear market protector, reinvesting dividends turns into a "return accelerator" once stock prices turn up. This is why dividend-paying stocks provide the highest return over stock market cycles.

The Bear Market Protector: The Case of Philip Morris

The theory that dividends are a bear market protector is equally as valid for individual stocks as it is for the market. In Chapter 4 we saw that Philip Morris had the best return of all the original S&P 500 stocks over the last half century. There is no better example of a company that proves bad news causing its price to go down could actually turn into good news for long-term shareholders.

In the early 1960s, Philip Morris was dead last in sales among the six major American cigarette producers. But the development and promotion of Marlboro cigarettes was a marketing coup that propelled the brand to be the world's best-selling cigarette in 1972. In 1983 the firm overtook R.J. Reynolds Tobacco, which had been the leading cigarette producer for a quarter century.

With rising health concerns about tobacco and increasing cash flowing in from cigarette sales, Philip Morris decided to diversify its operations. The company purchased General Foods in 1985 and Kraft in 1988, successfully integrating food products into its other lines of business. From 1957 through 1992, investors in Philip Morris achieved an astounding annualized return of 22 percent.

But the future was not as bright as the past. Figure 10.2 shows the ups and downs of Philip Morris stock from 1992 through 2003.

The first bombshell for Philip Morris shareholders occurred on April 2, 1993. Smokers had begun to rebel against the steady rise in the price of premium brands by opting to buy generic cigarettes whose prices were half that of Philip Morris's brands.

But Philip Morris decided to fight fire with fire: it slashed its prices 40 cents a pack. The *New York Times* described this as a "crash campaign to keep smokers loyal." Yet crash is exactly what happened to its stock price. The stock fell 23 percent on the news that generics were finally making headway, cutting into brand loyalty critical for Philip Morris's success.[2] April 2, 1993, became known as "Marlboro Friday."

But tougher competition from the cheaper generics and newly imposed cigarette taxes were by no means the toughest test for Philip Morris. A wave of tobacco litigation threatened to bankrupt the entire industry.

Litigation worries always existed, but in the early 1990s tobacco companies were proud of the fact that they had never lost a single case.[3] However,

FIGURE 10.2: IMPORTANT DATES FOR
PHILIP MORRIS STOCK, 1992–2003

a Pandora's box was opened on March 13, 1996, when Bennett LeBow, the financier who in 1986 had taken over the Liggett Group (maker of Chester-field and L&M cigarettes), announced a settlement with five states that had sued the industry. This was the first time a cigarette company dissented from the industry's standard defense that tobacco products were not ad-dictive. The Liggett group agreed to give up 5 percent of its pretax income for the next twenty-five years to settle the class action lawsuits against it. But, instead of making problems go away, the lawsuits intensified. One by one, additional states started suing the tobacco companies to recoup money they paid out through Medicaid and Medicare to treat smoking-related illnesses.

These lawsuits kept the tobacco stocks under constant pressure. Big Tobacco finally agreed to settle lawsuits in 1998 that would pay the states a cumulative total of more than $206 billion over the next twenty-five years to make up for smoking-related health problems—a gigantic sum that far surpassed any other settlement in legal history. Philip Morris's share of the settlement was approximately $100 billion.

But the litigation did not stop there. In 1999 the U.S. government filed a massive lawsuit against the tobacco companies, and on July 14, 2000, Philip Morris was slapped with $74 billion in punitive damages to Florida smok-ers.[4] Then on June 6, 2001, a Los Angeles jury awarded Richard Boeken, a former smoker, $3 billion in punitive damages. Given that almost half a million deaths per year have been attributed to cancer and other smoking-related diseases, this award, if applied to others, would most certainly bankrupt the industry.

Facing all this bad news, the billions of dollars in lawsuits, rising ciga-rette taxes, increasing negative publicity about smoking, and share lost to generics, it will come as no surprise that Philip Morris significantly lagged the market in the 1990s.

In March 2003 Philip Morris, which in January of that year had changed its name to Altria Group, lost an Illinois lawsuit that claimed the company's use of the word *light* was misleading. The firm was ordered by a judge to pay $10 billion and post a $12 billion bond. Philip Morris claimed that forcing it to put up $12 billion constituted an unreasonable burden and that it might have to file for bankruptcy if the court insisted on such payment. Philip Morris stock sank to $28 a share, about the same level it had achieved twelve years earlier. During this period, when the S&P 500 Index soared from 380 to 800, Philip Morris's stock price went nowhere.

Despite these ups and down, during this twelve-year period Philip Morris never lowered its dividend; in fact, it raised its dividend every year except 1993 and 1997. As a result, from 1992 through April 4, 2003, investors who reinvested their dividends increased their shares by over 100 percent, and their total return was a healthy 7.15 percent per year. This return did trail the market, but investors were perfectly situated to receive sharply higher returns if and when Philip Morris's price recovered.

And they didn't have to wait long. The return accelerator was about to work its magic. When the Illinois judge relented on the company having to post a $12 billion bond, Philip Morris's shares jumped. By the end of the year, Philip Morris was selling at $50. Although the appreciation of Philip Morris shares did trail the S&P 500 Index, shareholders who reinvested increased their shares by 100 percent and the total return to Philip Morris's stockholders actually beat the famous benchmark. It is yet another case where bad news for a dividend-paying stock spelled good returns to long-term investors.

Dividends and the Top-Performing Stocks

Table 10.1 reproduces the list of 20 best-performing survivor stocks from the original S&P 500 firms that we examined in Chapter 3. The return of each of these companies beat the S&P 500 over the past forty-seven years by between 2.8 and 8.9 percent per year, and every one of them paid a dividend.

The basic principle of investor return indicates that returns are magnified when dividends are paid and earnings growth exceeds expectations.

All of these top twenty firms had their returns boosted by dividend reinvestment. In fact, every stock in Table 10.1 has raised its dividend continuously over the past twenty years except for Royal Dutch, Schering-Plough, and Kroger. Management's commitment to return cash to their shareholders propelled the return on these stocks upward.

The case of Kroger illustrates how reinvested dividends can supercharge returns. In 1988 Kroger borrowed $4.1 billion in order to fend off a corporate takeover from Kohlberg Kravis Roberts. With this money,

Kroger paid a $40 one-time special dividend in August of that year as well as a debenture valued at $8.50 in December. Because of the huge indebtedness, Kroger had to use all its earnings to pay interest on these bonds and subsequently stopped paying dividends, but those investors who reinvested the $48.50 distribution increased their shares of Kroger more than sixfold. The dividend accelerator then worked wonders when Kroger continued to grow. If investors did not reinvest their dividends, their accumulation in Kroger stock would have been 60 percent less.

Most of the companies in Table 10.1 had average dividend yields that were near or above the yield of the S&P 500. Only two, Pfizer and Merck, had yields more than one percentage point below the index. And five companies—Royal Dutch, Philip Morris, Wrigley, Crane, and Hershey Foods—put to rest the notion that companies cannot have high dividend yields and maintain strong growth. All five of these companies delivered both higher dividend yields and earnings growth than the S&P 500.

High Dividend Yield Investment Strategies

Strategies of investing in high-yielding stocks are not new. The "Dow 10" or "Dogs of the Dow" has been regarded as one of the most successful investment strategies of all time.[5]

The strategy calls for investors to buy the ten highest-yielding stocks of the thirty firms in the Dow Jones Industrial Average (the Dow 30) at the end of each year. Since management usually tries to maintain their dividend payouts during times of adversity, stocks with a high dividend yield are often those that have fallen in price and are out of favor with investors. For this reason the Dow 10 strategy is often called the "Dogs of the Dow."

Figure 10.3 shows the cumulative returns in various dividend strategies compared to their benchmarks. Since the S&P 500 Index was founded, the Dow Jones Industrial Average has actually outperformed the index, providing investors an average annual return of 12.00 percent versus 11.18 percent for the S&P.

But the return of the Dow 10 strategy is much better than the Dow industrials (the Dow 30), providing investors with a 14.43 percent return, about 2.5 percent per year higher than the Dow 30 and accumulating to $493,216, about two and a half times that in the Dow 30.

The Dow 10 high-dividend strategy works well during bear markets,

TABLE 10.1: DIVIDEND YIELD
ON TOP-TWENTY SURVIVOR FIRMS

Return Rank	2003 Name	Accumulation of $1,000	Return	Dividend Yield
1	Philip Morris	$ 4,626,402	19.75%	4.07%
2	Abbott Laboratories	$ 1,281,335	16.51%	2.25%
3	Bristol-Myers Squibb	$ 1,209,445	16.36%	2.87%
4	Tootsie Roll Industries	$ 1,090,955	16.11%	2.44%
5	Pfizer	$ 1,054,823	16.03%	2.45%
6	Coca-Cola	$ 1,051,646	16.02%	2.81%
7	Merck	$ 1,003,410	15.90%	2.37%
8	PepsiCo	$ 866,068	15.54%	2.53%
9	Colgate-Palmolive	$761,163	15.22%	3.39%
10	Crane	$ 736,796	15.14%	3.62%
11	H.J. Heinz	$635,988	14.78%	3.27%
12	Wrigley	$ 603,877	14.65%	4.02%
13	Fortune Brands	$ 580,025	14.55%	5.31%
14	Kroger	$ 546,793	14.41%	5.89%
15	Schering-Plough	$ 537,050	14.36%	2.57%
16	Procter & Gamble	$ 513,752	14.26%	2.75%
17	Hershey Foods	$ 507,001	14.22%	3.67%
18	Wyeth	$ 461,186	13.99%	3.32%
19	Royal Dutch Petroleum	$ 398,837	13.64%	5.24%
20	General Mills	$ 388,425	13.58%	3.20%
	TOP 20	$ 944,352	15.75%	3.40%
	S&P 500	$ 124,486	10.85%	3.27%

confirming that dividends serve as a bear market protector. In the 1973–74 bear market, when the Dow 30 was down by 26.4 percent and the S&P 500

FIGURE 10.3: HIGH-YIELD DIVIDEND STRATEGIES

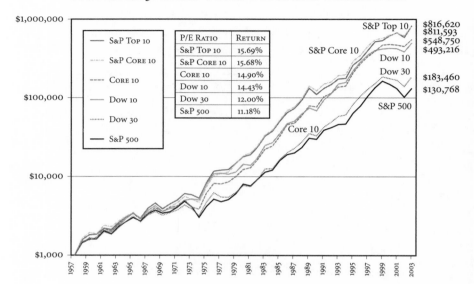

Index was down 37.2 percent, the Dow 10 high-yield strategy actually gained 1.4 percent! Similarly, in 2001 and 2002, the Dow 30 was down 20.4 percent and the S&P 500 Index was down 30.2 percent, but the Dow 10 fell only 9.9 percent. Clearly dividends cushioned the declines in the market, a feature that should be comforting to investors.

The S&P 10

A natural extension of the Dow 10 is to apply the high-dividend strategy to another group of large stocks, such as the 100 largest firms in the S&P 500 Index. After all, why should the strategy of choosing the ten best-yielding stocks be limited to the Dow industrials, which are only one quarter of the total market value of stocks?

Indeed, we find that choosing the ten highest-yielding stocks among the largest 100 S&P 500 stocks does even better than the Dow 10. These accumulations are also shown in Figure 10.3. A thousand dollars invested in these high yielders from the S&P 500 Index at the end of 1957 accumulates to more than $811,000 and beats the Dow 10 by more than 1 percent per year.

As with the Dow 10 strategy, the S&P 10 again demonstrates that dividends are a bear market protector. From 1998 through 2002, the largest 100 stocks in the S&P 500 were down a cumulative 20 percent. But the S&P 10 actually rose 13 percent over that same period. During the 1973–74 bear market, when the largest 100 stocks were also down 20 percent, the S&P 10 held steady and even gained 6 percent.

The Core 10

But there may be an even better high-yield strategy than the Dow 10 or S&P 10. Many investors, especially those with a long-term perspective, prefer to receive a steadily growing rather than fluctuating level of dividends. A policy of continually raising the dividend commits management to meet specific return requirements of its shareholders.

For this reason, we have also examined the ten highest-yielding stocks among those that have not reduced their dividend in the last fifteen years. A period of fifteen years was chosen because that means the firm must have passed through at least one recession. Managements that have not cut their dividend have demonstrated the consistent earning power and strength of their corporations. I call this strategy the Core 10 because management's commitment to dividends is seen as a basic or core strategy.

In Figure 10.3 we plot the accumulation of wealth by pursuing the Core 10 strategy in both the Dow industrials and among the top 100 market-value stocks in the S&P 500 Index. The Dow Core 10 does indeed outperform the Dow 10 by about 0.60 percentage point a year. Furthermore, the Dow Core 10 strategy permits a 20 percent reduction in the turnover of firms at year's end, which reduces both capital gains realization and transaction costs. The S&P Core 10 strategy reduces turnover, but performs about the same as the S&P 10.

Calibrating the Return Accelerator

Dividend-paying stocks do well through market cycles, since investors who reinvest dividends accumulate more shares during bear markets. Table 10.2 shows how many years it takes after a stock declines for investors to achieve the same return they would have received had the stock price not declined. These tables assume the firm maintains its dividend. The investor recoups the price loss because the lower price allows dividend-

reinvesting investors to accumulate more shares than they would have accumulated had the stock never declined. The value of these extra shares
eventually surpasses the magnitude of the price decline, making the investors better off.

As can be seen, the greater the dividend yield, the shorter the time
needed for investors to recover their losses. Surprisingly, the table also
shows that the greater the decline in price, the shorter the period of time
needed to break even, since reinvested dividends accumulate at an even
faster rate.

For example, take a stock that starts with a 5 percent dividend yield. If
the stock then declined by 50 percent and stayed down, investors who reinvest dividends will recover their loss in 14.9 years. This is because they
would have doubled the number of shares they hold, compensating for the
decline in the price.

A similar story held for Philip Morris. At the end of 1991, Philip Morris's dividend yield was only 2.8 percent. But with steadily rising dividends
and falling prices, its dividend yield rose throughout the decade and surpassed 7 percent in 2000. The extra shares accumulated at these high dividend yields were the major reason the return on Philip Morris's stock
return stayed high, despite its poor performance during the 1990s.

Table 10.3 illustrates the return accelerator. It shows the return investors

TABLE 10.2: YEARS TO BREAK EVEN AFTER PRICE DECLINES

		Dividend Yield								
		1%	2%	3%	4%	5%	6%	7%	8%	9%	10%
	10%	95.8	48.4	32.6	24.7	20.0	16.8	14.5	12.9	11.5	10.5
	20%	90.3	45.6	30.8	23.3	18.9	15.9	13.8	12.2	10.9	9.9
	30%	84.2	42.6	28.8	21.8	17.7	14.9	12.9	11.4	10.3	9.3
Price Decline	40%	77.6	39.3	26.6	20.2	16.3	13.8	12.0	10.6	9.5	8.7
	50%	70.4	35.7	24.1	18.4	14.9	12.6	10.9	9.7	8.7	8.0
	60%	62.2	31.6	21.4	16.3	13.3	11.2	9.8	8.7	7.8	7.2
	70%	52.7	26.9	18.3	14.0	11.4	9.7	8.5	7.6	6.8	6.3
	80%	41.4	21.3	14.6	11.2	9.2	7.9	6.9	6.2	5.6	5.2

would earn if the price of the stock returns to its original level after the number of years indicated in Table 10.2. We noted above that if a stock had a 5 percent dividend yield and declined by 50 percent, it would achieve the same return in 14.9 years as a stock that had not declined at all. If after 14.9 years, the stock that fell 50 percent recovers to its original price, the annual return on the stock over those 14.9 years would rise to 15.24 percent, a return that is 50 percent greater than what the stock would have been had the stock not fallen in price.

The return accelerator worked for Philip Morris when the stock staged a recovery in late 2003. Many other tobacco stocks, such as R.J. Reynolds and BAT Industries (formerly British-American Tobacco), experienced similar return accelerations when their prices recovered. Had these firms not paid dividends, their returns would have been far lower.

Share Repurchases

In recent years firms have used retained earnings to buy their shares in the open market rather than paying dividends. As noted earlier, despite recent legislation that reduced tax on dividend income to the same level as capital gains, share repurchase is still a superior way of delivering returns to shareholders in the most tax-efficient way. Using earnings to buy shares instead

TABLE 10.3: ANNUAL RETURN WHEN PRICE RECOVERS

		Dividend Yield								
	1%	2%	3%	4%	5%	6%	7%	8%	9%	10%
10%	10.12%	10.24%	10.36%	10.47%	10.58%	10.69%	10.80%	10.91%	11.01%	11.11%
20%	10.27%	10.54%	10.80%	11.06%	11.31%	11.56%	11.80%	12.04%	12.27%	12.50%
30%	10.47%	10.92%	11.37%	11.81%	12.24%	12.67%	13.08%	13.49%	13.89%	14.29%
40%	10.73%	11.44%	12.14%	12.82%	13.49%	14.15%	14.80%	15.43%	16.06%	16.67%
50%	11.09%	12.16%	13.20%	14.23%	15.24%	16.23%	17.20%	18.15%	19.08%	20.00%
60%	11.63%	13.24%	14.81%	16.35%	17.86%	19.34%	20.79%	22.22%	23.62%	25.00%
70%	12.54%	15.03%	17.48%	19.87%	22.22%	24.53%	26.79%	29.01%	31.19%	33.33%
80%	14.36%	18.63%	22.82%	26.92%	30.95%	34.91%	38.79%	42.59%	46.33%	50.00%

Price Decline

of paying dividends results in higher share prices, but these higher share prices are not taxed until the shares are sold. As a result, investors can defer the tax on the shares and may escape the tax completely if they are included in a non-taxable estate.

If a firm repurchases the same dollar amount of shares as it pays as dividends, both the bear market protector and return accelerator will work. If the price of the stock goes down, the number of shares repurchased rises over time. This reduces the number of shares outstanding and raises both earnings per share and the share price. In the case of dividend reinvestment, the investor gains by accumulating more shares. When share repurchase takes place, the per-share earnings of the firm will rise and boost the price of the stock. In either case, the figures shown in Tables 10.2 and 10.3 will hold.

It appears that share repurchases accomplish the same wonderful results as dividend reinvestment with the extra bonus of receiving tax-deferred capital gains. But this is often not the case. In practice, it has been shown that management is not as committed to a policy of repurchasing shares as it is to paying dividends.[6] Once a cash dividend level is established, management is often reluctant to lower its level. Reducing the dividend is universally regarded as a bad signal from the firm, and the market often takes the shares down sharply when a reduction is announced.

In contrast, share repurchases often occur in a haphazard fashion. It is true that the price of a stock often responds favorably when management pledges that it will repurchase shares, but shareholders have a harder time monitoring whether management in fact is fulfilling its pledge. Various studies have concluded that a large percentage of announced share repurchases are not completed.[7] Often management finds other uses for earnings and not all of them are in the interest of shareholders.

So although from a theoretical standpoint share repurchase will result in an identical pattern of returns as dividend reinvestment, in reality share repurchases have rarely served as a steady source of shareholder return. It is more reliable to have the investor purchase her own shares with the dividends that management returns to the shareholders than for management to serve as a stand-in for the investment that shareholders can do on their own.

Dollar Cost Averaging

Some sharp readers may have noted that the return-boosting qualities of dividend reinvestment are similar to what occurs when investors undertake a dollar cost averaging investment strategy. Dollar cost averaging involves the investment of a given stake in the market over regular intervals of time. Like dividend reinvestment, dollar cost averaging takes advantage of the fact that when prices are lower and prospective returns are higher, more shares are purchased. Similarly, when prices are higher and prospective returns are lower, fewer shares are purchased.

Can dollar cost averaging substitute for dividend reinvestment? The answer is yes *if* the firm is a long-term survivor. If the firm is not, then buying an increasing number of shares as the price sinks will be a losing proposition. Firms that have not cut their dividend tend to be long-term survivors and are therefore well suited for the strategy discussed here. The more speculative the stock, the less likely it is to be a survivor and the less likely it is that dollar cost averaging will lead to superior returns.

Other Cash-Generating Investments

The bear market protector and return accelerator work not only for stocks that pay a high dividend. They will also work with any investment that provides investors a large cash return. Other high-yielding investments, such as certain real estate investment trusts (REITs) or high-yielding (junk) bonds, qualify.

REITs are corporations whose income is derived from the ownership of real estate assets. REITs have special tax characteristics. If they pay out at least 90 percent of their income in the form of dividends to their shareholders, then the trusts are themselves exempt from corporate income taxes.[8] The average dividend yield from 1996 through 2003 for REITs has been 6.6 percent, more than four times that of the S&P 500 over that same period.

Junk bonds are bonds issued by corporations whose credit standing is below investment grade. These bonds carry substantially higher interest rates than bonds of investment-grade corporations or most government bonds.

The reinvestment of dividends from REITs or the reinvestment of interest payments from junk bonds also makes those assets bear market protectors and return accelerators. During every recession, prices on junk bonds fall as the risk that a corporation will default rises. Yet investors who are reinvesting their interest income will purchase more bonds, so when interest rates ease and the spread between risky and safe bonds falls, the return accelerator works wonders.

REITs offered particularly high yields when they fell out of favor during the late 1990s during the boom in technology stocks. When they regained popularity, the extra shares invested boosted the returns on REITs, so from the mid-1990s through 2003 they had one of the highest returns of any asset class.

Summary

Over the past decade dividends have received short shrift as investors sought capital gains. But examining the history of stock returns reveals the importance of cash dividends. Dividends not only protect investors in bear markets but have boosted returns significantly when the market rebounds.

Virtually all the best-performing stocks from the original 1957 S&P 500 pay dividends, and most have a dividend yield above the average.

The returns on many stocks, such as the tobacco manufacturers, have benefited greatly from cash dividends despite the fact that litigation risk has depressed the price of these stocks. Reinvestment of dividends has also helped the energy sector. The next chapter examines the source of dividends and earnings, and discusses how to measure them.

CHAPTER ELEVEN

Earnings:

THE BASIC SOURCE OF SHAREHOLDER RETURNS

In recent years, substantial capital arguably was wasted on a number of enterprises whose prospects appeared more promising than they turned out to be . . . [The] amount of waste becomes unnecessarily large when the earnings reports that help investors allocate investment are inaccurate.

—Alan Greenspan, 2002

The stock market had waited for this announcement with great anticipation. At 4:15 p.m., fifteen minutes after the market closed, Intel, the world's largest manufacturer of microprocessors, would report its quarterly earnings. Wall Street traders and analysts watched Intel's numbers like hawks. The firm was considered a bellwether not only for the technology sector but for the entire economy.

The announcement flashed across the screen: operating earnings came in at 47 cents a share, 5 cents above expectations, but those earnings excluded acquisition-related expenses, one-time charges for purchased R&D, and the amortization of goodwill. Reported earnings, or net income, the official earnings figure sanctioned by the Financial Accounting Standards Board (FASB), was actually much lower than expected.

But the market cared little about the official figure and focused on operating earnings because that is the number that analysts and Wall Street forecast. In response to the better-than-expected operating earnings, the price of Intel's shares surged in after-hours trading.

What is going on here? Why is the market ignoring official earnings and looking instead at an earnings figure that is neither defined nor sanctioned by the FASB? More important, what earnings measure should investors use to estimate the profitability of a firm?

Measurement of Earnings

Everyone who is into stocks talks about earnings because everyone knows that earnings drive stock prices. But when economists or analysts start discussing the details of these earnings, most investors' eyes begin to glaze over. Descriptions of deferred expenses, restructuring charges, pro forma earnings, pension costs, or accounting for employee stock options either bring up bad memories of a college accounting course or seem too complicated to be worth figuring out. For that reason I would not blame any reader who wants to jump to the next chapter to learn about the future of our economy and financial markets. But if you will take a few minutes to read this chapter, you will find some very worthwhile information that not only helps you pick stocks but also understand some critical issues impacting public policy and your pocketbook.

One of these issues, whether employee stock options should be expensed, has even moved into the political arena and sparked heated debate in the U.S. Senate. Technology firms have organized public demonstrations claiming that their workers would lose the very incentives that are critical to maintaining U.S. leadership in technology if these FASB proposals go through.

Another issue, how firms treat pension costs, is critical to whether pension benefits that corporations have promised to their retired workers will actually materialize. News reports are filled with the huge deficit of the Pension Benefit Guaranty Corporation, a government-sponsored enterprise that insures the pension of 55 million workers. Some fear that looming pension defaults could turn into another savings-and-loan fiasco, costing taxpayers hundreds of billions of dollars.

Are Current Earnings Real?

Robert Arnott, editor of the *Financial Analyst Journal,* clearly believes that corporate America's profit numbers are deceptive. In a debate with me in 2004, he said:

> I believe current reported earnings have a lot of fluff. [If we use proper accounting for pension funds] there goes between 15 percent and 20 percent of S&P earnings. If management stock options are fully expensed, there

goes another 10 percent to 15 percent of S&P earnings. So I would argue that 25 percent or thereabouts of S&P earnings are fictitious.[1]

If 25 percent of earnings are "fictitious" then investors are paying much more for stocks than they think and forward-looking prospects for the equity market are indeed poor.

In contrast, I do not believe that the overall earnings data that companies report materially misrepresent the profitability of the great majority of firms. There are biases that work in both directions, as I will show later in this chapter. If one is careful, earnings data do point in the right direction.

But in a nod to the skeptics, investors should indeed scrutinize earnings, particularly from firms that issue employee stock options or have large pension obligations. Standard & Poor's has made that scrutiny easier with its calculation of core earnings, a new earnings concept that I applaud and will also discuss later in this chapter. Examination of S&P core earnings reveals that employee stock options are concentrated in technology firms, while pension obligations are mainly found in older industrial firms, such as automobiles, airlines, and some energy companies.

Earnings Concepts

Earnings, which is sometimes called net income or profits, is simply the difference between revenues and costs. But the determination of earnings is not just a "cash in minus cash out" calculation, since many costs and revenues, such as capital expenditures, depreciation, and contracts for future delivery, extend over many years. Furthermore, some expenses and revenues are one-time or extraordinary items, such as capital gains and losses or major restructurings that do not give a good picture of the ongoing or sustainable earnings that are so important in valuing a firm. Because of these issues, there is no single "right" concept of earnings.

There are two principal ways that firms report their earnings. Net income or reported earnings are those earnings sanctioned by the FASB, an organization established in 1973 to establish accounting standards. These standards are called generally acceptable accounting principles or GAAP accounting. These are the earnings that appear in the annual report and are filed with government agencies.[2]

The other, more generous, concept of earnings is called operating earnings. Operating earnings represent ongoing revenues and expenses, omitting unusual items that occur on a one-time basis. For example, operating earnings often exclude restructuring charges (e.g., expenses associated with a firm closing a plant or selling a division), investment gains and losses, inventory write-offs, expenses associated with mergers and spin-offs, and depreciation of goodwill, among others.

Operating earnings are what Wall Street watches and what analysts forecast. The difference between the operating earnings the firm reports and what analysts expect them to report drives stocks during the "earning season," which occurs in the few weeks following the end of each quarter. When we hear that XYZ Corporation "beat the Street," it invariably means that its earnings came in above the average (or consensus) forecast of operating earnings.

In theory, operating earnings give a more accurate assessment of the long-term sustainable profits of a firm than reported earnings does. But the concept of operating earnings is not formally defined by the accounting profession, and its calculation involves much management discretion. As management has come under increasing pressure to beat the Street's earnings forecasts, they are motivated to "push the envelope" and exclude more expenses (or include more revenues) than are appropriate.

The data show the increased gap between reported and operating earnings in recent years. From 1970 to 1990, reported earnings averaged only 2 percent below operating earnings. Since 1991, the average difference between operating and reported earnings has widened to over 18 percent, nine times the previous average.[3] In 2002 the gap between the two earnings concepts widened to a record 67 percent.

During the latter phases of the bull market of the 1990s, some firms, particularly those in the technology sector, were rightly criticized for excluding too many expenses. For example, Cisco Systems wrote off inventories that the firm couldn't sell and used highly favorable accounting techniques to make acquisitions appear far more favorable than they were.

Some firms advanced earnings concepts that involved even more extreme assumptions. Amazon.com declared it was profitable in 2000 on a pro forma basis if the interest on nearly $2 billion of debt was ignored. This is like saying my vacation home doesn't cost me anything as long as I ignore my mortgage payments. Clearly standards had to be tightened.

The Employee Stock Option Controversy

One of the most controversial issues is accounting for employee stock options. In the last chapter we spoke of the options culture that technology firms, particularly Microsoft, fostered in the 1980s and 1990s. Employee stock options gave workers a right to buy stock at a given price if they worked for the firm for a given period of time. As I noted in Chapter 9, the proliferation of management stock options began after the IRS ruled that payment by options did not violate the compensation limitations set by Congress.

We have already showed that management stock options discourage dividends. But there was yet another reason why stock options became so popular. Not only did they bypass certain restrictions on management compensation, but most stock options, when granted, did not have to be accounted for as an expense in the firm's profit statements. Instead options were expensed if and when these options were exercised, which may be years after they are granted.

This convention, vigorously supported by technology firms, was allowed by the rules established years ago by the FASB. The board's position on options generated much debate within both the academic and professional communities. In 2000 the FASB reversed its position and, following the lead of the International Accounting Standards Board, decided that options should be expensed when granted. In 2004, expensing options would lower S&P 500 earnings by 5 percent, but earnings of the option-laden technology sector would fall substantially.

Technology firms lobbied Congress to block the FASB from instituting those rules. In one of the more shameful incidents of congressional meddling, Senator Joseph Lieberman of Connecticut led the Senate in 1993 to an 88–9 nonbinding "sense of the Senate" resolution disapproving FASB's proposal. After this vote, the FASB backed down on its proposed rule change.

But after the technology bubble broke, the FASB revisited the issue and set 2005 as the year that firms must expense options. As of this writing, technology firms are still seeking congressional help to block this rule.

Why Stock Options Should Be Expensed

On this issue, the FASB is right and the technology industry and the politicians that support them are wrong. Nobody put the case for expensing options better than Warren Buffett, who stated in his 1992 annual report well before this issue took center stage: "If stock options are not a form of compensation, what are they? If compensation is not an expense, what is it? And if expenses shouldn't go into the income statement, where in the world should they go?"[4]

Options should be expensed when issued because earnings should reflect the firm's best determination of the sustainable flow of profits— profits that could be paid out as dividends to shareholders. If employees were not issued options, their regular cash compensation would have to be raised by the value of the options forgone. Whether the compensation is paid by cash, options, or in candy bars, it represents an expense to the firm.

When an option is exercised, the firm sells new shares to the option holder at a discounted price determined by the terms of the option. These new shares will reduce the per-share earnings and is called the dilution of earnings. Current shareholders are giving up part of the firm's profits to new shareholders who, through options, purchased the shares at below-market prices.

CRITICS OF OPTION EXPENSING

Some argue that options should not be expensed if management repurchases sufficient shares in the open market to offset the new shares issued when options are exercised. In this case there will be no dilution. But this argument ignores that fact that the funds used to buy back shares could have been distributed to shareholders or otherwise used to enhance shareholder value.

Critics of expensing also ask what happens if the option is expensed and then the stock price goes down and the option is never exercised. In that case the option expense would be reversed and be counted as a one-time or extraordinary gain. On the other hand, if the stock price goes up and the option is exercised for more than the expense recorded at the time of issuance, then the firm should take an additional extraordinary expense.

Critics also maintain that employee options cannot be properly valued. This is fallacious. Modern option pricing models can value options as well as, if not better than, the thousands of other estimates that go into an income statement, such as the useful life of capital expenditures, the market value of illiquid assets, or the write-down of intangible assets.

RISKS TO STOCKHOLDERS

There is a favorable side of options. The issuance of employee stock options reduces the risk borne by shareholders. If the firm experiences poor earnings and the share price declines, then the options will expire worthless and the firm, if it had expensed them, would realize a gain by reversing the expense. On the other hand, if there is good news and the share price rises, then the option will be exercised and per share earnings will decline because of the dilution.

The risk that employees shoulder when they accept options instead of cash compensation reduces the risk to the outside shareholders. This means that a firm that fully expenses the fair value of options paid to employees should, all other things being equal, be valued slightly more than firms that pay an equivalent amount of cash in lieu of options.

But this also means that much of the upside of many technology stocks that heavily issue employee stock options is enjoyed first by the employees, not the outside shareholders. This is an important consideration not always appreciated by those buying stocks in this option-saturated sector.

FIRMS EXPENSING OPTIONS

As of mid-2004, 176 firms in the S&P 500, representing over 40 percent of the market capitalization, have decided to expense options.[5] Coca-Cola was one of the first large firms to eliminate its employee stock plan. Microsoft terminated its employee stock option plan in 2003, substituting stock grants for dividends.

Might Warren Buffett's influence have a bearing on these cases? Buffett is a major stockholder of Coca-Cola and has struck up a close friendship with Bill Gates, chairman of Microsoft. Whatever the reason, the tide of professional opinion is clearly moving toward expensing as the FASB proposes.

Employees do not need options to motivate them to work for tech firms. Clearly in the 1990s workers thought options were the guaranteed road to riches. But the decline in the market has shattered many of those dreams. For employees, accepting options in lieu of cash is like accepting pay in lottery tickets. When they saw others winning, it looked like a good idea. But in the long run, these options are a risk that many employees can ill afford.

Controversies in Accounting for Pension Costs
DEFINED-BENEFIT AND DEFINED-CONTRIBUTION PLANS

Almost as contentious as the treatment of options is the accounting treatment of pension costs. There are two major types of pension plans: defined-benefit (DB) plans and defined-contribution (DC) plans.

Defined-contribution plans, which gained enormous popularity in the 1990s bull market, place both the employee's and employer's pension contributions directly into assets that are owned by the employees. In these plans, the firm does not guarantee any benefits. In contrast, in defined-benefit plans the employer spells out the income and health care benefits that will be paid and the assets backing these plans are not chosen by or directly owned by individual employees.

Under government regulations, DB plans must be funded. This means the firm must place aside assets that will cover the expected benefits associated with these plans. In contrast, in DC plans, the risk that the value of the plan at retirement will not cover retirement expenses is taken by the employees, and they must decide where to place their investment dollars.

There were two reasons for the tremendous increase in the popularity of the defined-contribution plans over the past two decades. One was the great bull market of the 1990s that made many employees believe that they could obtain a better return on their own investments than the benfits promised by the firm.

But a second reason was that contributions in a DC plan were immediately vested, that is, became the property of the employee. If an employee left the firm, he could take his 401(k) assets with him to another job. In contrast, it normally takes a number of years before the benefits of a DB plan belong to the employee. If an employee left the firm before these benefits became vested, then no benefits would be received.

PROBLEM AND RISKS IN DEFINED BENEFIT PLANS

Current rules for calculating the returns on the assets backing defined benefit plans are generous to the corporations. FASB allows firms to choose their own estimate of the rate of return on the assets in their portfolio, and often these estimates are too high. These estimated returns are credited to income whether they are earned or not. Furthermore, if the value of the assets falls below the pension liabilities (and the fund is called underfunded), FASB allows firms to close this gap over a substantial period of time.

While the government requires firms to build a fund for retirement income benefits, it does *not* require them to fund for other pension-related benefits, particularly health benefits. In 2003 a Goldman Sachs analyst estimated the health care liabilities of the three Detroit automakers at $92 billion, roughly 50 percent greater than their combined market capitalizations.[6]

Most investors are fully cognizant of these unfunded liabilities and have taken down the value of the auto manufacturers, as well as that of other firms with large underfunded pension plans. In March 2003, the twenty-five companies identified as having the most serious pension-funding issues comprised only 1.4 percent of the market value of the S&P 500. The bankruptcies of the steel manufacturers and airlines over the last decade are related to their pension obligations.

Since virtually all pension plans started in the last twenty years are defined-contribution plans, the corporate pension problem will disappear over time as the risk of funding retirement is shifted to individuals instead of corporations. Nevertheless, it behooves investors to take a close look at the stock of firms with large defined-benefit plans, as they can be a serious claim on future earnings.

Standard & Poor's Core Earnings

The dismay over the treatment of pension and options and the ever-widening definition of operating earnings led Standard & Poor's in 2001 to propose a uniform method of calculating earnings that they called core earnings. The objective was to define and measure earnings from a firm's principal or core businesses and to exclude from earnings revenues or expenses that are incurred for other reasons. Core earnings expenses employee stock options, recalculates pension costs, and excludes unrelated capital gains and losses, goodwill impairments, and one-time litigations gains and losses, among others.

One cannot underestimate the importance of finding a good measure of sustainable earnings. A typical firm in today's market sells for about twenty times yearly earnings. This means that only 5 percent of its price depends on what happens in the next twelve months, and 95 percent of its price depends on what happens after that. That is why when we calculate

earnings, accounting decisions should distinguish between any one-time
gains and losses that are not expected to be repeated and those that have
implications for future profitability. This goal led Standard and Poor's to
develop core earnings.

This was an unusual and bold stance taken by a nonregulatory, private-
sector firm that is the keeper of the world's most replicated benchmark,
the S&P 500 Index. The *New York Times* called core earnings one of the
best ideas in 2002.[7] Warren Buffett applauded S&P's stance, stating in an
open letter, "Your move is both courageous and correct. In the future, investors will look back at your action as a milestone event."[8]

I also strongly support core earnings and applaud the work done by
David Blitzer, managing director and chairman of the Index Committee,
Robert Friedman, Howard Silverblatt, and others. Although I quibble with
their estimation of pension costs (a notoriously difficult accounting issue),
I believe core earnings makes a significant move in the direction of stan-
dardizing profit statements and is a very good way to measure a firm's
profitability.

Earnings Quality

Can a better read on earnings quality be profitable to investors?
Most certainly. One way to measure the quality of earnings is by examining a firm's *accruals,* which is defined as accounting earnings minus
cash flows.

A firm with high accruals may be manipulating its earnings and
this could be a warning of future problems. Alternatively, a firm that
has low accruals may be a sign that earnings are being conservatively
estimated.

Richard Sloan, a professor at the University of Michigan, determined
that a high level of accruals was related to subsequent low stock returns.[9]
Sloan found that from 1962 through 2001, the difference between the returns to firms with the highest quality earnings (lowest accruals) and the
poorest quality earnings (highest accruals) was a staggering 18 percent *per
year.* Further research indicated that despite the importance of accruals,
Wall Street analysts did not take this into account when forecasting future
earnings growth.[10]

Determining earnings will always be fraught with estimates, even if made in good faith. That is why cash flows, as well as dividends, are objective measures of firm profitability that must supplement earnings data.

Earning Biases: Up and Down

The accounting treatment of pensions and employee stock options overestimates corporate earnings. But there are accounting conventions that work in the opposite direction.

For example, research and development costs are routinely expensed although there is good reason to capitalize these expenditures and then depreciate them over time. This means that the reported earnings of firms with a high level of R&D expenditures, such as the pharmaceutical industry, may be understating their true earnings.

Take Pfizer, the largest drug stock in the world and one of the five largest companies in the S&P 500 in 2004. In 2003, Pfizer spent $7.6 billion on research and development for drugs and almost $3 billion on plants and equipment. Governed by current accounting rules, Pfizer deducted from its earnings 5 percent of the $3 billion it spent on plant and equipment as depreciation, as the remainder would be deducted over the useful life of these assets.

But 100 percent of the $7.6 billion Pfizer spent on research and development was deducted from its current earnings. This is because Pfizer's R&D is not considered an "asset" in accounting and must be expensed when the expenditures are made

Does this make sense? Is Pfizer's R&D less of an asset than its property, plants, and equipment? Considering Pfizer's value largely stems directly from the patents it gains through its research and development expenditures, this accounting treatment seems to cast too negative a shadow on Pfizer's performance.

Leonard Nakamura, an economist at the Federal Reserve Bank of Philadelphia, concurs. He stated, "It's really those [R&D] expenditures that are going to drive long-run corporate performance."[11] Current earnings practices understate the future earnings potential of industries with extensive research and development.

Another understatement of earnings comes from the treatment of interest expenses. Full interest expenses are deducted from corporate earnings even though inflation, which raises interest costs, causes a corresponding reduction in the real value of corporate debt. In inflationary times, the impact of rising prices on fixed corporate liabilities could be substantial.

The bottom line is that not all conventional accounting practices overstate corporate earnings.

A Final Word and a Look to the Future

This chapter evaluates corporate earning practices. While it is true there is some "fluff" in reported earnings, on balance, the earnings data for the entire economy are not materially misleading.

The inherent ambiguities in calculating earnings support the case for paying close attention to dividends. If a firm pays a dividend, you know what you are getting. It is much harder to fake a dividend payment than it is to misrepresent an earnings statement.

Although there is much justifiable concern about management manipulating earnings data, before we shake our fingers at these companies, we should know that the U.S. government plays accounting tricks with its pension programs that would never pass muster with any corporation or regulatory body. Social Security and Medicare have unfunded liabilities that measure in the tens of *trillions* of dollars, dwarfing those of the corporate sector. These shortfalls pose a much larger risk for our economy than underfunded corporate pension plans and are the subject of the next section of this book.

PART FOUR

The Aging Crisis and the Coming Shift in Global Economic Power

CHAPTER TWELVE

Is the Past Prologue?

THE PAST AND FUTURE CASE FOR STOCKS

I have but one lamp by which my feet are guided, and that is the lamp of experience. I know no way of judging of the future but by the past.

—Patrick Henry, 1775

Paul Samuelson, a Nobel Prize–winning economist and my graduate-school mentor, once said, "You have but one sample of history." And the history that we have all lived through is replete with twists and turns that would never be repeated if we could run the world again.

Yet history is all we have. And history must have value, since our brains are programmed to learn by observing the past. Studying how markets have reacted to past events gives us insights into how they will behave in the future.

It is with these thoughts in mind that in the early 1990s I began collecting long-term historical data on U.S. stocks and bonds with the goal of discerning whether there were any trends that I could use to predict future returns. The data I analyzed showed that since 1802, the after-inflation rate of return on a diversified portfolio of common stocks was between 6.5 and 7 percent per year over all long-term periods. This finding served as the foundation of my book *Stocks for the Long Run*. There I wrote:

> The long-term stability of these returns is all the more surprising when one reflects on the dramatic changes that have taken place in our society during the last two centuries. The United States evolved from an agricultural to an industrial economy and now to a postindustrial service- and technology-oriented economy. The world shifted from a gold standard to a paper money standard. And information, which once took weeks to cross the country, can now be transmitted instantaneously and broadcast

simultaneously around the world. Yet, despite mammoth changes in the basic factors generating wealth for shareholders, equity returns have shown an astounding persistence.[1]

But looming in the future are changes more fundamental and long-lasting than all the crises that have confronted our economy in the past. The "astounding persistence" of long-term equity returns that I referred to above is threatened by an unprecedented demographic realignment—the age wave—that will soon impact the world economy. The dramatic increase in the number of retirees and the pending sale of trillions of dollars of stocks and bonds threatens to crush asset prices and drown the baby boomers' hopes of a comfortable and lengthy retirement.

Before analyzing the reality of this threat, it is important to review the historical case for equities in light of new historical data.

Historical Asset Returns

Figure 12.1 is the single most important graph that I have produced from my past studies of financial market returns. It displays the total cumulative return (including capital gains, dividends, and interest) on stocks, long-term government bonds, Treasury bills, gold, and the dollar over the last two centuries after the effects of inflation have been removed.

A single dollar invested in stocks in 1802 grows to $597,485 of purchasing power by the end of 2003, far ahead of the $1,072 in bonds or $301 in Treasury bills. And a single dollar of gold bullion, an asset so beloved by many investors, would be worth only $1.39 two centuries later after the effects of inflation are removed. The cumulative effect of inflation has been substantial; the dollar that we hold today can buy only 7 cents' worth of what it commanded two centuries earlier.

The dominance of stocks over other assets is overwhelming. Swings in investor sentiment, as well as political and economic crises, can throw stocks off their long-term path, but the fundamental forces generating economic growth have always enabled equities to regain their footing. Despite our history of depressions, wars, financial panics, and most recently the terrorist attacks and scandals that we faced in 2001 and 2002, the resiliency of stock returns is indisputable.

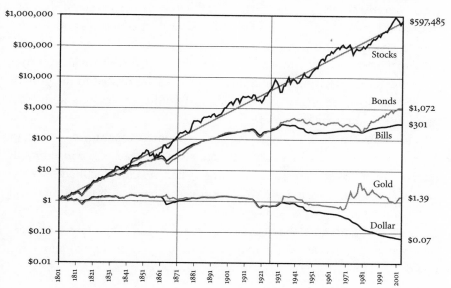

FIGURE 12.1: TOTAL REAL RETURN INDEXES 1802–2003

Siegel's Constant: 6.5 to 7 Percent Real Equity Returns

The most important statistic culled from these data is the long-term average after-inflation rate of return on stocks. That return has ranged between 6.5 and 7 percent over all long-term periods examined. This return means that investors' wealth, measured in purchasing power, has doubled on average every decade over the last two centuries in the stock market.

It matters not if you take the early period of U.S. economic development, from 1802 to 1870; the middle period, from 1871 to 1926, when comprehensive data on stock returns, dividends, and earnings became available; the period since 1926, which includes the worst stock crash and the Great Depression; or even the period since the end of the Second World War, when all the inflation our country has suffered has occurred. Real stock returns during all these periods remained between 6.5 and 7 percent. No other asset—not bonds, not Treasury bills, not gold, and certainly not the dollar—displays anywhere near the constancy of the real return on stocks.

I was flattered when Andrew Smithers, a British money manager, and

Stephen Wright, a professor at Cambridge University, authors of *Valuing Wall Street*, named the long-run equity return "Siegel's constant." They found it remarkable, just as I had, that this return has persisted through the radical transformations of both the American economy and society over the past two centuries.

The reason why the real equity return falls just short of 7 percent is not well understood. Certainly the returns on stocks are related to the growth of the economy, the quantity of capital, the liquidity of stocks, and the risk premium required by investors.

The return on fixed-income assets, the major competitor to stocks in investors' portfolios, told a very different story. Instead of a constant real return, the after-inflation return on bonds had steadily declined over the last two centuries. During the entire 200-year period, average annual real bonds returns, at 3.5 percent, are barely one-half of real stock returns. Treasury bills and other short-term money market assets averaged 2.9 percent real return, while gold managed a bare 0.1 percent return above the rate of inflation.

The Equity Risk Premium

What accounts for the premium return that stocks earn over bonds? At the most basic level, stock market returns depend on the willingness of investors to abandon the short-term safety of fixed-income assets and assume the risk of stock investing.

Such risks will not be undertaken freely. Investors must be compensated to take on risk, to give up, as the proverb says, a bird in the hand today for the chance to obtain two in the bush tomorrow. The extra return that stocks earn above safe investments, such as government bonds, is called the *equity risk premium*.

Over the past two hundred years, the equity risk premium has averaged about 3 percent.

Mean Reversion of Equity Returns

Very few disagree that stocks have higher returns than bonds in the long run. But many still shun stocks because of their higher volatility. Yet the risk of stocks is critically dependent on the time period over which you hold equities.

Go back to Figure 12.1. A statistical trend line has been drawn through the cumulative stock returns. Note how closely real stock returns cling to the trend line. This tendency of the stock market to follow the trend indicates what statisticians call the *mean reversion* of equity returns. Mean reversion refers to a variable that can be quite volatile in the short run but far more stable over longer periods. An example of a mean-reverting series is average rainfall, which can vary substantially day to day but is far more stable month to month.

Mean reversion completely changes the way that investors should look at risk. This is shown in Figure 12.2. The bars in Figure 12.2 show the risk (measured as the standard deviation) of the average after-inflation returns of stocks, bonds, and Treasury bills over all one-, five-, ten-, twenty-, and thirty-year periods from 1802 through 2003.

Over short periods, stocks are undoubtedly riskier than bonds. But as the holding period increases to between fifteen and twenty years, the riskiness of stocks falls below that of fixed-income assets. And over thirty-year periods, stock risk falls to less than three-quarters that of bonds or bills. As the holding period increases, the risk of average stock returns falls nearly twice as fast as fixed-income returns.

The reason for this surprising result is the instability of the rate of inflation. Inflation afflicts real bond returns far more than real stock returns. Bonds are promises to pay dollars, not goods or purchasing power. Only recently has the U.S. Treasury issued inflation-indexed bonds that adjust bond return for inflation, but these bonds constitute a small fraction of the total fixed income market.

Stocks, on the other hand, are claims on real assets, such as property, machines, factories, and ideas. Over time the price of these assets will rise with inflation. The behavior of equity returns confirms that over long periods of time, stocks fully incorporate realized inflation, while bonds, by their very nature, cannot.

This evidence supports the proposition that stocks, with their superior returns and lower long-term risk, should be the cornerstone of all long-horizon portfolios. Bonds are demanded by those wanting refuge from the short-term volatility of the stock market and therefore offer much lower

FIGURE 12.2: AVERAGE ANNUAL RISK
OF AFTER-INFLATION RETURNS

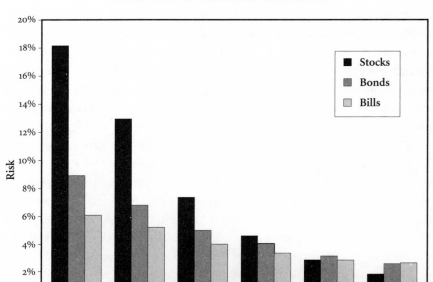

returns. But bonds do not hedge the inflation risk that is inherent in our paper money economy, where long-term changes in the price level are unpredictable.

Worldwide Equity Returns

When I published *Stocks for the Long Run* in 1994, some economists questioned whether my conclusions, drawn from data from the United States, might overstate equity returns measured on a worldwide basis.

Several economists emphasized the existence of a *survivorship bias* in international returns, a bias caused by the fact that long-term returns are intensively studied in successful equity markets, such as the United States, but ignored in markets such as Russia or Argentina, where stocks have faltered or disappeared outright.[2] This bias suggested that stock returns in the

United States were unique and perhaps historical equity returns in other countries were lower.

Three U.K. economists examined the historical stock and bond returns from sixteen countries over the past century and put to bed concerns about survivorship bias. Elroy Dimson and Paul Marsh, professors at the London Business School, and Michael Staunton, director of the London Share Price Database, published their research in a book entitled *Triumph of the Optimists: 101 Years of Global Investment Return.* This book provides a rigorous yet readable account of worldwide financial market returns in sixteen separate countries.

Despite the major disasters visited on many of these countries, such as war, hyperinflation, and depressions, all sixteen countries offered substantially positive, after-inflation stock returns. Furthermore, fixed-income returns in countries that experienced major wartime dislocations, such as Italy, Germany, and Japan, were decidedly negative, so that the superiority of equities relative to other financial assets was decisive in all countries.

Figure 12.3 shows the average annual real stock, bond, and bill returns of the sixteen countries analyzed from 1900 through 2003.[3] Real equity returns ranged from a low of 1.9 percent in Belgium to a high of 7.5 percent in Sweden and Australia. Stock returns in the United States, although quite good, were not exceptional. U.S. stock returns were exceeded by the returns in Sweden, Australia, and South Africa. And the average real return on stocks worldwide is not far from the U.S. return.[4]

When all the information was analyzed, *Triumph of the Optimists* concludes "that the US experience of equities outperforming bonds and bills has been mirrored in all sixteen countries examined. . . . Every country achieved equity performance that was better than that of bonds. Over the 101 years as a whole, there were only two bond markets and just one bill market that provided a better return than our *worst* performing equity market."[5]

Furthermore, "While the US and the UK have indeed performed well . . . there is no indication that they are hugely out of line with other countries. . . . . Concerns about success and survivorship bias, while legitimate, may therefore have been somewhat overstated [and] investors may have not been materially misled by a focus on the US."[6]

This last statement is of extreme importance. More studies have been made of the U.S. equity markets than of any other country in the world.

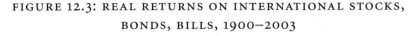

FIGURE 12.3: REAL RETURNS ON INTERNATIONAL STOCKS,
BONDS, BILLS, 1900–2003

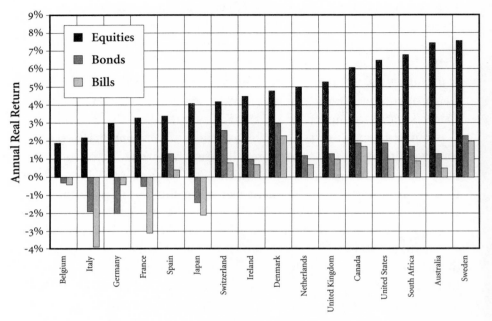

Dimson, Staunton, and Marsh are saying that the results found in the United States have relevance to all investors in all countries. The superior performance of U.S. equities over the past two centuries is not a special case. Stocks have outperformed fixed-income assets in every country examined, often by an overwhelming margin. International studies have reinforced, not diminished, the case for equities.

Is the Past Prologue?

Despite stocks' outstanding historical record, there are those who claim that looking at the past can be positively misleading. They claim that the most optimistic case for stocks, or in fact for any asset class, is always made at the absolute top of the market, when the returns looking backward are so good but returns looking forward are so abysmal.

There is much truth to this argument. For example, the past returns on

Japanese stocks were extraordinary if measured in December 1989, when the Nikkei average hit 39,000. In the 1980s, annual returns on Japanese stocks soared to nearly 30 percent per year, and international portfolios based on historical risk and return analysis allocated a large fraction to Japanese stocks, particularly the Japanese banking sector. But the Japanese market was on the verge of a great bear market; fourteen years later, the Japanese stocks were less than one-quarter of their level at the market peak. Similarly if you examined historical returns of U.S. market sectors in January 2000 and extrapolated the lessons of the past, all your money would no doubt be put in Internet stocks that had stratospheric returns. Two years later, you would be lucky to be left with ten cents on your dollar.

The Demographic Challenge

Are these wrongheaded predictions happening again? Will the case for equities be destroyed by baby boomers who will soon begin to sell their stocks and bonds?

Robert Arnott, editor of the *Financial Analyst Journal* whose skepticism about earnings I noted in Chapter 11, flatly stated that the 2000–2002 decline was just the first roar of a long bear market. Arnott said:

> I would argue that the impact of demographics is now and that the breaking of the bubble and the ensuing bear market were the first lurch into a demographics-driven future. The immense bull market from 1975 to 1999—which turned $1 into $50—was also, most likely, largely demographics-driven. The number of retirees will soar so much in the coming 20 years that capital markets are already starting to look ahead to [poor returns].[7]

These demographic arguments clearly challenge the bullish case for stocks. The next three chapters of this book dissect the demographic challenge and what it means to the economy and the capital markets. Chapter 13 puts forward the stark demographic facts. There is little doubt that the developed world is going to see an unprecedented decline in the number of workers per retiree. If current trends are continued, this decline will bankrupt the U.S. Social Security and Medicare programs and bring about both a dramatic increase in the retirement age and reduction in the retirement period. Most important, this chapter shows that not only the Social

Security trust fund but also your personal assets are threatened by the age wave.

Chapter 14 will analyze the solutions currently proposed to counteract the age wave. One by one, the conventional solutions are examined and found wanting. Increased saving by the boomers, faster productivity growth in the developed countries, or even increased immigration will not alone solve the problem.

But one future development confronts and neutralizes the age wave: the rapid economic growth in the world's developing nations. I have determined that the economic development of China, India, and other emerging nations can indeed provide the aging nations with the goods and services that they need to enjoy a comfortable retirement.

I call this the global solution. The global solution simultaneously provides the world with sufficient goods and—just as important—the capital markets with sufficient buyers to support stock prices into the distant future.

Why am I confident that this solution will become reality? This is the subject of the last chapter of this section: the Global Solution: The True New Economy. The true spark that ignites economic growth comes from the spread of information, knowledge, and ideas to the largest number of people. The communications revolution and development of the Internet, the very inventions that caused so much pain to investors, are set to become the foundation of the most rapid economic growth that the world has ever known.

CHAPTER THIRTEEN

The Future That Cannot Be Changed:

THE COMING AGE WAVE

"It is said that the present is pregnant with the future."

—Voltaire

When it comes to predicting the future, economists, like those in every other profession, have notoriously poor records. John Kenneth Galbraith, an emeritus professor of economics from Harvard, said of his profession: "We have two classes of forecasters: Those who don't know—and those who don't know they don't know."

But there are professionals who know a lot about the future: demographers, who study population trends. The reason for their foresight is straightforward. If there are 20 million Americans currently between the ages of thirty and thirty-four, five years from now these same 20 million people will be between thirty-five and thirty-nine, and ten years from now they will be forty to forty-four years of age. Of course, as we go forward, the mortality of this population must be factored in, but mortality rates are very low until the population becomes considerably older.

Since we know the age profile today, we can predict with great accuracy the age profile in the future. Following the end of the Second World War, specifically between 1946 and 1964, there was a burst in the birth rate that leveled off and then declined to record low levels. The baby boom turned into a baby bust.

As a result, the wave of 80 million Americans that is the baby boom generation is edging toward a hoped-for lengthy and prosperous retirement at the same time the workforce is declining.

These facts are immutable. This is the future that cannot be changed.

Why Should Investors Care?

The impact of the age wave is enormous. The most visible repercussions of aging will be felt on public pension funds. Years ago the United States and most other developed countries set up Social Security and medical plans for their senior citizens. Starting in the next decade, the baby boom generation will put unprecedented strains on these government programs. And as bad off as the United States is, most European countries and Japan are in worse shape and have pension obligations that are far greater.

There is a looming problem of supply and demand in the capital markets reminiscent of an old Wall Street story. A broker recommends that his client buy a small speculative stock with good earnings prospects. The investor purchases the stock, accumulating thousands of shares at ever-rising prices. Patting himself on the back, he phones his broker, instructing him to sell all his shares. His broker snaps back, "Sell? Sell to whom? You're the only one who has been buying the stock!"

The words "Sell? Sell to whom?" could haunt the baby boomers in the coming years. Who will be the buyers of the trillions of dollars of assets that boomers have patiently accumulated over the past several decades? The generation that has swept politics, fashion, and the media in the last half of the twentieth century has been part of an age wave that threatens to drown the economy in financial assets. The consequences could be disastrous not only for the boomers' retirement, but also for the economic well-being of the entire population.

Peter Peterson, author of *Gray Dawn* and *Running on Empty*, has been sounding the alarm for years. He warns, "There's an iceberg dead ahead. It's called global aging, and it threatens to bankrupt the great powers."[1]

Peterson calculates that the developed countries have unfunded pensions of about $35 trillion and health care liabilities of at least twice that. As he says, "To paraphrase the old quiz show, this makes the global issue at least a '$64 trillion dollar question.'" He cautions that unless significant action is taken to rectify the crisis, "personal living standards will stagnate or decline."[2]

These demographic realities could spell disaster for the financial markets. The baby boomers must begin selling their assets to fund their retirement needs: family vacations with grandchildren, medical bills, and everyday living expenses. But assets such as stocks and bonds have no intrinsic value—you cannot eat your stock certificates. The only way their value can be realized is by selling them, and you can sell them only if there are enough willing buyers. These buyers have traditionally come from the working-age population, and in the past the number of these workers has been much greater than the number of retirees. Now, however, because of the baby bust, there are not nearly enough Generation Xers (the generation born in the late 1960s and 1970s) with sufficient wealth to absorb the boomers' substantial portfolio of stocks and bonds at the prices the boomers paid for them. With a lack of buyers, asset prices must fall, and they may fall dramatically.

Many investors do not understand the gravity of this situation. Some acknowledge that Social Security and Medicare may not be available to them when they retire, but they comfort themselves by believing that their own portfolio of stocks, bonds, and real estate is adequate to support them during their retirement.

But this confidence is unwarranted. The age wave impacts the value of personal assets just as it will impact the government pension and medical programs. If the age wave plays out as the pessimists assert, asset values will fall, the retirement age will rise, and benefits will be cut across the board. The "remarkable persistence" of strong equity returns that we reported in the previous chapter will be a relic of the past.

Because the age wave is the biggest threat to investors' wealth in the coming decades, this chapter spells out its origins and consequences in much greater detail. We will show how much the retirement age will have to increase so that retirees can maintain their consumption levels if current trends continue. We will also expose the public's misunderstanding of the Social Security trust fund and show why problems will arise well before that fund's assets are depleted. Finally, we shall discuss what actions investors should take if the age wave hits us with full force. This chapter will set the stage for a critical analysis of the many "solutions" offered to solve the Social Security crisis and related age wave problems.

The Aging World

The aging of the world's economy is taking place in nearly every developed country, especially in Europe and Japan. Take Germany, the world's third-largest economy. By 2030, people over sixty-five will account for almost half of the German adult population, compared to one-fifth now. The number of workers will fall by 25 percent. Japan's population will peak at about 125 million in just a few years, and by midcentury, according to the more pessimistic forecasts of the government, it will shrink to below 100 million, with the number of workers falling even more.[3]

Figure 13.1 shows the projection of the age distribution in Japan in 2005 and at the middle of this century. These data are based on the demographics data provided by the U.N. Demographic Project and constitute the most extensive compilation of population data ever assembled. The age data for Japan are equally applicable to many European countries such as Italy, Spain, and Greece.

By midcentury, the most populated five-year age bracket in these countries will be seventy-five to eighty years old. The number of people over eighty will almost equal those under twenty. Although centenarians are rare enough to be newsworthy today, by 2050 for every four children under

FIGURE 13.1: POPULATION PROFILE IN JAPAN
IN 2005 AND 2050

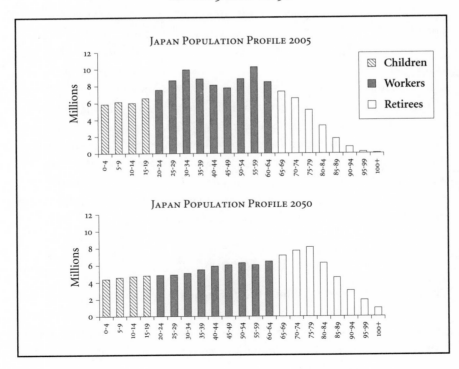

the age of five, there will be a Japanese man (or most probably a woman) over the age of one hundred.

The data for the United States, shown in Figure 13.2, are slightly more encouraging. The fertility rate, the number of children born to a woman, is the key variable that determines population growth. The rate needed to keep the population constant is about 2.1, slightly higher than 2 because of infant and childhood mortality.

Following the U.S. baby boom, the period of high births that occurred from 1946 to 1964, the fertility rate in the United States and Europe dropped below 2. But the European rate continued to fall, while the U.S. rate stabilized and is now just below the replacement rate. The U.S. fertility rate stabilized because U.S. baby boomers were having more children than their European and Japanese counterparts, and immigrants, with higher fertility rates, contributed to U.S. population growth. Nevertheless, there is a large

FIGURE 13.2: POPULATION PROFILE
FOR THE UNITED STATES IN 2005 AND 2050

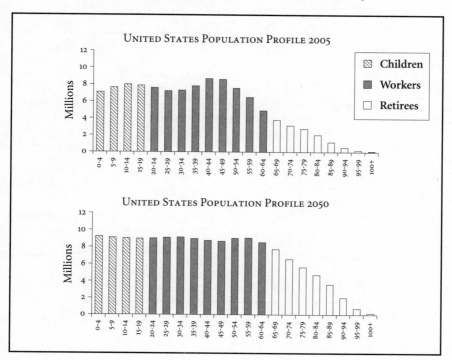

number of baby boomers who are now in their late forties and fifties and moving toward retirement.

The term "age wave," which has been applied to these bulges in population, is made visible in the population profiles in Figures 13.1 and 13.2. Beginning in less than a decade and continuing for the next twenty years, the baby boomers will move into retirement, collect pensions, cash in their assets, and consume goods, services, and especially medical care.

The Dearth of Workers

All the goods and services distributed to a given population must be produced by those who are in their working years. There is very limited ability to transfer output from one year to the next. This is where the problems lie: the working population is shrinking dramatically relative to the retired population. Take a look at Figure 13.3, which shows the number of workers

FIGURE 13.3: DECLINING WORKERS PER RETIREE
IN UNITED STATES AND JAPAN

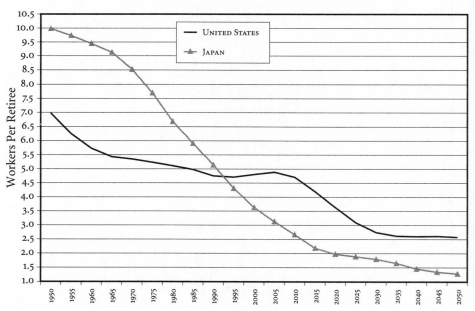

per retiree over the past fifty years and over the next fifty years in both Japan and the United States.[4]

In 1950, there were seven workers for every retired person in the United States. This shrank to 4.9 workers per retiree in 2005, and by 2050 it is expected to fall to 2.6 workers per retiree. In Japan the problem is even more severe. The number of workers per retiree was 10.0 in 1950 and 3.1 in 2005, and it is projected to fall to 1.3 by 2050. And these numbers assume that the retirement age in Japan is raised to sixty-five. If the retirement age remains in the low sixties, the number of workers will fall below the number of retirees. This will also happen in Spain, Italy, and a number of other European nations.

The Rise and Fall in Fertility

Why are we undergoing such extreme demographic changes? Economic forces and medical advances provide most of the explanation. Until recently, the world was forever young. Not only was life expectancy much shorter and mortality much higher, but children were viewed as prized assets: workers who could plow the land, fish the seas, and take care of the elderly.

Three hundred years ago, as North America was being settled, widows with children were much sought after. In 1776, the year America became an independent country, Adam Smith noted that women were "frequently courted as a sort of future. The value of children is the greatest of all encouragements to marriage." Today, single women with children are often spurned by potential suitors.[5]

In the twentieth century, as mortality was reduced through better nutrition and health care, populations in much of the world exploded. As late as 1970, Paul Ehrlich wrote the best-seller *The Population Explosion,* claiming that the rapidly rising population would strain the world's resources.

Ehrlich could be described as a modern Thomas Malthus, a nineteenth-century British economist who claimed that population increases condemn much of humanity to subsistence levels. Malthus believed the world was destined to experience a vicious circle: every technology improvement would lead to higher food output, which would lead to higher birth rates and more people, who would again exhaust available resources until starvation pushed the population down.

But the advances in the standard of living had an impact very different from what both Malthus and Ehrlich predicted. As economies developed and the level of incomes rose, adults decided to have fewer children, not more. The fertility rate fell dramatically in Europe from more than 2.5 in 1960 to less than 1.4 currently. And in some countries, such as Spain, Italy, and Greece, the level has fallen to between 1.1 and 1.3. Even the fertility rate of China has fallen, hastened by the Communist Party's one-child policies, from 6.1 in the late 1960s to 1.8 today.[6]

The reasons for the fall in fertility are not hard to find. In China it was the dictates of the Communist Party, but elsewhere, changing social norms and the shift in the nature of work from physical activity to intellectual activity favored women entering the labor force. As women's wages increased, the opportunity cost of staying home and raising children rose.

Preparing children for today's more highly skilled jobs requires extensive and expensive education. Even if tuition is paid for by the government, parental support is still needed. Furthermore, the increase in government pensions, such as Social Security, means that in their old age parents are less dependent on, and less likely to receive support from, their children.[7] As parents with sons and daughters in college already know, instead of being the prized assets that Adam Smith wrote about in 1776, children can become expensive burdens.

Rising Longevity

But the fact that parents are having fewer children is only one factor contributing to the age wave. People are living longer than ever before, and this rise in longevity means that individuals are living well past the historically accepted retirement age of sixty-five.

Longer life expectancies are nothing new, as death rates have generally been falling since the Industrial Revolution. Until the middle of the twentieth century, life expectancy rose primarily because infant and childhood deaths declined. Between 1901 and 1961, male life expectancy at birth rose by more than twenty years, but the life expectancy for men age 60 rose by less than two years.[8]

But now life expectancy is being extended by advances in medicine that treat, and sometimes cure, the afflictions of old age. The fastest growing age bracket today is those age one hundred and above. This helps explain why from 1961 onward, the increase in life expectancy for sixty-year olds rose at three times the rate of the previous sixty years. Looking forward to all of the advances in biotechnology and advanced medicine, the trend toward longer lives will likely accelerate.

The mapping of the human genome has spawned hopes that scientists are close to turning Ponce de Leon's dream of discovering the "Fountain of Youth" into a reality. Some scientists are debating whether the aging process can be slowed dramatically or even stopped.

James Vaupel, the director of the Max Planck Institute for Demographic Research, observed in the summer of 2000, "Half of the girls born today in Minneapolis, Tokyo, Bologna, and Berlin will probably celebrate the dawn of the twenty-second century as centenarians."[9]

Vaupel's projection is probably optimistic, although he will tell you he is "middle of the road."[10] But most demographers believe that most official U.S. government estimates of life expectancy, such as those made by the Social Security Administration and the trustees that project the health of that program, are far too low. For example, the Social Security Administration's forecast for U.S. life expectancy is eighty-one for both sexes in 2070, up only four years from the current seventy-seven.

In testimony before a Senate special committee on aging, Vaupel asked, "Is it realistic to assume that the United States will fail to catch up in half a century with expectations of life already exceeded in Japan and France? Is it realistic to assume that the United States will fall more than a decade behind Japan and France?"[11] These are very good questions. The increase in life expectancy forecasted by Social Security is far smaller than what has occurred in the past. Vaupel, with his colleague James Oeppen of Cambridge University, found that since 1840 life expectancy in the developed world has increased at a remarkably constant rate of 3 months per year, or 2.5 years per decade.[12] The increase has been remarkably stable and has shown no signs of abating. If this trend persists, life expectancy at birth will almost reach ninety by the middle of this century and hit ninety-five by 2070. Furthermore, the number of "old old," defined as those over eighty-five years of age, is likely to be two to three times as large as the 18 million predicted by the Social Security Administration.

These statistics mean that the predictions about the pending bankruptcy of public pension and medical care programs likely understate, by a wide margin, the magnitude of the aging problem.

Falling Retirement Age

While we are living longer, we are retiring earlier. In the past, men and women worked until they died or were too ill to work. In 1935, when Social Security was passed, the average retirement age was sixty-nine and the average life expectancy at age sixty-five was less than twelve years. Now the typical worker at age sixty-five lives another 17.9 years, and a far higher percentage of the working population reach retirement.[13] Yet the average retirement age has actually gone down from sixty-nine to sixty-three years.[14] Over the last fifty years there has been an ever-widening gap between retirement and death, and many today express their desire to retire even earlier.[15]

In Europe the decline in the age of retirement is even more extreme. In the early 1970s European governments lowered the minimum retirement age from sixty-five to sixty.[16] When doing this, most countries created no incentives for those considering retirement to stay in the workforce. A researcher for the Organisation for Economic Co-operation and Development (OECD) found that in eleven of twenty-six developed countries, a person age fifty-five who had worked for thirty-five years would receive the same pension as someone ten years older who had worked an extra ten years.[17] The incentives to retire earlier were so strong that Europeans responded en masse. In France, the proportion of men aged sixty to sixty-four in the workforce fell from about 70 percent to under 20 percent, and in West Germany it fell from over 70 percent to 30 percent.[18]

With the coming age wave the question is no longer whether these trends will continue but when they will be reversed. The question is how much longer people must work, not how much earlier they will retire, and if they do retire early, how much will their living standards have to decline.

The Social Security Crisis

How does the age wave impact government pension programs? I recall a number of years ago reading that the two most popular government programs in the United States over the past century were Social Security and the interstate highway system. Looking ahead, it seems that our highway system is in much better shape than our retirement system. Almost every American has driven on the interstate highway system, but tens of millions of baby boomers have yet to collect from Social Security and Medicare. As the age wave crests through retirement, the pressures put on our governmental pension systems will be worse than the worst traffic jam ever experienced on our interstate highways.

I can picture some of you reading this and thinking, "I don't especially care about the solvency of Social Security because I have enough wealth saved up in my retirement accounts to take care of my old age." But the truth is, you had better care. The forces that threaten the Social Security system threaten the assets of *all* pension plans, public and private. What happens with Social Security, especially the Social Security trust fund, will directly impact the levels of your wealth.

Social Security: A Perpetual Money Machine?

Let us stand back and try to understand what the Social Security system does and what policies can or cannot solve those problems. Social Security was passed in 1935 in the depths of the Great Depression as part of President Roosevelt's New Deal legislation. Social Security was designed as a "pay-as-you-go" system, which means that Congress decides on the level of benefits and then adjusts the tax rate or wages so that tax revenues will fund these expenditures.[19] The pay-as-you-go system worked well for many decades. Congress greatly expanded the Social Security benefits, but the number of workers was always growing to fund the system with moderate tax increases. As a result, retirees usually received far more benefits than they contributed in taxes, even granting a generous rate of return on the amount they paid into the system.

The Social Security system seemed like a perpetual money machine, year after year yielding a return on participants' contributions that were far greater than they could have received in the private market. Could this continue indefinitely? Believe it or not, it could. Paul Samuelson, America's first Nobel Prize winner in economics, made this point when he wrote:

> The beauty of social insurance is that it is *actuarially* unsound. Everyone who reaches retirement age is given benefit privileges that far exceed anything he has paid in. . . . How is this possible? . . . . Always there are more youths than old folks in a growing population. More important, with real

incomes growing at some 3 per cent per year, the taxable base upon which benefits rest in any periods are much greater than the taxes paid historically by the generation now retired. . . . A growing nation is the greatest Ponzi scheme ever contrived."[20]

Samuelson's reference to the Ponzi scheme refers to Charles Ponzi, an Italian immigrant who offered investment schemes that promised fantastic returns and paid off early investors with money put in by later investors. When this scam was uncovered, everyone demanded their money and the scheme collapsed.

But Social Security is a legal and a sustainable Ponzi scheme *as long as population and incomes are growing.* Then there will always be more coming into the system than money paid as benefits. But if the population and income fail to grow, the game is over.

The Social Security Trust Fund

Heeding the threatening demographic trends, President Reagan convened a blue-ribbon panel in 1982 to study the issue and recommend solutions. The commission, headed by Alan Greenspan, recognized that the baby boom was going to cause severe problems with a pay-as-you-go system down the road. As the baby boomers retired, tax rates would have to be boosted dramatically on younger workers to pay the ballooning retirement benefits of the boomer generation. Higher payroll taxes could set the stage for a generational conflict and discourage entry into the labor force at the same time as the number of workers decline.

The proposed solution was to abandon the pay-as-you-go system, raise current Social Security taxes above the current level of benefits, and use the excess to buy U.S. Treasury bonds. These bonds, which accrued interest at the ongoing market rate, would be placed in a special trust fund that could be sold to generate funds when the boomers retired. This would presumably avoid the need to impose crushing taxes on the working population in order to pay retirees benefits.

Congress abided by the Commission's recommendation and raised Social Security taxes sharply in 1983. The Social Security trust fund was designed to have sufficient bonds to keep Social Security solvent until well past the middle of this century, abiding by the seventy-five-year horizon that the trustees were obliged to use to measure the program's solvency.

But in the years following the commission's recommendations, fertility rates dropped, productivity lagged, and life expectancy increased beyond the commission's expectations. These trends meant the trust fund would not collect sufficient funds to pay the benefits promised. In their 2004 report, the trustees predicted that by 2018 the fund would begin selling its huge hoard of government bonds, and by 2042 these funds would be exhausted. In 2042, unless taxes were raised dramatically, Social Security payments would have to be cut by almost 30 percent.

But even this forecast is too optimistic. The day of reckoning of the Social Security system is actually much closer than 2042, the date when the trust fund runs dry. This is because hundreds of billions of dollars worth of government bonds will have to be sold into the market well before 2042 to meet the surging benefit levels. These sales from the trust fund will hit the market at the same time individual investors are trying to liquidate their own assets to fund their own retirement. This tidal wave of stocks and bonds hitting the market will have a huge impact on asset prices. This is why everyone who has wealth in stocks or bonds must care about what happens to Social Security and the age wave.

Investor Strategies if the Age Wave Hits

If the age wave hits full force, we can expect a significant impact on asset prices. Inflation will increase as the demand for goods by the retirees outstrips the dwindling supply produced by the decreasing number of workers. This will make conventional bonds, which pay a fixed-dollar coupon and principal, a very poor investment.[21] But stocks will not fare much better. It is true that stocks will weather inflation better than bonds, as corporate revenues will grow along with rising prices, but the shortage of workers will put upward pressure on wages, squeezing corporate profits and lowering the rates of return on equity capital.

Does this mean that investors should retreat to inflation hedges such as gold, silver, and perhaps natural resources? The short answer is no. As indicated in the last chapter, precious metals have provided investors no real return over long periods of time. Natural resources firms will not fare much better. The value of their land and energy reserves may keep up with the rate of inflation, but they will also be caught in the profits pinch as wages rise relative to the return on capital. Returns on real estate will not be any better as the aging of the population shrinks demand.

The best investment if the age wave strikes full force will be Treasury Inflation-Protected Securities, or TIPs. These securities, first offered in the United States in 1997, pay guaranteed fixed coupons and principal that are automatically adjusted by any changes in the price level.

When TIPs were first offered, their inflation-protected yield was 3 percent, a bit less than half the 6.8 percent average long-term real return on stocks. TIPs yields increased to 4 percent during the latter stages of the stock market boom, but they have subsequently fallen below 2 percent. If the age wave hits with full force, expect the TIPs yields to fall much further and their real yield will likely go below zero as everyone fights to preserve their capital. Certainly in a normal environment, TIPs returns are not competitive with stocks or real estate. But if the age wave strikes, these inflation-protected bonds will be the best of a bad lot.

What can be done, if anything, to prevent this depressing scenario from playing itself out both in the economy and in the financial markets? Is increased saving the answer? Higher payroll taxes? More immigration? Or is there something else, something far more hopeful, that can save us from drowning in the age wave? The answers will be found in the next two chapters.

CHAPTER FOURTEEN

Conquering the Age Wave:

WHICH POLICIES WILL WORK AND WHICH WON'T

"Results? Why, man, I have gotten a lot of results. I know several thousand things that won't work."

—Thomas Alva Edison

If current trends continue unabated, the developed world faces higher retirement ages, lower living standards, or a future where the old will fight with the young to get the benefits they believe they deserve. In the coming decade, these issues will spur political debate as the stark reality of underfunded public and private pension funds jolts investors and politicians to search for answers.

Pete Peterson, former secretary of commerce and author of the bestseller *Running on Empty,* advocates three measures: reduce benefits, increase taxes, and establish government-mandated savings accounts. He writes persuasively:

> Some of these reforms do require some sacrifices: yes, more taxes than we like to pay, and yes, fewer benefits than we expect. But these sacrifices are truly minor compared to what we have endured before in our history and to what we and our children are likely to endure tomorrow if we fail to live within our means.[1]

But are these really the only answers to the aging crisis? Clearly, reducing benefits will "solve" the problem, but that is a solution by default. And I believe the other measures advanced by Peterson also fall short. In fact, many of the espoused solutions to the aging crisis, such as increasing payroll taxes, increasing immigration, and even increasing the savings rate, will do little to alleviate the problem, and some, such as increasing taxes, will make the situation worse.

Understanding why these proposals won't work is the subject of this chapter. But don't throw your hands up in despair. There is a solution. You shall see that our economy, in contrast to what Peterson claims, is not "running on empty."

Modeling the Retirement Age

To study the impact of these proposed solutions I built a model of the world economy using population data from the U.N. Demographic Project. The model assumes that over time the output produced by the workers in an economy is sufficient to cover not only their own consumption but the consumption of the retirees as well. The model shows how the retirement age must rise to ensure enough goods are provided for all the retirees. When combined with assumptions about productivity growth, consumption patterns, and the aging of the population, the model provides a rich opportunity to study the dynamics of the world economy into the future.

On our current path, workers will have no choice but to work many more years than they do now if they wish to maintain their standard of living during retirement. Figure 14.1 shows how much longer Americans will have to work to achieve that goal.

Between 2005 and 2010, the trend of earlier retirement that has prevailed through modern history will be reversed. In the next several decades, not only will the retirement age be forced to increase from sixty-two to seventy-three, but that increase will be greater than the increase in life expectancy. Therefore, the time workers spend in retirement will decrease by nearly 25 percent. Because of their more severely aging populations, in Europe and Japan the retirement age must rise even faster.

These projections are based on a conservative estimate of the increase in life expectancy made by the U.N. demographers. If life expectancy increases at a more rapid rate, which many experts expect (see page 187), then the retirement age in the United States may need to rise to eighty or even higher.

Consequences of Earlier Retirement

Although some accept extending their working years as a natural consequence of a rising life expectancy, few realize how dramatic these changes

FIGURE 14.1: PAST AND PROJECTED U.S. LIFE EXPECTANCY
AND RETIREMENT AGE

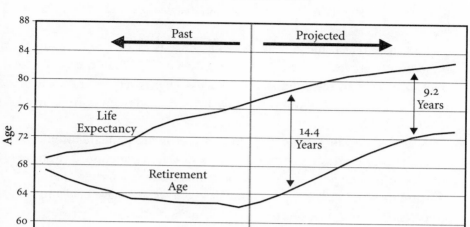

will be. Since the Industrial Revolution, workers have achieved shorter workweeks and longer retirements, and they view these developments as inherent benefits of economic progress.

In Europe, which has an older population than the United States, some of the public and private pension plans start paying retirees benefits in their fifties. A shift to a retirement age of seventy or more would be a dramatic turn of events. Even if workers accepted the increase in the retirement age, there are legitimate questions whether the older workforce would be competitive in the labor market and whether they could achieve the same productivity levels that are expected from younger workers.

The fact that demographic trends in the United States are significantly better than those in Europe or Japan should give Americans no solace. For many goods and services, the price is determined in a world market, and the retirees in Europe and Japan will be active bidders. Prices will be determined by the total demand for goods from retirees worldwide, not just demand in a single country.

What happens if Americans still insist on retiring at sixty-two, the current retirement age? Real asset prices will fall as boomers try to convert their stocks, bonds, and real estate into consumption goods. Retirees will not be able to generate nearly enough income from the sale of their assets to maintain a standard of living that they reached during their working years.

I estimate that if the current retirement age is maintained, the living standard of retirees who retire at midcentury will decline drastically to only 50 percent of the living standard they achieved at the end of their working life. Clearly few will accept this outcome, and many will be forced to return to work to raise their income.

A final option that could maintain retirees' living standards would be to sharply raise taxes on the future working-age population to transfer monies to the burgeoning number of retirees. But younger workers will demand to know why they are subsidizing retirees who have inadequately prepared for their own future. This will inevitably create a generational conflict that will manifest itself in a bitter political battle, pitting the large number of nonworking retirees against a smaller number of workers.

The three painful choices described here—increasing retirement age, accepting lower standards of living, or raising taxes on the working young—are inevitable unless other measures are taken. What can be done?

Greater Productivity Growth

Policies that increase the productivity of workers have the greatest potential to mitigate the impact of the age wave. Productivity, or output per hour worked, is the basic measure of our standard of living.[2] Increases in productivity raise incomes and boost the amount of goods and services available to both workers and retirees.

Productivity growth mitigates the problems caused by the age wave because, while workers both produce and consume more goods, the consumption of retirees remains relatively stable during retirement. This means the output associated with the productivity increases can be spread across a greater number of retirees.

Government pension programs reflect retirees' consumption patterns. While working, pension benefits are linked to average wages, but after retirement, pension benefits are indexed only to inflation. This is how Social Security and the great majority of private and governmental pension systems work around the world.[3] A boost of productivity acts like an increase in the number of workers and offsets the population imbalances caused by the age wave.

The Sources of Productivity Growth

If productivity is the key to solving the aging crisis, what policies can increase productivity? Throughout history, productivity was enhanced by the creation of new machines: the cotton gin, the steam engine, railroads, automobiles, and telephones. Since these machines required capital to build, and this capital had to come from savings, many assumed that increases in saving would spur capital formation and hence productivity growth. This is why economists suggest that the United States increase savings to increase productivity and mitigate the impact of the age wave.

But this hypothesis, that extra savings will significantly boost productivity, was put to the test in the mid-1950s by the pathbreaking work of Professor Robert Solow of the Massachusetts Institute of Technology, for which he received the Nobel Prize in 1987.[4] I studied under Professor Solow when I received my doctorate in economics at MIT, and I was fascinated with his finding that capital investment—all those machines, plants, and equipment that firms buy and utilize for production—is responsible for only a small part of the increase in productivity throughout history.

As noted above, most economists had previously thought that increases in the capital stock—the sum of all machines, factories, and other fixed assets—were the major source of productivity growth. But Solow's research showed that productivity growth primarily came from other sources such as invention, discovery, innovative management philosophies, or just plain old learning by doing. Most of these sources did not require heavy capital expenditures or higher savings.

When capital was needed in our entrepreneurial economy, venture capitalists always were able to attract funds for promising new ideas, no matter what the savings rate. The development of the Internet and the fiber-optic revolution began in the United States when our personal savings rate was extremely low. Japan, which has one of the highest savings rates in the world, had very low productivity growth in the 1990s, while the United States, with a low savings rate, had strong productivity growth.

Japan also shows that it is possible for countries to save too much and actually reduce living standards. This was considered a theoretical curiosity when I was studying at MIT. But recent evidence has convinced me that the high savings rate in Japan has done little to boost its economy. In the 1990s the Japanese government, in a vain attempt to stimulate economic activity, sharply boosted public investment in bridges and roads, but these had very low returns. There is also evidence that much of the investment undertaken by the private sector in Japan also had a low, if not negative, rate of return.[5]

If savings were the answer to our demographic problem, then Japan, the country with the highest savings rate in the developed world, should have absolutely no worry about the aging of its population. But that is not the case. Paul Hewitt, an economist who has researched global aging, declares, "Most of Japan's economic ills either arise directly out of, or are being exacerbated by its demography."[6] *The Economist* further states, "The bad news, however, is that even though the economy has sped up for a bit, Japan's runaway demographic trends still threaten to leave it in the dust."[7]

If increasing savings isn't the answer, what is? Paul Romer, an economist from Stanford University and founder of "new-growth" theory, suggests that the most important source of productivity growth is the stock of ideas and inventions. My own research supports this view. Very few innovations are developed from scratch, where no previous knowledge or information is assumed. In fact, most inventions are simply extensions, combinations, and rearrangements of past inventions.

Romer believes that to spur invention and productivity growth, the government should either grant tax subsidies for research or direct more of its own funds toward this end. But government-directed research has its own pitfalls. Take the significant funds devoted to government-directed research in the U.S. space program. Putting a man on the moon was a wondrous technological achievement that gave Americans great pride in our country. But it is arguable whether the NASA space program has delivered significant private benefits, especially compared to a similar amount of funds funneled into private research. Academic research also suggests that indicative planning, a practice whereby the government sector tries picking "winning" industries and directs public funds to that end, has been unsuccessful.[8]

Historically, bursts of innovation, from the railroad to the automobile to the Internet, have come from the private sector, and investors willingly fund projects believed to be commercially profitable. Even though private capital markets go through euphoric and depressive episodes, they have proven to be the most efficient allocators of capital. Certainly productivity growth needs capital, but an increase in capital, by itself, produces little productivity growth.

Productivity Growth and the Age Wave

The bottom line is that increased saving has, at most, a modest effect on productivity. Moreover, productivity growth would have to increase dramatically to have a meaningful impact on the age wave.

The rate of productivity growth required to keep the retirement age at sixty-three in the United States is staggering, on the order of 7 percent per year.[9] This is more than three times the historical rate of productivity growth, and a rate that has never been sustained beyond a short period of time. If we can raise the rate of domestic productivity growth to 3.5 percent—and this is the maximum the United States has achieved over *any* ten-year period since the end of the Second World War—the retirement age by 2050 would fall from only three years. Productivity growth *within* the United States (and most of the developed world) does not solve the problem because retirement benefits are linked to productivity through wages.

This pessimistic assessment of the impact of productivity growth on the age wave in the developed world has been echoed by Alan Greenspan and the Federal Reserve in its studies on productivity growth and the reform of the Social Security System.[10] Certainly productivity growth determines the buying power of wages, but the rate at which the developed countries, already at the technological frontier, can increase their productivity is far short of what is needed to solve the aging crisis.

Higher Social Security Taxes Are Not the Answer

Many believe that the age wave crisis can be relieved by boosting payroll taxes today, thereby increasing revenues to the Social Security trust fund. The argument goes that if the Social Security trust fund held more government bonds, this would decrease the amount of government debt held by private investors, allowing these investors to use their savings to fund more productive projects in the private sector.

This solution suffers from two problems. We have already shown that it is unlikely that an increase in the personal savings rate can increase productivity sufficiently to offset the age wave, so an increase in government savings, which is what increased funding of the trust fund accomplishes, is also unlikely to work.

But increasing payroll taxes has another, more pernicious impact on the economy's ability to cope with the growing number of retirees. Taxes that lower take-home pay discourage workers from working, and taxes that raise employment costs discourage firms from hiring. Just when we need more workers, we would be getting less.

There has been much written in economics on the effect of income and payroll taxes on the incentive to work. Recent evidence strongly supports the proposition that payroll taxes can have a significantly negative impact on the incentive to work. Edward Prescott, a recent Nobel Laureate in economics, wrote a paper entitled "Why Do Americans Work so Much More than Europeans?"[11] In it he reported that Americans not only work 50 percent more hours than the Germans, the Italians, and the French, but Americans also take about ten days of vacation a year, while Europeans take six to seven weeks. There is a popular perception that the contrasting work ethics stem from differing cultures; it is widely believed that Europeans have different priorities and simply enjoy their leisure time more than Americans do. As Jeremy Rifkin, author of *The European Dream,* wrote, "The American Dream pays homage to work ethic. The European Dream is more attuned to leisure and play."[12] But Prescott finds otherwise. Currently European tax rates on wages and salaries are much higher than rates in the United States. But in the early 1970s, when European and U.S. tax rates were comparable, European and U.S. workweeks were roughly equal. Prescott finds the reduced workweek directly related to the rise in payroll taxes.

Confirming this work, Steven Davis at the University of Chicago and Magnus Henrekson of the Stockholm School of Economics, conducted an econometric study of rich countries in the mid-1990s. They also found that higher tax rates are negatively correlated with the number of people working as well as with the number of hours each employee works.[13]

Perhaps if workers saw these payroll taxes directing flowing into their pension benefits, then the negative impact of higher Social Security taxes on employment would be reduced. But surveys overwhelmingly indicate that workers see the deductions taken from their paycheck as taxes, not as "contributions."

And from a legal standpoint, they are perfectly right. Two Supreme Court cases have confirmed that the Social Security (and Medicare) taxes carry no implied right to a future benefit. In 1937 the Supreme Court wrote, "The proceeds of both [employee and employer] taxes are to be paid into the Treasury like any other internal-revenue taxes generally, and are not earmarked in any way." In 1960 the Court further affirmed, "To engraft upon the Social Security system a concept of 'accrued property rights' would deprive it of the flexibility and boldness in adjustment to ever-changing conditions which it demands."[14]

The perception of Social Security being a tax instead of a contribution to a personal retirement account carries much significance. If the current 12.4 percent tax on the first $87,900 of wages (2004 levels) were allowed to accrue directly to a worker's savings account that could be used for retirement or even major purchases such as a home, the positive incentive effects on work effort, not to say savings, could be significant.

Although I do not believe that an increase in the savings rate will solve the problem caused by the age wave, personal accounts are a far more attractive option than trying to increase government savings through higher taxes.

Immigration

Because the decrease in the number of workers causes the scarcity of output, immigration might be seen as the answer to the problem. If workers are added at a young enough age, they could provide labor services for many years before collecting pension benefits.

The number of immigrants needed to keep the retirement age of Americans at sixty-three depends on assumptions such as the average age of the immigrant, the average number of dependents per worker, and the workers' skill level. Assuming that the average immigrant upon arriving in the United States earns one-half of the average per capita income of Americans, the number of immigrants needed over the next forty-five years to keep the retirement age constant is over 400 million, far in excess of the current U.S. population. The reason the number is so high is that immigrants also have dependents, use government services, and receive pension benefits upon retirement, putting more strain on the system.

There is much debate over the right immigration policy, and I personally favor liberalizing the laws governing immigration. However, it is unreasonable to expect that immigration can by itself solve the aging problem of the developed world.

What to Do?

The traditionally offered solutions to the aging crisis are seriously flawed. Although increased savings is a worthy goal, it will have limited impact on reducing the retirement age. Productivity growth, the commonly cited answer to the problem, has limited impact because benefits are themselves largely tied to productivity, offsetting its ability to solve the crisis. Higher taxes and increased immigration are also not the answers. Like Thomas Edison, quoted at the head of this chapter, I believe we have found many results that won't work.

But this does not mean that we should be resigned to the consequences of the age wave. There *is* a source of productivity growth that offers much hope. Not only do China, India, and other developing countries stand on the brink of rapid economic expansion, but their huge populations have an age profile that is sharply different from that of the developed world. Bringing more people into the production process can solve the age wave crisis. Immigration was needed in the 19th and early 20th century to bring workers to the most advanced technology. Now state-of-the-art capital is being brought to the workers anywhere in the world.

Can the growth in the developing world, which today produces only a fraction of the world's output, truly offset the pernicious impact of the age wave? That is the topic of the next chapter.

CHAPTER FIFTEEN

The Global Solution:

THE TRUE NEW ECONOMY

Some men see things as they are and say, "Why?" I dream of things that never were and say, "Why not?"

—George Bernard Shaw, 1949

Has demography—the future that cannot be changed—doomed the developed world to a much shorter and less affluent retirement and investors to falling asset prices? After analyzing our aging economy, a good case could be made for this dismal scenario. But this grim conclusion is based on a far too narrow view of the world.

Historically, the young have earned enough to provide both for themselves and the elderly. Some of this income is transferred through government pension programs, such as Social Security. But in the rich countries, the elderly largely finance their retirement by selling their assets and using the proceeds to fund their needs. This symbiotic exchange of the young's earnings for the older generation's assets is how the young generation accumulates its wealth and the retirees support their lifestyles.

Markets for financial assets allow this exchange to work over wide geographic areas. For example, no one fears that the state of Florida will fall into an economic slump because there are not enough workers in the state to provide for its huge retirement population. We know that the consumption of Florida's elderly can be supported by importing goods and services from the younger population in the remaining forty-nine states. Furthermore, Florida retirees have no problem selling their assets to younger investors in the rest of the country.

But very soon, the elderly will reside in all fifty states and in Canada, Europe, and Japan. Who will buy their assets when they retire?

Expand your horizons and think of the world as one economy instead of separate nations, each one attempting to provide goods for its own citizens. Although the developed world is aging rapidly, the rest of the world is very young. Take a look at Figure 15 1. This shows the age profile of India, China, and the rest of the developing world. The young of the world can produce the goods for, and buy the assets from, the retirees of the developed world. For more than 80 percent of the world's population, there is no age wave.

Can the aging populations in the richer countries in fact be supported by the young workers in the developing world? Right now the answer is no. The developing countries, despite having more than 80 percent of the world's population, produce less than one-quarter of the world output measured in dollars.

But something extraordinary is happening in these young, developing countries. For the first time, China and now India have launched into a sustained period of rapid growth. Their growth, if it can continue at

FIGURE 15.1: DEVELOPING WORLD POPULATION
PROFILE 2005 AND 2050

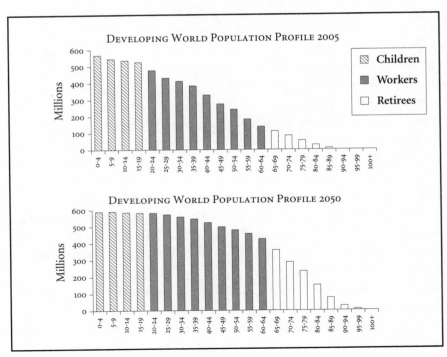

the levels achieved over the past decade, will have an extremely significant effect not only on their countries but on the rest of the world as well.

Figure 15.2 shows how higher productivity growth rates in these developing countries can impact the retirement age in the rich countries. And the impact is dramatic.

If the developing world can increase productivity at 6 percent per year over the next several decades—and this rate has long been surpassed in China and has now been achieved in India—then the retirement age of the boomer population need rise only modestly. On the other hand, if the developing world stops growing, the retirement age in the United States would have to rise from sixty-two to seventy-seven. As can be seen in Figure 15.2, each 1 percent increase in developing-world growth rates equates to about two extra years of retirement for the developed world.

Growth in the developing world will be fueled by the explosive growth of exports to the aging world. These young countries must find an outlet for the dollars, yen, and euros they receive from their exports. Despite the rapid growth in their own economies, they will find U.S., European, and

FIGURE 15.2: PROJECTED RETIREMENT AGE FOR DIFFERENT GROWTH RATES OF DEVELOPING COUNTRIES

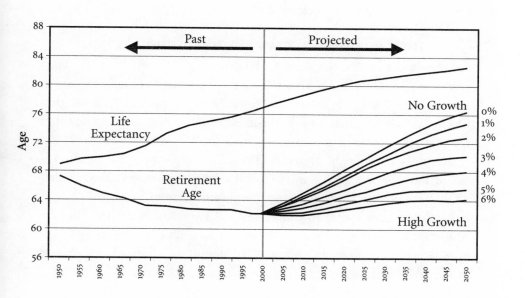

Japanese assets attractive for their brand names and their managerial, marketing, and technical know-how. The Indian-based Tata Tea's acquisition of the global giant Tetley and the Chinese Lenovo's acquisition of IBM's personal computers are just the tip of the iceberg. The next half century will see a massive exchange of goods for assets that will not only shift the center of the world economy eastward but also negate the destructive impact of the age wave on asset prices and retirement opportunities.

I call this the global solution.

I admit that the global solution is not the conventional wisdom. It depends on sustained rapid growth in the developing countries. Doubters can point to flashes of growth in many parts of the globe that subsequently died out. At the turn of the twentieth century, Argentina was one of the ten richest countries in the world before going into a long decline. More recently the "Asian tigers"—Thailand, Taiwan, the Philippines, and South Korea—stumbled during the currency crises of the late 1990s. Communism, socialism, and other anti-market policies have squelched much development throughout history.

But something very different is happening today. I believe the world is ripe for a dramatic change. The communications revolution, which caused so much pain to investors in the telecom industries, ultimately planted the seeds for the global solution.

The study of history shows us why the communications revolution is such a positive force for worldwide growth.

THE CREATION AND TRANSMISSION OF DISCOVERIES

Let's begin our analysis by going far back in time. Michael Kremer, a Harvard economist, wrote an article in the prestigious *Quarterly Journal of Economics* with the grandiose title "Population Growth and Technological Change 1,000,000 B.C. to 1990." Of course, economic output data does not stretch back that far in time, but data on human population do exist.

Kremer convincingly argues that throughout most of history, the number of humans was a very good indicator of economic progress. Higher population density led to increased communication of ideas, greater specialization, better tools, and increased food production. The ability to communicate from one person to another and from one generation to another was of paramount importance. Greater information led to increased productivity and the ability to support larger populations.

Until the onset of the Industrial Revolution, productivity and population growth inched ahead extremely slowly. In fact, productivity backtracked as often as it moved forward. Discoveries and inventions were made, but many were lost to the next generation. For example, Rome of AD 100 is said to have had a better infrastructure (roads, sewage systems, and water distribution) than many European cities in the 1800s.[1]

Joel Mokyr, a professor of economics and history at Northwestern University, claims "the paradox is that whereas it might have been expected that these losses [in knowledge] would occur in illiterate societies with low geographic mobility, classical civilization was relatively literate and mobile, and ideas of all kinds disseminated through the movements of people and books. Yet many of the classical discoveries did not survive."[2]

Why did this happen? Why did important discoveries occur but then get lost? There is one reason that stands out: The inability to communicate ideas within and across generations.

THE IMPORTANCE OF COMMUNICATIONS

Evidence demonstrating the importance of communications shows up repeatedly in the historical data. Kremer found that when populations were isolated from one another, their standard of living not only stopped increasing but actually declined. When the land bridge between ancient Britain and Europe was cut off, around 5500 B.C., Britain fell technologically behind Europe. Similarly, there is evidence that the Paleolithic population in Japan was quite primitive after Japan's bridge with mainland Asia was lost.

Kremer believed that population density, which facilitated the communication of ideas and division of labor, was correlated with technological progress. He held that the melting of the polar ice caps at the end of the Ice Age, around 10,000 B.C., and the consequent flooding of land bridges, provide a natural experiment that isolated the Old World (Asia and Europe), the Americas, mainland Australia, Tasmania, and Flinders Island [a small island near Tasmania].

The course of development confirmed Kremer's hypothesis:

As the model predicts, [around 1500] the Old World had the highest technological level. The Americas followed, with the agriculture, cities, and elaborate calendars of the Aztec and Mayan civilizations. Mainland Australia was third, with a population of hunters and gatherers. Tasmania, lacked even such mainland Australian technologies as the boomerang, fire-making, the spear-thrower, [and others]. . . . Flinders Island . . . last inhabitants died out about 4000 years after they were cut off by the rising seas—suggesting possible technological regress.[3]

William Nordhaus, an economics professor at Yale University, provides another example of how crucial knowledge was lost in his fascinating history of man-made light: "As Europe declined into the Dark Ages, there was a clear deterioration in the lighting technology, with lighting returning to the Paleolithic open saucer that performed more poorly than the wicked Roman lamps." Nordhaus describes the medieval peasant's practice of burning pine splinters, holding the torn branches in his mouth so as to leave the hands free, a practice that harkened back to prehistoric times.[4]

It is astonishing that this knowledge of lighting technology that is so central to one's life could not be passed on from one generation to the next. Even in relatively modern times, vital information was lost because there was no easy way to record and transmit it. For example, the importance of fresh fruit in the prevention of scurvy had been realized before James Lind published his *Treatise on Scurvy* in 1746. The Dutch East India Company kept citrus trees on the Cape of Good Hope in the middle of the seventeenth century so that their sailors could partake of food that would prevent the disease. Nevertheless, as Roy Porter noted, the remedy "kept on being rediscovered and lost."[5]

CHINA: THE RISE AND FALL

The rise and fall of China over the last millennium demonstrates both the power of communication to create new ideas and how the suppression of those ideas by the reigning authorities led to decline.

China in the thirteenth and fourteenth centuries was generally recognized as the most advanced civilization on earth. Some of the credit for this advance goes all the way back to the first century AD, when China invented paper. In his fascinating book ranking the one hundred most influential persons in history, Michael Hart places Ts'ai Lun, the Chinese inventor of paper, as the seventh most important person in world history, behind Muhammad, Isaac Newton, Jesus Christ, Buddha, Confucius, and St. Paul and just ahead of Johannes Gutenberg. It was not until the middle of the eighth century that papermaking spread to Arabs in the Middle East, and it took another 400 years for Europeans to learn the art. "Prior to the second century A.D.," Hart writes, "Chinese civilization was consistently less advanced than Western civilization. During the next millennium, China's accomplishments exceeded those of the West, and for a period of seven or eight centuries, Chinese civilization was by most standards the most advanced on earth."[6] China's dominance was clearly facilitated by its ability to record and transmit information.

But this technological superiority did not last. Mokyr, in *The Lever of Riches,* describes the significant discoveries made by the Chinese that were later lost. The first timepieces were invented by Su Sung in 1086, but the Chinese had to be reintroduced to clocks when the Jesuits came in the sixteenth century. The Chinese developed moveable type in the ninth century, 500 years before Gutenberg's invention of the printing press, but they never developed an active press. The Chinese used silk reeling machines as early as 1090, but as late as the nineteenth century, raw silk, which accounted for about 25 percent of China's exports, was entirely hand-reeled. The Chinese invented gunpowder for use in rockets and bombs in the tenth century, but they then had to relearn the use of the cannon from the West in the middle of the fourteenth century.

Why did this happen? David Hume, a great British economist of the eighteenth century, believed that the despotism of the Ming Dynasty, which ruled China from 1368 to 1644, stymied growth in China: "An unlimited despotism . . . effectually puts a stop to all improvements, and keeps men from attaining . . . knowledge."[7] The Ming rulers preferred a stable and controlled environment and therefore squelched invention and discovery. Subsequently China fell into a long period of stagnation.

The Ming rulers rejected anything that disturbed the status quo. Although China's naval technology was far superior to the West's and the Chinese could have easily sailed to America, they did not. Chinese geographic exploration was completely halted after 1433 because the emperor considered naval exploration an "expensive adventure."[8]

Many books of knowledge vanished during the Ming Dynasty. Sung Ying Hsing's great technical encyclopedia, *Exploitation of the Works of Nature,* was written in 1637 and provided an excellent summary of advanced Chinese technology, from weaving to hydraulics to jade working. But the work was soon destroyed, most likely because Sung Ying Hsing's political views differed from those of the rulers.[9]

As Mokyr boldly put it, "The Chinese were, so to speak, within reach of world domination, and then shied away." Echoing this conclusion, Charles Jones, an economics professor at Stanford University, wrote, "China came within a hair's breadth of industrializing in the 14th century, yet in 1600 their technological backwardness was apparent to most visitors; by the nineteenth century the Chinese themselves found it intolerable."[10]

THE PRECURSOR TO THE INDUSTRIAL REVOLUTION:
THE PRINTING PRESS

Michael Hart may have placed Ts'ai Lun, the inventor of paper, ahead of Johannes Gutenberg, the inventor of the printing press, but most historians would say the printing press was the one invention, more than any other, that fundamentally transformed how information was accessed and transmitted.

Before Gutenberg invented the printing press in 1455, it took a scribe six months to copy a book. The printing press was fifty times as productive, thereby reducing printing costs by 98 percent.[11] Michael Rotschild, in his book *Bionomics*, discusses how the dissemination of information facilitated by the printing press sparked tremendous growth in the useful stock of knowledge. By the year 1500, just forty-five years after Gutenberg's first Bibles were printed, more than 1,000 presses had produced about 10 million copies of 35,000 different titles. The written word and the knowledge it conveyed went from being a luxury good, available to a privileged few, to a commodity cheaply available to all.

> [O]ne cannot help but notice that prior to 1500, major discoveries were few and far between. Except for Gutenberg's invention of movable type printing, scant scientific or technological progress had been made since the decline of Greece 1700 years earlier. But after 1500, once Gutenberg's technology had become commonplace, a sudden rush of scientific achievement laid the foundations of modern knowledge.
>
> In 1512, Copernicus first argued that the earth revolves around the sun. In the following 25 years, Anthony Fitzherbert published the first English manual on agriculture, Albert Durer compiled the first German treaty on geometry, Paracelsus published the first book on surgery, George Agricola

produced the first treatise on mineralogy, and Andreas Vesalius issued the first anatomical charts of the human body."[12]

But the invention of the printing press had to wait at least two centuries before these discoveries could be turned into the building blocks of the Industrial Revolution. The Industrial Revolution had to be preceded by the Scientific Revolution and the Age of Reason, which marked the beginning of "open science."

COMPETING NATION-STATES: EUROPE VERSUS CHINA

During the Scientific Revolution knowledge about the natural world became increasingly public and scientific advances and discoveries were freely shared between the leading universities and the general population. In the West there was little or no ideological opposition to using rational analysis to explain natural phenomena, a situation that was aided by the spread of the Enlightenment from continental Europe in the late seventeenth century. The ideological intolerance displayed by the Ming Dynasty did not have any counterpart in Europe. In the West, the competing nation-states provided a much more receptive climate for discovery; as David Hume observed in 1777, Europe succeeded while China stagnated because "the divisions into small states are favorable to learning, by stopping the progress of authority as well as that of power."[13]

The total ban on shipbuilding that occurred in China could not have occurred throughout Europe. As Spanish exploration declined, for example, the Dutch, English, or Portuguese would quickly enter to fill the void. Martin Luther's Protestant Reformation provided competition among religious sects. Although new ideas were sometimes squelched—recall the Catholic attack on Copernicus's heliocentric theories of the universe—the lack of religious or political hegemony in Europe ensured that new ideas could not be completely suppressed.

Christopher Columbus's search for a sponsor for his voyages, reported by Jared Diamond in *Guns, Germs, and Steel,* aptly illustrates the difference between Europe and China:

> Christopher Columbus, an Italian by birth, switched his allegiance to the duke of Anjou in France, then to the king of Portugal. When the latter refused his request for ships in which to explore westward, Columbus

turned to the duke of Medina Sedonia, who also refused, then to the count of Medina Celi, who did likewise, and finally to the king and queen of Spain, who denied his first request but granted his renewed appeal.[14]

Had there been only one nation-state, Columbus never would have secured funding and his voyage to the New World would not have been possible. The hegemony in China gave an innovator only one chance, while the competition in Europe gave him many.

The Industrial Revolution

Following the Enlightenment and the Scientific Revolution of the eighteenth century, both population and economic growth accelerated sharply. The onset of the Industrial Revolution ushered in the world's first sustained period of rapid economic growth.

Charles Jones provides a good analogy to understand how recent this sustained growth has been in the course of human history.[15] Jones says to imagine the period from 1 million BC to the present as the length of a football field.

Humans lived as hunters and gatherers throughout most of history; this period represented 99 of the 100 yards. Humans did not develop agriculture until the one-yard line (10,000 years ago). And the Industrial Revolution, which ushered in the first and only period of sustained economic growth in the entire one million years of human history, was essentially the "width of a golf ball perched at the end of a football field."

What happened between 200 and 300 years ago that sparked the revolution in productivity? Two factors came together: a significant leap in the ability to communicate combined with openness on the part of those in power to accept these new ideas.

Most important, these are the very forces that define today's true new economy.

The True New Economy

Throughout history, communication was the critical factor shaping economic growth and the wealth of nations. That is why the Communications Revolution makes the prospects for our world economy so bright.

The Internet can play a role today akin to Ts'ai Lun's discovery of paper in the first century and Johannes Guttenberg's invention of the printing press in the fifteenth. The global network is the key to unlocking the global solution.

Soon virtually everything that has ever been written and recorded—on tape or film, in print, or digitally—will be instantly accessible online. Although countries can still censor and direct information, this will become increasingly difficult as the years pass. For the first time in human history, there will be virtually free and unlimited access to the world's knowledge.

Isaac Newton is quoted as saying, "If I have seen farther than others, it is because I was standing on the shoulders of giants."[16] Now hundreds of millions of people, if not billions, can stand on the shoulders of giants with a click of their mouse.

INNOVATION AND THE FUTURE OF THE INTERNET

Examples of how the Internet has already stimulated invention abound. The *Wall Street Journal* reported that Professor Manindra Agarwal, a computer scientist at the Indian Institute of Technology in Kanpur, recently discovered a relationship that determines with complete certainty if a number is prime—solving a math problem that had puzzled mathematicians for over two thousand years.[17] One of the primary tools Professor Agarwal used to bolster his understanding of complex number theory was the search engine Google. Instead of contacting the top mathematicians around the globe, Professor Agarwal just turned on his computer and typed in a description of what he was looking for. He was able to access up-to-date information on the progress toward a solution and was able to complete his proof.

Alan Cohen, vice president of marketing and product management at Airespace, a private company specializing in wireless networking platforms, shares his view of Google's impact:

> If I can operate Google, I can find anything. And with wireless, it means I will be able to find anything, anywhere, anytime. Which is why I say that Google, combined with Wi-Fi, is a little bit like God. God is wireless, God is everywhere and God sees and knows everything. Throughout history, people connected to God without wires. Now, for many questions in the world, you ask Google, and increasingly, you can do it without wires, too.[18]

Of course, Cohen's take on Google is sensationalist. But pause a moment and think where technology is leading us. Soon all search engines will be voice-activated and will be designed to answer any question, not just spew forth Web sites with associated words. These engines along with advanced navigational systems and voice and digital transmission will be embedded in devices no larger than today's cell phones.

Tiny earpieces will connect to these devices, which will access and process all information and answer all questions. All known information will literally be at your beck and call. All foreign languages will be instantly and idiomatically translated, so language will no longer be a barrier in international communication. Anyone will be able to link with the global stock of knowledge and build on the advances of others.

These electronic and digital advances not only shrink distances but also save time. This allows individuals to communicate with a worldwide network of individuals working on the same problem. This interaction sets up a self-reinforcing feedback: as more people contribute, more progress is made, which in turn stimulates even more discovery, which accelerates productivity growth.

CHINA AND INDIA

Anyone who has any doubt about how fast the world is changing need only go to Shanghai, the largest city in China. I was there in June 2004 as a speaker with the Wharton Global Alumni Forum.

Pudong, the new part of the city on the east side of the Huangpu River, looks like the City of Tomorrow. I have never seen anything like it anywhere else in the world. With soaring commercial and residential high-rises and wide boulevards, the city is clearly seeking to outclass its longtime rival, Hong Kong—and it is succeeding.

Locals love to tell you that Pudong was a rice paddy ten years ago. The conversation at the cocktail party before one of the dinners could have taken place in any high-society soiree in Manhattan. Everyone was talking about real estate, and many predicted sharply higher prices in select areas, such as the former French and English concessions. Shanghai was clearly the place to be if you wished to tap China's enormous potential.

Given the country's huge area and population, it is clear the Chinese wish to harness the power of the Internet to advance the economy. Despite the threat that the free flow of information from the Internet will undermine its authority, the government has embraced a technology initiative intended to expand the Internet's presence and influence across China. As the Chinese Ministry of Information Industry declared:

> [I]nformatization is the key in promoting industrial advancement, industrialization and modernization. . . . It is the very first time for the Central Committee of the Communist Party of China to put informatization in such a high strategic position. . . .
>
> By 2010, China will become an information society, raising the breadth and the depth of using information resources and the development in information services will accelerate and meet the demand from the public. The information industry will be the most important industry in the national economy, achieving a large scale and technologically advanced national information infrastructure.[19]

These goals are not just wishful thinking by the government. I noted that the Chinese, who now have more mobile-phone users than any country on earth, use their phones in the subways, something that is currently impossible in most of the United States. In many instances, China's technology is far superior to what is available in the the developed world.

As Morgan Stanley economists Steve Roach and Andy Xie write, "We are enthusiastic about the outlook because of the role the Internet should play in helping the Chinese economy develop and because of the wealth-creation opportunities we see over the long term. . . . The Internet is the only cost-efficient way that China can push into central and western parts of the nation, while simultaneously striving for transnational connectivity. . . . It is going to be a fascinating decade or two."[20]

Intel, one of the world's premiere technology companies, agrees that China is the place to be when it comes to technology. In 2003, Intel received $3.7 billion or 12 percent of its revenue from China and predicted double-digit increases in demand far into the future. Intel's president and chief operating officer Paul Otellini, said, "I come back from visiting China, and I feel as if I've visited the fountain of youth of computing."[21]

In India the communication revolution is being led by the private sector. Bangalore is the prototype of the future world economy, and Infosys

Technologies is the prototypical Indian software company. The firm is headquartered on a self-sufficient, twenty-nine-acre campus that is marked by software development centers, dormitories, and an auditorium with a forty-screen video wall that allows Infosys's global supply chain (American managers, Indian software programmers, and Asian manufacturers) to conduct a "virtual meeting." Thomas Friedman, author and *New York Times* columnist, characterizes how management feels:

> All the walls have been blown away in the world, so now we, an Indian software company, can use the Internet, fiber optic telecommunications and e-mail to get super-empowered and compete anywhere that our smarts and energy can take us. And we can be part of a global supply chain that produces profit for Indians, Americans and Asians.[22]

India has a number of natural advantages. Wide use of English is certainly one of them. And because India is located on the other side of the globe from the United States, Indians can take advantage of time sharing. When Americans are leaving work for the day, Indians are arriving in the office to start their day. Because of the Internet's ability to transmit data instantly, Americans can e-mail a project they are working on to their counterparts in India, who can send their work back over to Americans the next morning. All of a sudden, you now have a twenty-four-hour workday.

But India had better watch its northern neighbor. English is spreading rapidly in China, and with the advent of computer-based translators, China will be a formidable competitor.

The World at Midcentury

The wide impact of China and India on the future world economy is inevitable. By 2050 China is projected to have about 1.5 billion people, nearly four times the 400 million inhabitants projected in the United States.

When I was in China, I asked economists and top executives whether they saw any reason why China could not achieve at least half the per capita income of the United States by the middle of this century. This would put China on the same footing that Portugal and South Korea have relative to the United States today. Not one person I talked to thought that goal impossible, and in fact a few believed that Chinese development might be even greater. If China achieved that feat, the Chinese economy would be almost twice the size of the U.S. economy by midcentury.

Is this possible? Most certainly. Over the last forty years, Japan has gone from 20 percent of the U.S. per capita income to 96 percent, Hong Kong from 16 to 70 percent, and Singapore from 14 to 58 percent. And over the last twenty-five years South Korea has gone from 17 percent to nearly 50 percent.[23] China could reach that goal with a productivity growth rate of 3 percent a year above the United States. By comparison, over the past twenty-five years China has achieved a per capita growth rate of 7.7 percent, almost six percentage points above the United States.

Putting this into perspective, Angus Maddison, an economic historian at the University of Groningen in the Netherlands, points out that during much of the 1800s, China accounted for as much as a third of the world's total economic output. But during most of the twentieth century, China's economy sank. So what is happening now is that China is living up to its potential and returning to its previous levels.[24]

India's economy will also eclipse the United States' in size. India, starting from a lower base than China, would need to grow about four percentage points faster than the United States if it wants to achieve half the U.S. standard of living by midcentury. This growth rate would still be well below China's growth over the past twenty-five years. If both India and China can achieve these growth rates, then their combined economies will be almost four times the size of the U.S. economy by midcentury.

IT'S NOT JUST CHINA AND INDIA

While China and India rank at the top in prospects for growth, their growth alone will not entirely offset the burdens levied by the age wave. Without any help from other nations, a successful China and India can, in my demographic model, offset about half of the increase in retirement ages, gaining Americans about five extra years of retirement by midcentury.

But prospects are bright in other countries as well. Goldman Sachs believes that in addition to India and China, Brazil and Russia also will show remarkable growth over the next half century.[25] Brazil currently makes up one-third of Latin America's 555 million people. If Brazil, Mexico, and the rest of Latin America embark on a catch-up period, as Goldman Sachs believes Brazil is apt to do, the Latin American economies will produce more output than the United States by 2030.

Indonesia, with the world's fourth largest population, is another Asian country with a very young population and much growth potential. With over 230 million inhabitants, Indonesia has a median age of twenty-six but a per capita income that is only 9 percent of America's. Many multinational companies, such as Coke, Unilever, Heinz, and Campbell Soup, have already flocked to Indonesia as an export base for their Southeastern Asia operations.[26] I expect this trend to continue well into the future, as the Asian economies continue their rapid expansion.

One of the regions with potential to have a huge impact is sub-Saharan Africa. The region has over 735 million people, or 11 percent of the world's population, but it accounts for only 3 percent of the world's economic production. This part of the world also has the youngest population and the highest birth rates, so that by 2050 sub-Saharan Africa will have 1.8 billion people, making up almost 20 percent of the globe's population. The sheer size of this population means that its growth path will be important for the rest of the world.

THE TRADE DEFICIT AND THE FOREIGN TAKEOVER
OF WESTERN FIRMS

In Chapter 1 I posed the fundamental questions facing the developed world over the next half century: who will produce the goods that the retirees need, and who will buy the assets that they sell during their retirement? We have found the answer in this chapter: workers and investors from developing countries. The aging populations will import the goods and services they need, and finance these purchases by selling their stocks and bonds to the investors in the developing world.

These coming patterns of world commerce will cause increasing trade deficits in both the United States and the rest of the developed world. But these deficits are not necessarily a cause for concern, no more than the state of Florida running a trade deficit with the other forty-nine states. They will arise as part of the inevitable demographic trends that dictate the exchange of goods for assets that are part of the global solution.

As most of the world's output will be produced by the developing nations, eventually most of the assets in the United States, Europe, and Japan will be owned by investors in the developing world. By the middle of this century, I believe the Chinese, Indians, and other investors from these young countries will gain majority ownership in most of the large global corporations.

There is evidence that this unprecedented shift in ownership has already begun. Consider the story of Lakshimi Mittal, an Indian-born billionaire, who in 2004 turned his family business into the world's largest steel producer by acquiring the assets of American companies LTV Corp. and Bethlehem Steel. There is also Wipro, an Indian IT services company, which recently bought an American consulting firm as well as GE Medical Systems' IT department. In 2000, the Indian firm Tata Tea took over Tetley Tea, the second biggest tea company in the world and a firm twice its size.

The Chinese are also playing in the global M&A game. Chinese brands are little known outside their home country, so Chinese firms are starting to buy the global brands that they traditionally manufactured. The highest profile acquisition thus far was conducted by Lenovo Group, China's leading computer company. Lenovo shook up the industry by acquiring IBM's personal computer division in 2004, forming the world's third largest PC business and giving the Chinese manufacturer access to IBM's global presence. Hong Kong–based Li & Fung, whose primary business is sourcing and coordinating manufacturing for big retailers such as Kohl's and Bed Bath & Beyond, recently acquired the rights to both design and manufacture Levi Strauss's Signature brand, which is sold at Wal-Mart and Target.[27]

The American firm Royal Appliance Manufacturing, which had made the popular Dirt Devil vacuum cleaners in Cleveland, Ohio, since 1905, was forced to close its American factories and pay a Chinese firm to produce its products. But in 2003 the Chinese company Techtronic acquired the entire company and the brand.[28] Similarly, the Chinese electronics company TCL acquired the French firm Thomson's rights to the RCA brand name, and went on to become the largest television manufacturer in the world.[29] Look for this trend to continue well into the future. Stocks such as Sinopec, Infosys Technologies, Wipro, Asia Mobile, and Indotel will be found in the portfolios of investors who now own only U.S.-based or European firms.

The beauty of capital is that it flows to the most efficient producer with the greatest profit potential. Firms that cannot compete in the global marketplace will be bought by firms that can—and those firms are increasingly going to be Indian, Chinese, or Indonesian.

JOB LOSS AND JOB CREATION

I acknowledge that there are political forces that wish to erect barriers to prevent the integration of world markets, which would threaten this outcome. Change is never easy. Undoubtedly there will be jobs lost in the process, but history has convincingly shown that if we allow change to occur, ultimately many more jobs will be gained.

In the late nineteenth and early twentieth centuries manufacturing jobs left the northern half of the United States and headed to the South, where labor was cheaper. In the late twentieth century jobs migrated to Japan and then across the border into Mexico. Now they are going to China, and in the future, I hope, to Africa. But those who bemoan the loss of manufacturing jobs fail to see the big picture. During the decade of the 1990s U.S. trade went from balanced to a huge deficit, while Europe and Japan remained in surplus. But during the same period, the great American job machine turned out job growth rates that were four times higher than Europe's and created over 20 million jobs, roughly the same number as Europe and Japan combined.[30] By taking advantage of the lower prices of imported goods, Americans had more money left in their wallets. This extra cash increases demand for other goods and services, leading to the creation of new jobs.

Furthermore, most of the job loss is due to higher productivity, not one country "stealing" jobs from another. The productivity growth of American farmers provides a perfect example. At the turn of the twentieth century, about 40 percent of the United States' population still worked on a farm. Now, although less than 0.5 percent of the American labor force works in farming, the United States is still a world exporter of food.[31]

The Conference Board reports that between 1995 and 2002, global manufacturing lost 22 million jobs, but output soared 30 percent.[32] During that period the United States lost 2 million manufacturing jobs, but the Chinese lost 15 million! Admittedly, most of these losses came from the closing of inefficient state-owned enterprises; nevertheless, technological growth, wherever it occurs, changes the patterns of demand and the mix of employment.

The same thing has happened in the steel industry. Although the industry and unions representing steelworkers have called for tariffs to keep cheap foreign steel out, it turns out that cheap foreign steel is not the source of the loss of jobs. In 1980 a ton of domestically produced steel required 10 man-hours to produce; today the industry average is less than 4 man-hours. That means it takes 60 percent fewer workers to produce the same amount of steel, regardless of whether it is imported.

The absolute wrong way to go about protecting American jobs and prosperity is by hiking tariffs and establishing quotas on imported goods. The cost of these measures, in terms of the higher cost of goods to consumers, is enormous. A 1984 government report showed that consumers paid $42,000 annually for each textile job that was preserved by quotas, $105,000 for each automobile job, and $750,000 for each job saved in the steel industry.[33] These sums far exceed the wages of workers in these industries. In every case consumers would be better off paying the lost wages of displaced workers rather than accepting the higher costs of protectionism. The route politicians find so easy to take is costing the American consumer dearly.

OPPORTUNITIES, NOT THREATS

We must look to these changes taking place in our global economy as opportunities and not as threats. Huge markets await those willing to tackle them. The demands from developing nations for infrastructure, health care, education, financial services, and managerial and technical expertise, to name just a few, are enormous and growing.

As Thomas Friedman learned after taking a trip to Bangalore, what goes around, comes around. Friedman visited a company called 24/7 Customer and witnessed young Indians answering phone calls, providing technical computer support, and selling credit cards. He queried the founder of 24/7, Shanmugam Nagarajan, how the growth of India benefits Americans.

"Well," Nagarajan answered patiently, "look around this office. All the computers are from Compaq. The basic software is from Microsoft. The phones are from Lucent. The air-conditioning is by Carrier, and even the bottled water is by Coke, because when it comes to drinking water in India, people want a trusted brand."[34]

Our Future

The future of the world economy is bright. The communication revolution has set the stage for the entire world to experience robust economic growth. This growth will permit us to achieve the global solution, which will enable the aging nations to enjoy a longer and ever more prosperous retirement.

The emergence of the developing world is critical to everyone. If China and India falter, a dimmer future faces us. If they succeed, and if the rest of the developing world copies their success, there will be enough goods and services to support an ever-lengthening retirement without any reduction in the standard of living.

Some countries have erected barricades to global competition. But all those that have resisted change have ultimately failed. The free flow of information combined with the powerful economic incentives created by the division of labor and increasing productivity growth has always triumphed over the forces of isolation and protectionism.

But this is no time to become complacent. Clearly we must encourage free trade, lift tariff barriers, promote foreign direct investment, and advance the globalization of the world's economic system. The gains will more than cover the costs of helping those that are displaced from their jobs and cannot be retrained for any other position in our growing economy. If we descend to protectionism and fragment the world economy, it is our own future that will be most at risk.

As more and more doomsayers intone about coming economic and financial crises, remember the global solution: the young in the developing world will be the ones producing the goods and buying the retirees' assets. The economic success of these countries is not only good for their people but essential to the continued prosperity of our society.

As we look ahead to our and our children's welfare, there is no other economic goal that should have higher priority. We must embrace this future.

PART FIVE

Portfolio Strategies

CHAPTER SIXTEEN

Global Markets and the World Portfolio

"Today let's talk about a growth industry. Because investing world-wide is a growth industry. The great growth industry is international portfolio investing."

—John Templeton

My optimism about the growth in developing countries raises an important question: what does the global solution mean for your portfolio? Most investors, lured by the heady growth prospects in China and India, reflexively want to buy stocks from these rapidly growing countries.

But that would be a mistake. Recall the growth trap that we illustrated in Parts 1 and 2 of this book. Strong growth does not imply better returns for foreign firms any more than it does for domestic firms. As the basic principle of investor return states, what matters is growth relative to expectations, not growth alone. The evidence from the study of international returns strongly supports this proposition and is not comforting to the growth enthusiasts.

This does not mean that you should ignore foreign investing. Quite the contrary. Today, almost half the world's equity is headquartered outside the United States. To ignore the foreign markets would be akin to forming a domestic portfolio filled only with firms that begin with the letters *A* through *L*. Unbalanced portfolios increase risk without increasing returns.

But before we learn how to structure an international portfolio, I want to again emphasize the difference between growth and returns by examining the recent history of two countries, China and Brazil. This case is parallel to the tale of two companies, IBM and Standard Oil of New Jersey, that I presented in the very first chapter of this book.

China and Brazil

Travel back in time to the end of 1992. The global economy looks ripe for growth. The Berlin Wall fell three years ago, and Eastern Europe is anxious to integrate with the West. The First Gulf War ended in a big victory for the West—the United States, with its coalition allies, ousted Saddam Hussein from Kuwait and has emerged as the world's sole superpower. Russia relinquished parts of its former empire, and the onetime beacon of world communism shifted to a capitalist economy.

Your investment advisor suggests stocks in either China or Brazil to capitalize on this growth. China is the most populous country in the world, and Brazil has the largest economy in the Americas outside the United States. Both countries have enormous economic potential. Which country presents you with the greatest potential to build your wealth? Let us examine the record.

CHINA

China's economic growth had already taken off by the early 1990s. Ten years earlier, the Chinese government, under the leadership of Deng Xiaoping, began implementing an economic reform program that would catapult its economy from an inefficient Soviet-style centrally planned state to a market-oriented system. In 1990, the Chinese economy, already clicking on all cylinders, went into overdrive.

That year the Shenzhen and Shanghai stock exchanges were opened, to the tremendous excitement of both Chinese and foreign investors. In 1992 the number of listed stocks increased from twenty to seventy and had an aggregate market value of over 100 billion yuan ($20 billion). Trading volume expanded nearly thirtyfold over the previous year, and in December 1992 Morgan Stanley began calculating its China stock index of total returns.[1]

After a slow start, Chinese stocks soared in the second half of 1993, and American investors responded eagerly. *Newsweek* reported:

> In China, it's the year of the Rooster. But in America, 1993 has become the year of China. Out in Peoria, Mom and Pop are pouring their savings into mutual funds that pursue heady gains in China's booming market. For

those who don't get the message, President Jiang Zemin touts the fact that his country is now Boeing's biggest customer.[2]

Those who predicted that China's economy was going to surge ahead were absolutely right. Real GDP growth in the following eleven years averaged 9.3 percent a year, far above that of any other country in the world and nearly three times the rate in the United States. By 2003 China, in terms of purchasing power, had become the second largest economy in the world, and it was the world leader in foreign direct investment.

BRAZIL

Brazil, on the other hand, began the 1990s in political and economic crisis. In 1992 President Fernando Collor de Mello was impeached by the Chamber of Deputies and forced to resign. Brazil faced economic chaos as inflation soared to over 1,100 percent by year's end.

Those expecting things to get worse were right. By 1994 inflation surpassed 5,000 percent and real output dropped. Fernando Cardosa, who was elected president in October 1994, temporarily stabilized inflation but was forced to devalue the currency in January 1999 when increasing budget deficits prompted a flight of international reserves.

Then came a series of corruption scandals and an energy crisis that led the government to order widespread cuts in electrical consumption. Popular dissatisfaction with these austerities brought Luiz Inacio Lula da Silva, an avowed leftist of the opposition Workers' Party, to the presidency in 2002.

During these troubled years, Brazil's GDP grew at only 1.8 percent per year, among the lowest in the developing world and less than one-fifth the growth rate of China. While the Chinese economy expanded by a cumulative 166 percent over these eleven years, Brazil's increased by only 22 percent.

Once again Brazil's huge potential was squandered. Frustrated optimists bemoaned, "Brazil is the country for the future . . . and it always will be."

THE VERDICT

Those who predicted China's economy would grow faster than Brazil were right; China outpaced Brazil by a wide margin in virtually every category of economic output. China also enjoyed a stable currency, low inflation, and relative political stability, while Brazil had none of these.

But as Figure 16.1 shows, the returns to stock investors tell a very different story. From 1992 onward, China experienced the world's *worst* stock returns as investors saw their portfolio shrink, on average, by almost 10 percent per year. A $1,000 investment in China at the end of 1992 shrank to $320 by the end of 2003. Brazil, on the other hand, produced extraordinarily good returns of over 15 percent per year, with the same $1,000 investment in 1992 accumulating to $4,781, handily beating U.S. stocks.

How could this happen? For the same reason, as we learned in Chapter 1, that Standard Oil of New Jersey had better returns than IBM even though IBM beat Standard Oil on every measure of growth. Low prices and high dividend yield were the keys to Jersey's better returns and the reason why Brazilian investors outpaced the Chinese investors.

The conventional wisdom that investors should buy stocks in the fastest-growing countries is wrong for the same reason that buying the fastest-growing firms is wrong. China was indisputably the world's fastest-growing

FIGURE 16.1: A TALE OF TWO COUNTRIES:
CHINA AND BRAZIL STOCK RETURNS AND GDP GROWTH

country, but investors in China realized horrible returns because of the overvaluation of Chinese shares.

On the other hand, stock prices in Brazil were cheap in 1992, and all its economic troubles kept its prices low over the subsequent decade. As a result, the dividend yield on Brazilian stocks stayed high. Patient investors, buying value instead of hype, won out.

The Conventional Wisdom Is Wrong Again

The failure of economic growth to produce good stock returns extends far beyond the case of Brazil and China. Figure 16.2 plots the economic growth and stock returns in twenty-five emerging markets.[3] Countries with reasonably priced markets, such as Brazil, Mexico, and Argentina, gave investors the highest returns, although their economic growth was among the slowest. Even if we exclude China (the fastest grower and worst performer) and Brazil (the second slowest grower with the third best returns), the relation between real GDP growth and return in these countries is still negative.

FIGURE 16.2: GDP GROWTH AND STOCK RETURNS
IN EMERGING MARKETS, 1987–2003

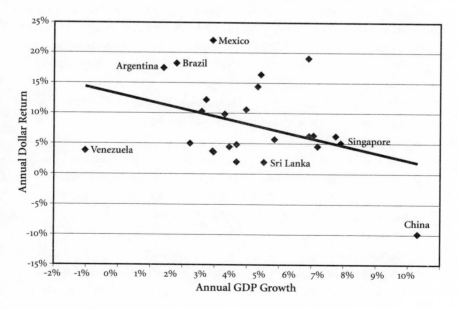

The same conclusion holds for developed economies. When Dimson, Marsh, and Staunton, in their landmark study *Triumph of the Optimists,* analyzed the data from sixteen countries from 1900 forward, they also found a negative relation between GDP growth and real stock returns.[4] Japan had the highest growth of real GDP but poor stock returns. South Africa had the lowest GDP growth but the third highest stock returns, surpassing returns in the faster growing United States. Australia and the United Kingdom had among the weaker real GDP growth rates but relatively high stock returns. Growth is not enough to sustain a profitable investment strategy.

Growth and Stock Returns

At this point you may be confused. In Chapter 15 I extolled growth as the global solution to the developing world's economic and financial problems. Now I claim that growth may be bad for the stock returns of individual countries. These claims seem contradictory, but they are not. Growth does produce more output, more income, and more buying power. This tends to support stock prices. But the prospect of growth often creates too much excitement and results in overpricing, especially in newly emerging economies.

That is what happened in China, when too much money chased too few shares. This caused overvaluation and poor future returns. Given the opportunity, many Chinese would have preferred to invest in U.S., European, or even Japanese firms. But they could not, so all the demand for shares was focused on a relatively small group of stocks.

Fortune magazine gave an insightful view of the pandemonium that broke loose when the Shenzhen market was opened in 1992:

> To buy stock in the West, you pick up the phone. To buy stock in China, you must first secure a permit to enter Shenzhen, the special economic zone near Hong Kong. You then bring 100 yuan, or half a month's wages, and wait in line for three days and nights. Then you get mad.
>
> Chinese police used batons and tear gas to contain parts of a fractious crowd of a million people attempting to buy application forms to purchase shares in the exchange's new listings. China's "savings overhang," all that money stuffed in mattresses or tied up in savings accounts earning 2% a

year, is estimated at one trillion yuan, or $185 billion. The old stock market was shut down more than 40 years ago, and there are simply too few shares available on the new markets to meet demand.[5]

The crowd erupted because some had accused government officials of hoarding the application forms. Imagine one million Chinese waiting in line for three days hoping to buy stock. The frenzy at the opening of the markets in China was like the South Sea bubble in England in 1708 or an IPO during the Internet craze in 1999. Insiders made out like bandits, whereas almost everyone else lost. The prices for Chinese firms priced in Hong Kong, where investors were free to buy foreign assets, were much cheaper than the prices of the same shares in Shenzhen or Shanghai.

As restrictions on share ownership are lifted, the Chinese will be able to buy foreign stocks and bonds as opportunities arise in the foreign markets. Chinese shares will become more moderately priced and the demand for investments outside of China will increase. As the age wave hits the developed world, the Chinese investors will have what the American, European, and Japanese retirees need: willing buyers of financial assets.

The World Portfolio

What does all this say about how much of your stock portfolio should be invested in foreign markets? Before we answer that question, it is important to look at the numbers in Table 16.1, which reports what percent of the market value of world equities are headquartered in each major region of the world.

As of September 17, 2004, the Morgan Stanley All-World Index, which contains most of the largest, most liquid firms in each country, had a market capitalization of $19.2 trillion. The value of firms headquartered in the United States is 52.3 percent of the world's market value; the figure for developed Europe is 27.8 percent and that for Japan 9.1 percent. Developed Asia (Hong Kong, Singapore, Australia, and New Zealand) contains 3.2 percent, while Canada has 2.6 percent. All these above named countries contain 13 percent of the world's population, although they serve as headquarters for firms that comprise 95.1 percent of the world's firms based on market value. The rest of the countries, or 87 percent of the world's population, are headquarters for firms with only 4.9 percent of the world's market value.

TABLE 16.1: ALLOCATION OF WORLD'S EQUITY
VALUES, SEPTEMBER 17, 2004

Region	Percentage
North America	54.9%
United States	52.3%
Canada	2.6%
Europe	27.8%
United Kingdom	10.2%
France	3.8%
Germany	2.7%
Other Developed Europe	11.1%
Japan	9.1%
Developed Asia Excluding Japan	3.2%
Australia	2.0%
Hong Kong	0.7%
Singapore, New Zealand	0.5%
Emerging Markets	4.9%
Korea	0.9%
Taiwan	0.5%
China	0.4%
Brazil	0.4%
Mexico	0.3%
India	0.3%
Russia	0.2%
Other Emerging Markets	1.9%

Finance theory dictates that investors should hold the broadest of all possible portfolios, each country weighted by its market value, to achieve maximal diversification. If these precepts were followed, then

U.S.-based investors would hold nearly half of their stock portfolio in non-U.S. companies.

Home Equity Bias

But the reality of most investors' portfolios is very different from this market value–based allocation. Recent data show that U.S. investors, both professional and individual, hold only 14 percent of their stocks in non-U.S.-based companies, less than one-third of the indexed proportion.[6] The reluctance to invest in assets outside the home country is called the home equity bias. Why does this bias exist?

The following reasons have been cited: (1) the additional risks incurred by currency fluctuations, since the prices of most foreign firms in their primary markets are quoted in foreign currencies, (2) higher transaction costs for investing abroad, and (3) investors' greater knowledge of, and therefore greater comfort in buying, domestic companies.

Currency fluctuations appear to be a valid reason to prefer equities denominated in your home currency. Exchange rates between countries can be very unstable. From 1997 through July 2001 the dollar rose 35 percent relative to a basket of foreign currencies but fell 30 percent from the peak through 2003. If Americans had bought foreign stocks in 1997, they would have had to deal with a strong headwind of foreign currency depreciation for four years before the tide turned in their favor.

Despite short-term exchange rate fluctuations, there is very strong evidence that in the long run the returns on foreign stocks cancel out these currency movements. Over the long run, movements in exchange rates are determined by relative inflation between the countries, and stock returns will compensate investors for this difference in inflation.

Brazil and China illustrate this point. Since 1992 the Brazilian currency has depreciated more than eighty times relative to the dollar, but this was more than compensated for by appreciation of Brazilian stocks. Brazilian stock prices held up well because when inflation hits, investors run to tangible assets, such as real estate, precious metals, and stocks. The impact on foreign investors of the depreciating currency is offset by the rising price of output and increasing profit margins, as wages generally lag inflation.

On the other hand, China, which for the last decade maintained an extremely stable exchange rate with the dollar (it was fixed at 8.25 yuan to the dollar in 1995), has offered investors extremely poor returns. Currency stability does not guarantee good performance.

The importance of transaction costs and the unfamiliarity with foreign stocks, the other two factors cited in favor of overweighting home equities, has declined over time. Transaction costs in international funds have fallen dramatically, and the annual fees of internationally based exchange-traded and indexed mutual funds are now not much higher than indexed products matching U.S. markets. Furthermore, it is now common for analysts to cover both foreign-based and domestic firms, so the information gap between U.S. and foreign-based firms has declined significantly.

Rising Correlations of International Markets

Recently another argument has been raised in favor of investors staying with domestic equities: the increasing correlations of the returns between the world's stock markets. Diversification is valuable because some stocks go up when others go down. If returns between stocks are increasingly correlated, the benefit from diversification is reduced.

The correlations between world stock returns are indeed rising. Figure 16.3 shows the correlation coefficient between annual stock market returns in the United States and the rest of the world over a nine-year moving period since 1970. When correlations are near zero (or even negative), diversification works well. But when correlations reach unity, all markets move together and there is no gain from diversification. One can see that since 1996, the correlation has been in a steady uptrend, reaching .75 in 2003.

The increased correlation between world financial markets is not surprising. The communications revolution has made the financial markets increasingly interconnected, as traders in one market react to news and developments in other markets. In Tokyo the day's trading often takes its cue from what happens in the United States the day before; the Europeans look at both the U.S. and Japanese markets; and before-market trading in the United States often takes its cue from Europe. Reactions to events and short-term fluctuations in investor sentiment, which in the past would have been confined to individual markets, now roll through the world's markets much like the wave of hands that rolls through sports stadiums.

These higher correlations should not, however, deter investors from in-

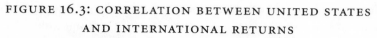

FIGURE 16.3: CORRELATION BETWEEN UNITED STATES
AND INTERNATIONAL RETURNS

ternational diversification. In the United States, many of the ten sectors highlighted in Chapter 4 have returns that are highly correlated, but I have not heard anyone suggest that one should refrain from investing in the industrials sector because, say, it is highly correlated with the materials sector. More important, where a firm is headquartered will become increasingly irrelevant to investors.

Sector Diversification versus Country Diversification

The most successful companies are going to be those that envision the global economic changes outlined in the last section. They will be headquartered anywhere in the world. In fact, the term "foreign investing," which is defined by where a firm keeps its home base, is a relic of the past. Why should we identify firms by where their headquarters are located and ignore where they produce or sell their goods?

Coca-Cola, ExxonMobil, Altria (formerly Philip Morris), Texas Instruments, and Intel sell at least two-thirds of their products abroad, but they are defined as U.S.-based firms. Similarly, Unilever is a Dutch firm, Nestlé is Swiss, Toyota and Sony are Japanese, and HSBC (Hong Kong Shanghai Bank Corporation) is English despite the fact that all these are global firms that buy, sell, and produce goods and services in international markets. For the S&P 500 Index, over 20 percent of all sales come from foreign markets, but that percentage will certainly increase as the global solution becomes a reality.

A Morgan Stanley report titled "How Global Is Your Industry" echoes these views: "We think that regional allocation is passé; indeed, research has shown that global industry influence has now surpassed country influence in explaining outcomes."[7] As noted in the chapter discussing sector returns, the Morgan Stanley report concludes that investors ought to focus their asset allocation strategies more prominently on global sectors. Unfortunately, investing by global sectors remains difficult because a complete set of global sector investment products is not yet available.[8]

Recommended Allocation

After considering all the factors, my recommended weight for foreign-based holdings of equity is 40 percent of the stock portfolio, somewhat short of the share of foreign stocks in the world markets. This is based on risk-return analysis that takes currency fluctuations into account, but uses a longer perspective than the standard risk analysis done in financial markets.

Investors may be persuaded to follow the crowd and underweight foreign holdings. The economist John Maynard Keynes perceptively maintained, "Worldly wisdom teaches that it is better to fail conventionally than succeed unconventionally."[9] If you make an investment that everyone else made and the investment fails, you have others with whom to commiserate, and misery loves company. If you fail by purchasing stocks that no one else buys, you bear the sole responsibility for the decline and will get little sympathy from others.[10]

Although copying the actions of others affords some psychological comfort, it pays to stand apart from the crowd. Conventional wisdom in the financial markets is generally wrong. We have seen that the future lies with the global market economy. Profits will flow to firms that take advantage of this growth. You should put your money to work in the international markets, no matter where the firms are headquartered.

How to Invest Abroad

How, then, should investors buy foreign-based firms for their stock portfolio? The best way to achieve broad-based international diversification is through global index funds. An index fund allows investors to match the returns of representative indexes at very low cost.

Index funds have gained popularity and should continue to do so because they have the lowest costs while still achieving excellent returns. There is much literature written on the underperformance of actively managed stock mutual funds. Jack Bogle, the founder of the Vanguard Group, the world leader in index products, has written extensively on the topic, as did I in *Stocks for the Long Run*.[11] The index funds noted below are available in mid 2004, but investors should be alert to new products that will become available.

Outside the United States the most popular indexes are those developed by Morgan Stanley's Capital Index Group. Vanguard's Total International Stock Index Fund (VGTSX), which is based on these Morgan Stanley Indexes, is the most inclusive non-U.S. indexed fund available. It includes stocks based in developed Europe[12] (around 60 percent of the fund), the Pacific[13] (nearly 30 percent), and an emerging-markets index (10 percent of the fund). The European, Pacific, and emerging-markets mutual funds can also be purchased separately.

Except for the emerging-markets segment, the Vanguard international fund is based on Morgan Stanley's EAFE Index, which stands for Europe, Australia, and the Far East. The EAFE Index constitutes the best-known and most widely cited non-U.S. index of the developed world's equities.[14]

Indexation of foreign stock markets, although more expensive than that in the United States, is no longer costly. The Vanguard Total International Stock Index charges 0.36 percent a year, twice the stated cost of Vanguard's S&P 500 or Total Stock Market Index funds.[15]

Vanguard has always been the undisputed low-cost and largest provider of indexed mutual funds. However, in the summer of 2004, Fidelity Mutual Funds of Boston, the world's largest mutual fund group, threw down the gauntlet and announced that its major index funds would slash fees to only 0.10 percent per year, lower than the stated fee on Vanguard.

This competition is great for investors. But investors should be fore-warned that *stated* fees may differ from actual fees and that Vanguard has offset most of its stated fees through its proprietary trading techniques. Tiny differences add up to significant dollars for the long-term investor.

Exchange-Traded Funds

In recent years an innovation, exchange-traded funds or ETFs, has sky-rocketed in popularity because of the funds' low fees and simple replica-tion of index products. ETFs, in contrast to mutual funds, can be bought and sold throughout the trading day. The annual costs of ETFs are even lower than the stated fees on indexed mutual funds, although a brokerage commission must be paid to buy and sell these funds.

For investors who seek exchange-traded funds, the Morgan Stanley EAFE Index has a very actively traded and liquid ETF (ticker EFA) that charges fees of 0.35 percent a year. The emerging-markets ETF is a separate fund (ticker EEM) with an annual expense ratio of 0.78 percent.

Unfortunately, our northern neighbor, Canada, is not included in the EAFE index because of its high correlation with U.S. stocks. But Canada should not be ignored, being home to such firms as Inco, Alcan, and New-mont Mining, which were eliminated from the S&P 500 Index in S&P's purge of non-U.S.-based firms in 2001. One can complete the non-U.S. portion of the international market by buying the Canadian exchange-traded fund (symbol EWC), which accounts for 2.6 percent of the equities in the world market.

Indexing at Home

For equity exposure to the United States, the best choice of index prod-ucts is the Dow Jones Wilshire Total Stock Market Index. This index is a capitalization-weighted index that contains all stocks that are traded on the major U.S. indexes. Vanguard's Total Stock Market Fund, which tracks the Wilshire Index, was founded in April 1992, and its average return, includ-ing all fees, has been only 0.19 percent per year less than its benchmark.[16]

Vanguard has a very strict policy against trading in and out of its index mutual funds. To satisfy those who wish to do so, Vanguard has instituted a group of exchange-traded funds called VIPERs (Vanguard Index Participation Equity Receipts). Each of Vanguard's VIPERs amounts to a new class of shares of one of the company's well-known index funds. This includes the Vanguard Total Stock Market Fund (VTI) as well as others.

There are two reasons why I prefer the Total Stock Market Fund to an index that covers part of the market, like the S&P 500 Index. First, I prefer to achieve the greatest diversification, and it is important to add small and midsized stocks, which make up about 20 percent of the U.S. stock market but are not in the S&P 500 Index. Second, investors should be wary of linking their wealth to very well known and widely replicated indexes that cover only part of the market. As I discussed in Chapter 2, these indexes advertise well ahead of time what stocks are being added or deleted. This enables speculators to buy stocks prior to their inclusion, pushing up their prices and putting the indexed investor at a disadvantage. With a fund linked to all stocks, this is impossible.

However, for those who prefer to decide their own allocations, one can add small and middle-sized capitalization indexes to the S&P 500 Index to achieve the total market or tilt the portfolio toward smaller or larger stocks. The S&P 400 midcap index (which contains about 7 percent of U.S. capitalization) and S&P 600 small-cap complement (which contains about 3 percent of the index) can be added to the S&P 500 Index to form the S&P 1500, an index that contains about 90 percent of the tradable U.S. market. Standard & Poor's monitors the entire U.S. market and chooses stocks in its index depending on market capitalization, industry representation, and liquidity, among other factors.

Alternatively, one could invest with the popular Russell indexes. The Russell indexes, in contrast to the Standard & Poor's indexes, are based almost exclusively on market capitalization.[17] The Russell 3000 contains the 3,000 largest stocks traded on all exchanges, comprising about 97 percent of the value of all U.S.-traded stocks. The Russell 1000 contains the 1,000 largest stocks by market value, and the Russell 2000 is a popular small-cap index comprising the 2,000 smallest of the 3,000 stocks belonging to the Russell universe. Russell has a host of exchange-traded funds.[18]

Again, for those who prefer ETFs, the two most popular exchange traded funds are those representing the S&P 500 Index, called spiders (after the acronym SPDR, for S&P Depository Receipts) and the Nasdaq 100, called cubes (after the ticker symbol QQQ), which represents a tech-heavy index of the 100 largest nonfinancial stocks traded on Nasdaq. Spiders and cubes are so popular that the average daily dollar volume in these issues often exceeds that of any listed stock on either the New York or Nasdaq exchange. Another popular exchange-traded fund is called diamonds, named after the symbol DIA, which represents the venerable Dow Jones Industrial Average.

International Indexation at the Core of the Portfolio

This chapter advances an international approach to holding equities. This approach emphasizes the importance of holding a substantial fraction of your equity assets—approximately 40 percent—in stocks that are headquartered outside the United States. This world indexed equity exposure should be considered the core of your portfolio.

We also learned that the growth trap is just as applicable to stocks of individual countries as it is to individual firms. Fast-growing countries such as China do not necessarily have the best-performing stocks. Broad-based diversification is the key to achieving the gains from global growth. In the next chapter we will talk about strategies investors can use to supplement this indexed core to achieve higher returns.

CHAPTER SEVENTEEN

Strategies for the Future:

THE D-I-V DIRECTIVES

Good thoughts are no better than good dreams, unless they be executed.

—Ralph Waldo Emerson, 1836

From Indexing to the D-I-V Directives

When I lecture to investors about the stock market, two questions invariably arise: "What will happen to the economy and my investments when the baby boomers retire?" and "Which stocks should I buy for the long run?"

The research that I undertook for this book confirms that the future is bright for equity investors. Growth in the developing world will provide both enough goods and enough demand for stocks to offset the impact of the age wave in the developed world. The future performance of stocks should easily outpace those of bonds, precious metals, and other inflation hedges.

On the second question, "Which stocks should I buy for the long run?" my answer has shifted since I conducted the research for this book. Formerly, I recommended that investors put all their money allocated to equity into a fund that tracked the broadest possible index of common stocks. Since the overwhelming evidence indicates that active equity managers and mutual funds, after fees, do not perform as well as low-cost index funds, I believed indexing was the best way for investors to accumulate wealth. Now I am convinced that there are strategies that can do even better.

Don't get me wrong. I still believe that indexing should be a core component of your stock portfolio. I spoke to the importance of indexing to the world markets in the last chapter. But my historical studies of the firms in the S&P 500, industry performance, IPOs, and dividends have revealed that investors may obtain better returns by supplementing their indexed portfolios with the strategies analyzed in this book.

I have distilled the portfolio implications of my new research into three directives, using the mnemonic D-I-V. The D-I-V directives are designed to help investors focus on strategies they can use to construct their stock portfolio.

Dividends: Buy stocks that have sustainable cash flows and return these cash flows to the shareholders as dividends.

International: Recognize the forces that will swing the balance of economic power away from the United States, Europe, and Japan toward China, India, and the rest of the developing world.

Valuation: Accumulate shares in firms with reasonable valuations relative to their expected growth and avoid IPOs, hot stocks, or other firms or industries that the consensus believes are "must-have" investments.

Dividends

HIGH-DIVIDEND STRATEGIES

This book emphasizes the importance of dividends in generating superior stock returns. The primary function of management should be to maximize current and future cash flows to shareholders. The payment of dividends has provided management with that discipline throughout most of the stock market's history, and I believe that stocks that pay good dividends will yield superior returns in the future.

Table 17.1 summarizes the risks and returns of the dividend strategies described in Chapters 9 and 10. All of these strategies beat both the S&P 500 Index and the Dow Jones Industrial Average.

The reward-risk ratios, which are the measure of the extra return per unit risk, are all superior to the indexing strategy.[1]

Which companies appeared on these dividend lists most often? The large integrated oil companies stand as high-yielding winners. In the top yielder strategy, which chooses firms in the S&P 500 with the highest (top 20 percent) dividend yields, Royal Dutch Petroleum has been in this group for twenty-nine years, and in those twenty-nine years it returned 17.11 per-

TABLE 17.1: DIVIDEND STRATEGIES, 1957–2003

Strategy	Description	Accumulation of $1,000	Annual Return	Risk	Reward-Risk Ratio
S&P 10	Ten Highest-Yielding Stocks of 100 Largest S&P 500 Stocks	$816,620	15.69%	17.70%	0.645
S&P Core 10	Ten Highest-Yielding Stocks of 100 Largest S&P 500 Stocks That Have Not Reduced Dividends in 15 Years	$811,593	15.68%	18.20%	0.628
Dow Core 10	Ten Highest-Yielding Dow Stocks That Have Not Reduced Dividends in 15 Years	$596,084	14.90%	15.82%	0.654
Dow 10	Ten Highest-Yielding Dow Industrial Stocks	$493,216	14.43%	15.38%	0.654
Top Yielders	Highest 20% Yielding Stocks in S&P 500	$462,750	14.27%	19.29%	0.530
S&P 500 Index	Indexing to 500 Largest U.S.-Based Stocks Chosen by S&P	$130,768	11.18%	17.02%	0.405
Dow 30 Average	Indexing to Dow Jones Industrial Index of 30 Stocks	$183,460	12.00%	16.64%	0.458

cent per year. This is over three percentage points more than its buy-and-hold annual return from 1957 to the present. ExxonMobil was on the list twenty-three years and returned almost 20 percent per year during that time, a full 6.5 percent above its buy-and-hold return. Mobil Oil (now merged with Exxon) earned 18 percent per year in its sixteen years in the strategy.

Oil stocks were also important in the Dow and S&P dividend strategies, as Standard Oil of New Jersey (now ExxonMobil) was in the Dow 10 strategy a record thirty-eight years, from 1957 through 2003.

Another industry that frequents these high yielding strategies are the cigarette manufacturers, such as Philip Morris and Fortune Brands (formerly American Tobacco). Philip Morris, which has never lowered its dividend payment, had a return of nearly 32 percent per year for the thirteen years that it was in the Core 10 strategy.

An important reason why these high-dividend strategies work so well is because of the basic principle of investor return. This principle, discussed in Chapter 3, states that stock returns are based not on earnings growth alone but on growth relative to expectations. For many of these dividend-paying stocks, investors became overly pessimistic at a dip in earnings growth, leading to lower-than-justified valuations and higher-than-average returns. For stocks paying a dividend, these lower valuations led to higher dividend yields, and investors were able to accumulate more shares at discounted prices. The return accelerator, described in Chapter 10, worked its magic on these stocks.

The evidence supporting dividends extends beyond the borders of the United States. Dimson, Marsh, and Staunton, authors of *Triumph of the Optimists*, found that the highest dividend yielding stocks in the U.K. outperformed the lowest-yielding stocks, just as I found for the United States. The divergence was substantial, amounting to 3 percent per year over the past 103 years.[2] I am certain that future research will find that dividend-based outperformance is present in other countries as well.

IMPLEMENTATION OF DIVIDEND STRATEGIES

The Dow 10, the S&P 10, and their associated core strategies involve just ten stocks, so they can be implemented by individual investors. For those who do not wish to purchase individual stocks, unit investment trusts that implement the Dow 10 strategy as well as similar strategies in other countries are available.

The list of companies in the 2004 portfolios of the Dow 10, Dow Core 10, S&P 10, and S&P Core 10 are found in Table 17. 2. Four of the Dow companies also appear on the S&P list: SBC Communications, Altria, General Motors, and J.P. Morgan Chase.

It should be emphasized that this list changes every year, and by the time you are reading this book, it is likely that some of these stocks will no longer be in these dividend strategies. You can find the stocks that currently make up the Dow 10 strategy, also known as "Dogs of the Dow," on the Internet.

While there are only a few dividend-related index funds available today, I am certain that as more investors learn of the power of dividends, there will be many more such investment vehicles in the future.

TABLE 17.2: MEMBERS OF DOW 10, DOW CORE 10, S&P 10, AND S&P CORE 10 DIVIDEND STRATEGIES IN 2004

Dow Strategies—2004 Companies				
Company	Ticker	Div Yld	Member of Dow 10	Member of Dow Core 10
SBC Communications	SBC	5.41%	✓	✓
Altria Group	MO	4.85%	✓	✓
AT&T	T	4.68%	✓	✓
General Motors	GM	3.75%	✓	
J.P. Morgan Chase	JPM	3.70%	✓	✓
Merck	MRK	3.20%	✓	✓
DuPont	DD	3.05%	✓	✓
Citigroup	C	2.88%	✓	✓
General Electric	GE	2.58%	✓	✓
ExxonMobil	XOM	2.44%	✓	✓
International Paper	IP	2.32%		✓

S&P Strategies—2004 Companies				
Company	Ticker	Div Yld	Member of S&P 10	Member of S&P Core 10
SBC Communications	SBC	5.41%	✓	✓
Altria Group	MO	4.85%	✓	✓
Verizon Communications	VZ	4.39%	✓	✓
Bristol-Meyers Squibb	BMY	3.92%	✓	✓
General Motors	GM	3.75%	✓	
J.P. Morgan Chase	JPM	3.70%	✓	✓
Washington Mutual	WM	3.49%	✓	✓
ChevronTexaco	CVX	3.31%	✓	✓
BellSouth Corp	BLS	3.25%	✓	✓
Schering-Plough	SGP	3.25%	✓	✓
Dow Chemical	DOW	3.22%		✓

Real estate investment trusts are companies that purchase and manage real estate or real estate loans. These trusts are not taxed as long as 90 percent of their net operating income is passed on as dividends to investors. For this reason, REITs are very high-yielding stocks. As of this writing, their yield is more than three times the 1.7 percent dividend yield on the S&P 500 Index.

Real estate, especially owner-occupied homes, is normally considered a separate asset class from corporate equity. However commercial, industrial, and multifamily residential properties are assets of considerable value that have publicly traded securities. As of the middle of 2004, publicly traded REITs owned more than $400 billion of the nearly $4 trillion worth of commercial real estate. The equity market value of these REITs is about $225 billion.

I believe that REITs should be a part of a well-balanced equity portfolio, especially one with a bias toward high-dividend stocks. There are many different index fund products, such as Vanguard's REIT (VGSIX) and two separate exchange-traded funds, iShares Dow Jones U.S. Real Estate Index Fund (IYR) and the streetTRACKS Wilshire REIT (RWR).

International

I have spoken of the dramatic shift in the relative wealth of the developed and developing world that I expect over the next half century. In the last chapter I recommended that investors have a substantial portion of their assets in an indexed world portfolio. For dollar-based investors I recommend 60 percent be in U.S.-headquartered firms and 40 percent in non-U.S.-based firms.

The evidence is strong against overweighting firms that are based solely in fast-growing countries, as these stocks are especially vulnerable to the growth trap. However, I do believe that firms that have committed to the global economy should be especially attractive to investors.

Table 17.3 is a list of the twenty largest non-U.S.-based firms that derive a substantial portion of their operating income from many different countries. One choice for investing in these global firms would be to buy the Standard & Poor's Global 100 exchange-traded fund (IOO), which repli-

TABLE 17.3: TWENTY LARGEST NON-U.S.-BASED FIRMS,
RANKED BY MARKET VALUE, SEPTEMBER 2004

Rank	Name	Sector	Headquarters Country
1	British Petroleum	Energy	United Kingdom
2	HSBC Holdings	Financial	United Kingdom
3	Vodafone Group	Telecom	United Kingdom
4	Total	Energy	France
5	GlaxoSmithKline	Health Care	United Kingdom
6	Novartis	Health Care	Switzerland
7	Royal Dutch Petroleum	Energy	Netherlands
8	Toyota	Consumer Disc	Japan
9	Nestlé	Consumer Staples	Switzerland
10	UBS	Financial	Switzerland
11	AstraZeneca	Health Care	United Kingdom
12	Telefonica	Telecom	Spain
13	Barclays	Financial	United Kingdom
14	Siemens	Industrials	Germany
15	Nokia	Information Tech	Finland
16	BNP Paribas	Financial	France
17	Banco Santander Central Hispano	Financial	Spain
18	Samsung Electronics	Information Tech	South Korea
19	Banco Bilbao	Financial	Spain
20	Canon Inc	Information Tech	Japan

cates the performance of 100 multinational companies. This index chooses large-cap firms based around the world whose businesses are global in nature and who derive a substantial portion of their operating income from many different countries. Currently the annual fee for this fund is

0.40 percent a year. Another global index is the Dow Jones Global Titans (DGT) 50 Index, a capitalization-weighted index of the fifty largest multinational companies.

In 2004, there was not yet any company based in China or India on this list. But it is only a matter of time before firms of China (such as China Mobile, Hutchison Whampoa, the Hang Seng Bank, and China Petroleum) and India (such as Infosys, Reliance Industries, Wipro, and others) join these global giants.

Dividend and valuation criteria are also important for international firms. In Part 3 we spoke of the importance of dividends to the corporate governance process. Since international standards of corporate accounting are so diverse, it is important to have tangible evidence of the profitability of firms. Dividends present just such evidence and are as important for foreign-based firms as they are for firms headquartered in the United States.

It is also critical that investors avoid the growth trap when buying international stocks, especially those from emerging countries. Investors should not choose the fastest-growing firms without attention to the price paid. No matter how fast firms are growing, there are limits to valuation. As always, the quality of the management and its commitment to expand those products within the company's core competencies will always be a critical criterion for investor success.

Valuations

If anyone doubted that valuation is important when buying stocks, the experience following the Internet and technology bubbles of 1999–2000 should have erased any doubts. Valuation always matters when buying stocks.

Table 17.4 summarizes the valuation strategies that are discussed in the book. Three are based on investments in global sector funds that are linked to the energy, health care, and consumer staples industries that we described in Chapter 4. One of these strategies, introduced in Chapter 3, chooses stocks with the lowest 20 percent of all P/E ratios in the S&P 500 Index and rebalances annually. Another strategy chooses the top-performing survivor stocks of the original S&P 500, which I have called the corporate El Dorados. I also recap the investment performance of Warren Buffett, first the partnership and then Berkshire Hathaway.

TABLE 17.4: VALUATION STRATEGIES, 1957–2003

Strategy	Description	Accumulation of $1,000	Annual Return	Risk	Reward-Risk Ratio
Buffett/ Berkshire	Invests in Warren Buffett's Partnership and then Berkshire Hathaway	$51,356,784	26.59%	33.53%	0.753
Top Performers	Invests in 20 Best-Performing Survivors of the Original S&P 500 Stocks	$840,291	15.76%	18.92%	0.619
Lowest P/E Stocks	Lowest 20% of P/E Ratios of S&P 500 Stocks	$425,703	14.07%	15.92%	0.600
Health Care	Invests in the Health Care Sector of S&P 500	$375,969	13.76%	21.64%	0.467
Consumer Staples	Invests in the Consumer Staples Sector of S&P 500	$319,776	13.36%	18.52%	0.500
Energy	Invests in the Energy Sector of S&P 500	$221,230	12.45%	18.01%	0.459
S&P 500 Index	Indexing to the 500 Largest U.S.-Based Stocks Chosen by S&P	$130,768	11.18%	17.02%	0.405

Sector Strategies

OIL

There is no question that there will be great strides in finding alternative energy sources over the next fifty years. But it is extremely unlikely that there will be a sudden reduction in the demand for oil and its distillates. The energy needs of the developing countries are huge and China and India consume more energy per unit of GDP than the developed countries of the world. That demand will clearly grow as these economies expand.

The oil sector of the S&P 500 Index has had a historical return of 12.45 percent since the founding of the S&P 500 Index, more than a percentage point above the overall index. Stocks in the oil sector also have the lowest correlation with the other sectors of the economy. This means that oil stocks can be viewed as a hedge: if their price goes up, it hurts economic growth, particularly for such countries as the United States that import oil, but the rise in price helps petroleum producers who hold large oil reserves. This countercyclical behavior of the energy sector's returns is a valuable diversifying tool for investors.

In addition to the large U.S.-based companies, such as ExxonMobil and ChevronTexaco, the international sector includes BP, Total of France, Royal Dutch Petroleum and Shell Trading and Transport of the Netherlands, ENI from Italy, and others.

HEALTH CARE AND CONSUMER STAPLES

The two best-performing sectors of the economy over the past half century have been health care and consumer staples. Their respective returns, at 13.76 percent and 13.36 percent annually, outpace the S&P 500 Index by more than two percentage points per year. In Chapter 3 I showed that 90 percent of the best-performing stocks—our corporate El Dorados— have come from those sectors.

The communications revolution makes it certain that consumers' preferences will be shaped by the global media. People who travel today are struck by the similarities and not the differences in what consumers, especially those in the higher income brackets, purchase—upscale shopping malls in Beijing, New Delhi, and St. Petersburg look strikingly similar.

Many bemoan the homogenization of cultures. Yet as global travel for business and pleasure booms, individuals seek out both the unique and the familiar. The very same people who are buying the Gucci bags and Mercedes cars are showcasing their country's own unique history and culture to foreign tourists.

Reputation and trust, attributes that brand-name producers feed on, are held in high esteem by the developing world. There is no reason why those trends should not continue. Although many brand-name firms are headquartered in the United States, the Swiss-based Nestlé and the U.K.-based Diageo, which manufactures such alcoholic beverages as Johnnie Walker, Seagrams, and Guinness, stand out.

Certainly the health care industry faces challenges. The cost of developing new drugs has skyrocketed, litigation threats abound, and price pressures from generics remain fierce. Nevertheless, the aging of the population will ensure the future demand for health care: drugs, hospitals, and nursing homes, as well as medical devices. Furthermore, the proliferation of discretionary medical treatments to offset the aging process is bound to increase.

Despite the hand-wringing over the high percentage of the U.S.'s output that goes to health care, it is hard to imagine that that proportion of GDP devoted to this sector will decline in coming decades. As long as the valuations in this sector do not stray far from the historical average, firms in health care are likely to outperform the market over the next fifty years. In the pharmaceutical sector, there are many foreign-based giants, such as GlaxoSmithKline and AstraZeneca from the United Kingdom and Novartis and Roche from Switzerland.

LOWEST-P/E STRATEGY

The lowest-P/E strategy sorts the S&P 500 Index each December 31 and invests in the 100 stocks (20 percent) with the lowest price-to-earnings ratios. Currently, there is no direct investment product that mimics this strategy, but I am hopeful that one will become available in the future.

The return on this strategy is slightly lower than the one using dividend yields, but it still beats the S&P 500 Index by nearly three percentage points a year, and its reward-to-risk ratio is higher. Royal Dutch Petroleum was a part of this strategy for forty-four years. There is a mix of utilities and consumer discretionary stocks that appear on the list when they are heavily discounted in the market.

The low-P/E strategy works similarly to the high-dividend-yield strategy. In the short run investors often overreact to unfavorable news, sending the price of stocks below their true values. As long as the firm is still earning profits, these overreactions will show up as a low P/E ratio, giving investors the opportunity to pick up discounted shares.

TOP SURVIVORS

The top-performing survivors include the twenty best-performing surviving stocks from the original group of the S&P 500 Index. These were the firms we identified in Chapter 3 as standing the test of time: they maintained dividend yields that were near the average for the index, slightly higher-than-average P/E ratios, and strong and committed managements devoted to expanding their markets globally. These are the tried-and-true companies that triumphed over the past half century.

It should be noted that the firms on this list do not result from an explicit strategy that investors could have pursued over the past forty-six years, since it presupposes that one knew in 1957 what the twenty best-performing survivor firms would be. However, it does suggest what returns investors could realize in the future if they are successful in seeking out the tried-and-true firms described throughout this book.

BERKSHIRE HATHAWAY

My list would not be complete without adding Warren Buffett's investment vehicle, Berkshire Hathaway. It is noteworthy that Buffett started his investment partnership in 1957, the same year that the S&P 500 Index was founded. An investment of $1,000 put in a hypothetical no-cost S&P 500 Index fund would have accumulated to $130,700 at the end of 2003, for an 11.18 percent annual return, whereas $1,000 placed with Warren Buffett would today be worth more than $51,356,000, for a 26.59 percent annual return.

Buffett has followed all the tenets of sound investment practice advocated in this book. He is fiercely loyal to his shareholders and ever mindful of valuation, and he avoids "story" stocks, IPOs, and those firms in fields outside of his range of expertise. Yet Berkshire pays no dividends. In Chapter 9 I go into great detail why the payments of dividends are not as important for Buffett's investors as they are for other firms.

If everyone were enthusiastic about Buffett's investment expertise, the price of Berkshire's stock would soar above the underlying value of the assets, taking into account his superior future investment prowess. That has happened on occasion, but as the superior returns on his stock indicate, Warren continues to work his magic beyond what the market expects. But the best person to ask whether to buy Berkshire is Warren Buffett—he will honestly tell you whether he thinks it is overpriced or not.

Indexation and Return Enhancement

The first decision that you as an investor must make is what proportion of your equity portfolio should be indexed to the broad international market and how much should be devoted to these return-enhancing strategies. There is no single percentage that is right for every investor. My recommendation is that 50 percent of the equity portfolio should be devoted to an internationally indexed portfolio and 50 percent should be devoted to these return-enhancing strategies. But the exact proportion will depend on a number of factors specific to the particular investor.

One of those factors is taxes. Because many of the return-enhancing strategies have a higher dividend yield and realize more capital gains, the tax status of the account—whether it is taxable or tax-sheltered—is an important factor. Return-enhancing strategies are generally better suited for tax-sheltered accounts. Although this recommendation is less important today, after recent congressional tax reform that has lowered the tax rate on dividend income, many investors still wish to realize capital gains in a tax-sheltered account.

Another important factor is investors' comfort level. No strategy can guarantee superior performance, and it is virtually certain that there will be periods of time when such strategies will underperform the market. If those periods would make an investor uncomfortable, then a lower fraction of the total portfolio should be devoted to these strategies and a higher fraction to indexation. These are issues that must be decided by each investor in conjunction with his or her financial planner. Remember that it is impossible to achieve better-than-average returns without taking some risk. Even straight equity indexation will, at times, underperform the fixed-income assets. One of the reasons stocks have returned so much more than bonds over history is the reluctance of investors to take this risk.

The Total Equity Portfolio

We are now ready to summarize the advice given in Chapters 15 and 16. These recommendations apply only to the stock allocation in your portfolio.*

I do not recommend an exact allocation to each return-enhancing strategy because this depends on market conditions and the risk tolerance of the individual investor. But an allocation of between 10 and 15 percent for each return-enhancing strategy would be reasonable.

---

* The proportion of your total portfolio that should be allocated to stocks is beyond the scope of this book (it is treated in *Stocks for the Long Run*).

ALLOCATION OF EQUITY FUNDS

Equity Holdings: 100%
World Index Funds: 50%
U.S.-Based Stocks   *30%*
Non-U.S.-Based Stocks   *20%*
Return-Enhancing Strategies: 50% (10% to 15% each)

- ■ *High-Dividend Strategies*
  - Highest-yielding dividend-paying stocks
  - Dow 10, S&P 10, Dow and S&P Core 10 Strategies
  - Real estate investment trusts
- ■ *Global Firms*
  - S&P Global 100
  - Dow Jones Global Titans
  - Diversified multinational equity firms
- ■ *Sector Strategies*
  - Oil and natural resources
  - Pharmaceuticals
  - Brand-name consumer staples
- ■ *Low Price Relative to Growth*
  - Lowest price-to-earnings ratio
  - Top survivors (growth relative to expectations)
  - Berkshire Hathaway

Conclusion

Forecasting financial market returns is never easy, but the next half century presents a particular challenge to those who look into the future. The world will simultaneously face two enormous forces: the aging of the rich countries and the rapid growth of the developing world.

Fortunately, these forces are working in tandem to stop the age wave from drowning future retirees in a sea of unsold stocks and bonds. The growth in world production made possible by the rapid spread of knowledge will create buyers who will support our financial markets well into this century.

The rapid pace of technological change will attract investors to firms using the latest technology to produce new and innovative goods and services. But most of the "story" stocks that arise from these new industries will disappoint investors. History has shown that those less exciting, tried-and-true firms whose managements have stuck with winning formulas and sold their products in the expanding global market will be better investments.

Because future economic growth will be robust, a strategy of indexing returns to the global equity market will no doubt serve investors well. But the strategies revealed in this book are likely to enhance investors' returns even further. These strategies are based on the innate propensity of investors to overpay for the "new" while ignoring the "old."

Some maintain that once these successful value-based strategies are well known, stock prices will adjust and nullify their advantage. But I disagree. Warren Buffett had it right when he said in 1985, "I have seen no trend toward value investing in the 35 years I've practiced it. There seems to be some perverse human characteristic that likes to make easy things difficult."[3]

Indeed, there is nothing difficult about successful long-term investing. Avoiding the growth trap and sticking with the tried and true has served investors very well in the past. And there is no reason why those strategies will not continue to serve investors well in our future.

APPENDIX

THE COMPLETE CORPORATE HISTORY AND
RETURNS OF THE ORIGINAL S&P 500 FIRMS

At the end of this appendix you will find the corporate histories and returns of each of the original S&P 500 stocks, ranked by their cumulative return from February 28, 1957, through December 31, 2003.

We first describe the twenty top-performing stocks that include all merged firms and spin-offs (with special attention to Philip Morris and RJR Nabisco), and then discuss the returns of the twenty largest stocks by market value in 1957.

Riding on Coattails: The Twenty Best-Performing Firms in the Total Descendants Portfolio

Table A1 lists the 20 best-performing firms of the Total Descendants portfolio, which includes those original firms that have merged with other firms as well as those survivor firms that remained intact. Surprisingly, fully two-thirds of the firms that make it to the top of the list do so not only because of their own success but because they rode the coattails of other successful firms. These investment successes did not require any active participation from investors; the shares of the acquiring firm were automatically credited to the shareholders of the acquired firm.

An example of how losers can become winners is found by following the investors in Thatcher Glass, a milk bottle manufacturer that was profitable in the early 1950s, during the early years of the U.S. baby boom. It is quite likely that many readers recall these bottles from when they were growing up, as Thatcher was the first milk-bottle producer and retained a dominant share of the market.

One might believe that holding on to stock in this firm would be a disaster. Births peaked in 1957 and then began to decline quickly. The baby boom turned into a baby bust. Glass milk bottles went the way of the dinosaur, soon to be replaced by waxed cardboard milk cartons, which were much cheaper, lighter, and more convenient. Today Thatcher Glass products can only be found in the memorabilia sector of eBay, going for a few dollars a bottle.

But this doesn't mean that those who bought and held Thatcher Glass for the next forty-seven years did not do well. The glass company was bought nine years later by Rexall Drug, which became Dart Industries, which merged with Kraft in 1980 and was eventually bought by Philip Mor-

TABLE A1: TWENTY BEST-PERFORMING FIRMS
IN TOTAL DESCENDANTS PORTFOLIO

Rank Return	Rank Market Cap 1957	Original Name — 2003 Name (— Merger; > Name Change)	Total Accumulation	Annual Return
1	215	Philip Morris > Altria (2003)	4,626.40	19.75%
2	473	Thatcher Glass — Rexall Drug (1966) > Dart Industries (1969) — Dart & Kraft (1980) > Kraft (1986) — Philip Morris (1988) > Altria (2003)	2,742.27	18.42%
3	447	National Can — Triangle Industries (1985) — Pechiney SA (1989)	2,628.72	18.31%
4	485	Dr Pepper — Private (1984) — Dr Pepper 7-Up (1993) — Cadbury Schweppes (1995)	2,392.22	18.07%
5	458	Lane Bryant — Limited Stores (1982) > Limited Inc. (1982)	1,997.87	17.62%
6	259	Celanese Corp. — Private (1987) — Celanese AG (1999)	1,520.68	16.93%
7	65	General Foods — Philip Morris (1985) > Altria (2003)	1,467.10	16.85%
8	197	Abbot Labs	1,281.33	16.51%
9	234	Warner-Lambert — Pfizer (2000)	1,225.25	16.40%
10	299	Bristol-Myers > Bristol-Meyers Squibb (1989)	1,209.44	16.36%
11	433	Columbia Pictures — Coca-Cola (1982)	1,154.27	16.25%
12	487	Sweets Co. > Tootsie Roll Industries (1966)	1,090.96	16.11%
13	274	American Chicle — Warner-Lambert (1962) — Pfizer (2000)	1,069.50	16.06%
14	143	Pfizer	1,054.82	16.03%
15	83	Coca-Cola	1,051.65	16.02%
16	267	California Packing Corp — Del Monte (1978) — R.J. Reynolds Industries (1979) — Private (1989) — RJR Nabisco Holdings (1991) — Philip Morris (2000) > Altria (2003)	1,050.10	16.01%
17	348	Lorillard — Loew's Theatres (1968) > Loew's (1971)	1,026.20	15.96%
18	66	National Dairy Products — Dart & Kraft (1980) > Kraft (1986) — Philip Morris (1988) > Altria (2003)	1,011.39	15.92%
19	117	Merck	1,003.41	15.90%
20	218	Standard Brands — Nabisco Brands (1981) — R.J. Reynolds Industries (1985) > RJR Nabisco (1986) — Private (1989) — RJR Nabisco Holdings (1991) — Philip Morris (2000) > Altria (2003)	1,002.98	15.90%

ris in 1988.[1] An investor who purchased only 100 shares of that company in 1957 would now have 140,000 shares of Philip Morris stock worth over $16 million!

You might exclaim how lucky that was. But such luck is not uncommon: *thirteen* of the twenty best-performing stocks of the original S&P 500 companies resulted from riding the coattails of other firms. Thatcher Glass was the second best-performing S&P 500 firm not because of its accomplishments alone, but also because of those of its successors.

It is most certain that in the next half century the acquiring firms will be global firms. Nearly 15 percent of the Total Descendants portfolio consists of companies that are headquartered outside the United States. Electrolux, the Swedish firm that is the world's largest producer of household appliances, bought Emerson Radio; British Petroleum bought former Dow industrial Anaconda Copper, Atlantic Richfield, and Amoco; Australian News purchased Twentieth Century–Fox; and Diageo, a British firm and the world's largest producer of alcoholic beverages, purchased the Liggett Group's food and tobacco interests, to name just a few.

R.J. Reynolds Tobacco and Philip Morris: The Cultivation of Winning Firms

Thatcher Glass became the second best-performing stock in the S&P 500 because of its purchase by Philip Morris. But Thatcher Glass is not the only firm to benefit from being purchased by the leading cigarette manufacturer: fully four original S&P 500 firms made it to the top twenty because of Philip Morris and its predecessors.

The full corporate story of Philip Morris is complex, but the outstanding performance of its stock makes its history worth retelling. Because of its acquisitions, Philip Morris winds up with the primary holdings of ten separate companies from the original S&P 500. Remarkably, all ten of these original S&P 500 companies outperformed the market.

Throughout the postwar period there were two prominent U.S. tobacco manufacturers, Philip Morris and R.J. Reynolds Tobacco. Philip Morris not only made Marlboro, the world's most successful brand, but also Parliament, Merit, Virginia Slims, and L&M (the flagship brand of Liggett and

Myers, which Philip Morris bought in 1999). Reynolds Tobacco made Camel, Winston, Doral, and Salem, four of the top ten leading brands.

As smoking declined and the threat of legal actions against cigarette manufacturers increased, both firms used their plentiful cash to acquire other firms, particularly in the food industry. In 1985, Philip Morris purchased General Foods, and R.J. Reynolds Tobacco bought Nabisco Brands, forming RJR Nabisco.[2] Nabisco Brands, through previous mergers and acquisitions, absorbed two other original S&P 500 firms, including Cream of Wheat in 1971 and Standard Brands in 1981. Reynolds also had purchased Penick & Ford in 1965, as well as Del Monte Foods in 1979, which had earlier purchased California packing in 1978. All six companies in the RJR lineage, including RJR itself, beat the market by more than 2 percent a year, and the top two, California Packing and Standard Brands, outperformed the S&P by over 5 percent a year.

In 1988 Philip Morris purchased Kraft for $13.5 billion. The following year RJR Nabisco was taken private by Kohlberg Kravis Roberts (KKR) in the largest leveraged buyout in history. KKR paid $29 billion for RJR Nabisco, and three years later, in 1991, sold a portion of the firm to the public in the form of RJR Nabisco Holdings.[3, 4]

FIGURE A1: CORPORATE EVOLUTION OF
PHILIP MORRIS FROM 1957

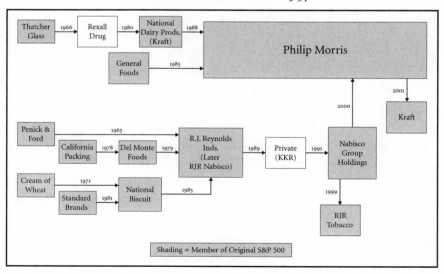

RJR Nabisco Holdings spun off its ownership of Reynolds Tobacco to shareholders in 1999, but due to the fact that RJR was a much smaller share of Nabisco Holdings than Nabisco, shareholders still had a majority of their investment in Nabisco Holdings. Nabisco Holdings was then bought by Philip Morris in 2001.

After this purchase, Philip Morris combined General Foods, Kraft, and Nabisco Holdings into one company called Kraft. Sixteen percent of Kraft was sold from Philip Morris in an IPO in 2001 (proceeds were over $8 billion).

From the direct Philip Morris lineage, General Foods became the seventh best-performing firm of the original S&P 500 firms, giving shareholders a return of 16.85 percent per year, 6 percent better than the S&P 500. Kraft Foods, whose original parent was National Dairy Products, is the same company I cited in Chapter 1 as having the best return among the largest fifty firms in 1950. National Dairy came up number eighteen on the list of the best original S&P 500 companies.

As a result, Philip Morris is the legacy firm for ten original S&P 500 firms: the six from the RJR lineage, General Foods, Kraft, Thatcher Glass, and Philip Morris itself. All ten of these companies ended up beating the S&P 500 Index, and four are among the twenty top-performing original stocks.

The Performance of the Twenty Largest Firms in 1957

Most of the companies that reached the top twenty (Table 3.1 in Chapter 3 and Table A2) started out quite small. None of the top-twenty performing stocks from the Total Descendants portfolio ranked larger than sixty-fifth in market capitalization in 1957. Since the S&P 500 index is, like most averages, capitalization-weighted, it is important to learn how large stocks performed.

The answer, as Table A2 shows, is "very well." The return to an equally weighted portfolio of the twenty largest companies, which constituted 47 percent of the market value of the S&P 500 in 1957, generated an 11.40 percent return for investors, identical to the performance of the Total Descendants portfolio and considerably above the return on the S&P 500 Index.

The Dominance of Oil

Nine of the twenty largest firms in 1957 were in the energy sector, which was the second largest sector after basic manufacturing (materials). It is surprising that despite the rapid shrinkage of the oil sector, the top five of the best-performing stocks from these twenty largest firms were all from the petroleum industry.

Number one was Royal Dutch Petroleum, a firm founded in the Netherlands, and one of the companies that Standard & Poor's deleted from its index in 2002 when it purged all foreign-based firms. The second best-performing firm was Shell Oil, a U.S.-based company that was purchased by Royal Dutch in 1985. Royal Dutch gave shareholders a handsome 13.6 percent annual return over the next forty-seven years, and Shell returned 13.1 percent, both far better than the S&P 500 Index.

Shell and Royal Dutch share a long history that extends back to 1892. Shell Transport & Trading, a London-based firm, built the world's first oil tanker, which on its maiden voyage delivered 4,000 tons of Russian kerosene to Singapore and Bangkok.

At the time, Royal Dutch was developing oil fields in Asia and commissioned an oil fleet of its own. In 1903, facing competition from the Standard Oil trust and John D. Rockefeller, the two European companies decided it would be better to merge their operations. While both Royal Dutch and Shell Transport remained independent companies, in 1907 the two companies formed the Royal Dutch Shell Group, with Royal Dutch owning 60 percent of the firm and Shell owning 40 percent.

The original oil companies that ranked third, fourth, and fifth were Socony Mobil (which first dropped the Socony [Standard Oil Co. of NY] name and later merged with Exxon), Standard Oil of Indiana (which merged into BP Amoco), and Standard Oil of New Jersey, which changed its name to Exxon in 1972. Each of these firms outperformed the S&P 500 Index by between 2 and 3 percent per year over the next forty-six years.

Gulf Oil, Standard Oil of California, and Texas Co. (Texaco) eventually merged to form ChevronTexaco, and both outperformed the S&P 500 Index, while Phillips Petroleum, which became part of ConocoPhillips, slightly underperformed the Index.

Of the remaining eleven firms in the top 20, the basic materials and manufacturing stocks, such as Union Carbide (now part of Dow Chemical), DuPont, General Motors, and Alcoa, lagged the market significantly. U.S. Steel would have given investors an even worse return had it not purchased and transformed itself into Marathon Oil. Bethlehem Steel, once the second largest steel manufacturer in the world behind U.S. Steel, went bankrupt in 2001 and is the only one of the original twenty largest S&P 500 stocks to lose money for investors.

It might be tempting to suggest that the outperformance of the original S&P portfolios is related to the superior returns in the oil sector, which constituted almost one-quarter of the original index. But that is not the case. Even when all firms from the oil sector are removed, all the S&P 500 portfolios of original stocks would still have outperformed the S&P 500 Index.

TABLE A2: RETURNS OF THE TWENTY LARGEST COMPANIES FROM THE ORIGINAL S&P 500

Rank Return	Rank Market Cap (1957)	Original Name — 2003 Name (— Merger; > Name Change)	Total Accumulation of $1 (including spin-offs)	Annual Return
1	12	Royal Dutch Petroleum	398.84	13.64%
2	14	Shell Oil — Royal Dutch Petroleum (1985)	323.96	13.14%
3	13	Socony Mobil Oil > Mobil (1966) — ExxonMobil (1999)	322.41	13.13%
4	16	Standard Oil of Indiana > Amoco (1985) — BP Amoco (1998)	285.31	12.83%
5	2	Standard Oil of New Jersey > Exxon (1972) > ExxonMobil (1999)	254.00	12.55%
6	5	General Electric	220.04	12.21%
7	6	Gulf Oil > Gulf — Chevron (1984) > ChevronTexaco (2001)	214.12	12.14%
8	11	International Business Machines	196.50	11.94%
9	10	Standard Oil of California > Chevron (1984) > ChevronTexaco (2001)	172.29	11.62%
10	15	Sears, Roebuck	151.51	11.32%
11	8	Texas Co. > Texaco (1959) — ChevronTexaco (2001)	128.63	10.93%
12	20	Phillips Petroleum > ConocoPhillips (2002)	119.61	10.76%
13	1	American Telephone & Telegraph > AT&T (1994)	107.16	10.50%
14	7	Union Carbide & Carbon > Union Carbide (1957) — Dow Chemical (2001)	86.20	9.98%
15	4	DuPont	41.82	8.30%
16	3	General Motors	41.47	8.28%
17	17	Aluminum Company of America > Alcoa (1999)	37.74	8.06%
18	19	Eastman Kodak	35.33	7.91%
19	9	U.S. Steel > USX Corp (1986) > USX Marathon (1991) > Marathon Oil (2000)	8.25	4.61%
20	18	Bethlehem Steel	0.001	−13.54%

THE RETURNS OF THE ORIGINAL S&P 500 FIRMS

Included in this list are the name changes, the mergers, and the year that they occurred. It is assumed that $1.00 is invested in each of the firms and that all dividends are reinvested and all spin-offs, if any, are held. If a firm goes private, the funds from privatization are assumed to be invested in the S&P 500 Index fund, with dividends reinvested. If the privatized firm goes public again, the total accumulated in the index fund is used to purchase the newly issued firm. These firms comprise the Total Descendants portfolio, as described in Chapter 2.

This list displays the breakdown of the accumulation of each dollar between the parent and spin-offs, and the percentage allocated to each. Included is the rank by market capitalization of each firm on February 28, 1957.

Returns of Original S&P 500 Firms

Results of investing $1 in each S&P 500 Company on March 1, 1957.

Returns measured through December 31, 2003

Rank Return	Rank Market Cap 1957	Original Name — 2003 Name (— Merger; > Name Change)	Total Accumulation	Percent Total	Annual Return
1	215	Philip Morris > Altria (2003)	$4,626.40	100.0%	19.75%
2	473	Thatcher Glass — Rexall Drug (1966) > Dart Industries (1969) — Dart & Kraft (1980) > Kraft (1986) — Philip Morris (1988) > Altria (2003)	$2,742.27	100.0%	18.42%
		Altria	$2,701.27	98.5%	
		Premark (1986) — Illinois Tool Works (1999)	$30.43	1.1%	
		Tupperware (1996)	$10.57	0.4%	
3	447	National Can — Triangle Industries (1985) — Pechiney SA (1989)	$2,628.72	100.0%	18.31%
4	485	Dr Pepper — Private (1984) — Dr Pepper 7-Up (1993) — Cadbury Schweppes (1995)	$2,392.22	100.0%	18.07%
5	458	Lane Bryant — Limited Stores (1982) > Limited Inc. (1982)	$1,997.87	100.0%	17.62%
		Limited	$1,399.23	70.0%	
		Too (1999)	$158.52	7.9%	
		Abercrombie (1998)	$20.33	1.0%	
6	234	Warner-Lambert — Pfizer (2000)	$1,225.25	100.0%	16.40%
		Aventis	$1,131.83	92.8%	
		Celanese AG (1999)	$88.33	7.2%	
7	65	General Foods — Philip Morris (1985) > Altria (2003)	$1,467.10	100.0%	16.85%

Rank Return	Rank Market Cap 1957	Original Name — 2003 Name (— Merger; > Name Change)	Total Accumu- lation	Percent Total	Annual Return
8	197	Abbot Labs	$1,281.33	100.0%	16.51%
9	259	Celanese — Hoechst AG (1987) — Aventis (1999)	$1,220.16	100.0%	16.39%
		Aventis	$1,131.83	92.8%	
		Celanese AG (1999)	$88.33	7.2%	
10	299	Bristol-Myers > Bristol-Myers Squibb (1989)	$1,209.44	100.0%	16.36%
		Bristol-Myers Squibb	$999.26	82.6%	
		Zimmer Holdings (2001)	$210.18	17.4%	
11	433	Columbia Pictures — Coca-Cola (1982)	$1,154.27	100.0%	16.25%
		Coca-Cola	$1,146.51	99.3%	
		Columbia Pictures (1988) — Sony (1989)	$7.76	0.7%	
12	487	Sweets Co. > Tootsie Roll Industries (1966)	$1,090.96	100.0%	16.11%
13	274	American Chicle — Warner-Lambert (1962) — Pfizer (2000)	$1,069.50	100.0%	16.06%
14	143	Pfizer	$1,054.82	100.0%	16.03%
15	83	Coca-Cola	$1,051.65	100.0%	16.02%
		Coca-Cola	$1,044.57	99.3%	
		Columbia Pictures (1988) — Sony (1989)	$7.07	0.7%	
16	267	California Packing Corp — Del Monte (1978) — R.J. Reynolds Industries (1979) — Private (1989) — RJR Nabisco Holdings (1991) — Philip Morris (2000) > Altria (2003)	$1,050.10	100.0%	16.01%
		Altria	$659.90	63.2%	
		R.J. Reynolds Tobacco (1999)	$373.10	35.5%	
		Sealand (1984) — CSX Corp (1986)	$17.10	1.6%	
17	117	Merck	$1,032.64	100.0%	15.97%
		Merck	$949.69	254.5%	
		Medco Health Solutions (2003)	$82.95	485.1%	
18	348	Lorillard — Loew's Theatres (1968) > Loew's (1971)	$1,026.20	100.0%	15.96%
19	66	National Dairy Products — Dart & Kraft (1980) > Kraft (1986) — Philip Morris (1988) > Altria (2003)	$1,011.39	100.0%	15.92%
		Altria	$970.38	95.9%	
		Premark (1986) — Illinois Tool Works (1999)	$30.43	3.0%	
		Tupperware (1996)	$10.57	1.0%	
20	218	Standard Brands — Nabisco Brands (1981) — R.J. Reynolds Industries (1985) >RJR Nabisco (1986) Private (1989) — RJR Nabisco Holdings (1991) — Philip Morris (2000) > Altria (2003)	$1,002.98	100.0%	15.90%
		Altria	$640.73	63.9%	
		R.J. Reynolds Tobacco (1999)	$362.26	36.1%	
21	298	Richardson Merrell — Richardson Vicks (1981) — Procter & Gamble (1985)	$992.50	100.0%	15.87%
		Procter & Gamble	$893.13	90.0%	
		Smuckers (2002)	$8.14	0.8%	
		Dow Chemical (1981)	$91.23	9.2%	
22	421	Houdaille Industries — Private (1979)	$950.02	100.0%	15.77%
23	474	Reeves Brothers — Private (1982)	$941.87	100.0%	15.74%
24	342	R.H. Macy — Private (1986)	$922.48	100.0%	15.69%
25	409	Stokely–Van Camp — Quaker Oats (1983) — Pepsi (2001)	$873.83	100.0%	15.56%
		PepsiCo	$813.10	93.1%	

Rank Return	Rank Market Cap 1957	Original Name — 2003 Name (— Merger; > Name Change)	Total Accumulation	Percent Total	Annual Return
		Fisher-Price (1991) — Mattel (1993)	$60.73	6.9%	
26	216	PepsiCo	$866.07	100.0%	15.54%
		PepsiCo	$761.09	87.9%	
		Tricon Global Restaurants (1997) > Yum Brands (2002)	$104.97	12.1%	
27	481	McCall — Norton Simon (1968) — Esmark (1983) — Beatrice Foods (1984) — Private (1986)	$798.48	100.0%	15.34%
28	239	Colgate-Palmolive	$761.16	100.0%	15.22%
29	60	R.J. Reynolds Industries (1985) >RJR Nabisco (1986) — Private (1989) — RJR Nabisco Holdings (1991) — Philip Morris (2000) > Altria (2003)	$743.83	100.0%	15.16%
		Altria	$467.44	58.5%	
		R.J. Reynolds Tobacco (1999)	$264.28	35.5%	
		Sealand (1984) — CSX Corp (1986)	$12.11	1.6%	
30	275	Crane Co.	$736.80	100.0%	15.14%
		Crane	$491.55	66.7%	
		Medusa Corp (1988) — Southdown (1998) — Cemex SA (2000)	$235.26	31.9%	
		Huttig Building Products (1999)	$9.98	1.4%	
31	441	Consolidated Cigar — Gulf & Western Industries (1968) > Paramount Communications (1989) Viacom (1994)	$697.82	100.0%	15.01%
		Viacom	$694.26	99.5%	
		GW Land/Private (1969)	$3.56	0.5%	
32	376	Penick & Ford — R.J. Reynolds Tobacco (1965) > RJR Nabisco (1986) — Private (1989) RJR Nabisco Holdings (1991) — Philip Morris (2000) > Altria (2003)	$694.81	100.0%	15.00%
		Altria	$436.63	62.9%	
		R.J. Reynolds Tobacco (1999)	$246.87	35.5%	
		Sealand (1984) — CSX Corp (1986)	$11.31	1.6%	
33	303	Bestfoods — Corn Products (1958) > C P C Int'l (1969) > Best Foods (1998) — Unilever (2000)	$688.20	100.0%	14.97%
		Unilever	$659.64	95.9%	
		Corn Products International (1998)	$28.56	4.1%	
34	296	Paramount Pictures — Gulf & Western Industries (1966) > Paramount Communications (1989) Viacom (1994)	$673.56	100.0%	14.92%
		Viacom	$670.12	99.5%	
		GW Land (1969) *	$3.44	0.5%	
35	443	General Cigars >Culbro (1976) — General Cigar Holdings (1997) — Swedish Match (2000)	$668.28	100.0%	14.90%
		Swedish Match	$256.88	59.3%	
		First Financial Caribbean (1988) — Doral Financial (1997)	$396.07	38.4%	
		Griffin Land and Nurseries (1999)	$15.34	2.3%	
36	471	Virginia Carolina Chemical — Socony Vacuum Oil (1963) > Mobil (1966) — ExxonMobil (1999)	$655.05	100.0%	14.85%
37	439	Congoleum-Nairn — Bath Industries (1968) > Congoleum (1975) — Private (1980)	$647.19	100.0%	14.82%
38	378	Truax-Traer Coal — Consolidation Coal (1962) — Continental Oil (1966) > Conoco (1969) —DuPont (1981)	$642.82	100.0%	14.80%
		DuPont	$496.29	77.2%	
		Conoco (1999) — Conoco Phillips (2002)	$146.54	22.8%	
39	374	American Agricultural Chemical— Consolidation Coal (1963) —			

Rank Return	Rank Market Cap 1957	Original Name — 2003 Name (— Merger; > Name Change)	Total Accumu-lation	Percent Total	Annual Return
		Continental Oil (1966) > Conoco (1969) — DuPont (1981)	$640.72	100.0%	14.80%
		DuPont	$494.66	77.2%	
		Conoco (1999) — Conoco Phillips (2002)	$146.06	22.8%	
40	432	Amalgamated Sugar — National City Lines (1982) — Private (1985)	$636.88	100.0%	14.78%
41	277	Heinz	$635.99	100.0%	14.78%
		Heinz	$566.10	89.0%	
		Del Monte (2002)	$69.88	11.0%	
42	148	Corn Products > C P C Int'l (1969) > Best Foods (1998) — Unilever (2000)	$619.00	100.0%	14.71%
		Unilever	$604.31	97.6%	
		Corn Products International (1998)	$26.63	4.3%	
43	188	Wrigley	$603.88	100.0%	14.65%
44	72	American Tobacco > American Brands (1969) > Fortune Brands (1997)	$580.03	100.0%	14.55%
		Fortune Brands	$348.98	60.2%	
		Gallaher Group (1997)	$231.05	39.8%	
45	329	Electric Auto-Lite — Eltra (1963) — Allied Corp.(1979) — Honeywell International (1999)	$572.28	100.0%	14.52%
		Honeywell International	$541.26	94.6%	
		Henley Group (1986) — Wheelaborator Group (1989) — Waste Management (1998)	$16.75	2.9%	
		Fisher Scientific (1987) — Wheelaborator Group (1989) — Waste Management (1998)			
		Henley Manufacturing (1987) — Private (1989)	$14.28	2.5%	
46	467	Bohn Aluminum & Brass (1963) — Gulf & Western Industries (1966) > Paramount Communications(1989) — Viacom (1994)	$571.01	100.0%	14.51%
		Viacom	$568.09	99.5%	
		GW Land (1969) *	$2.92	0.5%	
47	328	Flintkote — Genstar (1980) — Imasco (1986) — British American Tobacco (2000)	$562.93	100.0%	14.48%
48	226	Quaker Oats — PepsiCo (2001)	$556.73	100.0%	14.45%
		PepsiCo	$518.04	93.1%	
		Fisher Price (1991) — Mattel (1993)	$38.69	6.9%	
49	403	Gulf Mobile & Ohio RR — Illinois Central RR (1972) — Illinois Central Industries > Whitman (1988) > PepsiAmericas (2001)	$552.70	100.0%	14.43%
		PepsiAmericas	$59.86	10.8%	
		PetInc (1991) — Grand Metropolitan (1995) > Diageo (1997)	$236.32	42.8%	
		Illinois Central (1990) — Canadian National Railway (1998)	$151.33	27.4%	
		Hussman International (1998) — Ingersoll Rand (2000)	$86.12	15.6%	
		Midas (1998)	$8.21	1.5%	
		Prospect Group (1989) — Private (1997)	$3.16	0.6%	
		Banctec (1990) — Private (1999)	$3.28	0.6%	
		Sylvan Food Holdings (1990) > Sylvan (1994)	$1.46	0.3%	
		Knowledge Universe (1992) *	$2.38	0.4%	
		Forschner Group (1990) > Swiss Army Brands (1990) —			

Rank Return	Rank Market Cap 1957	Original Name — 2003 Name (— Merger; > Name Change)	Total Accumulation	Percent Total	Annual Return
		Victorinox (2002)	$0.58	0.1%	
50	180	Kroger	$546.79	100.0%	14.41%
51	255	Schering — Schering-Plough (1971)	$537.05	100.0%	14.36%
52	178	Container Corp. of America — Marcor (1968) — Mobil (1976) — ExxonMobil (1999)	$519.54	100.0%	14.28%
53	31	Procter & Gamble	$513.75	91.3%	14.26%
		Procter & Gamble	$509.11	99.1%	
		Smuckers (2002)	$4.64	0.9%	
54	164	Swift > Esmark (1973) — Beatrice Foods (1984) — Private (1986)	$513.12	100.0%	14.25%
55	227	Hershey Foods	$507.00	100.0%	14.22%
56	345	Norwich Pharmacal >Morton Norwich Prods (1969) >Morton Thiokol (1982) > Thiokol (1989) > Cordant Tech (1998) — Alcoa (2000)	$498.99	100.0%	14.19%
		Alcoa	$238.54	47.8%	
		Morton International (1989) — Rohm & Haas (1999)	$195.94	39.3%	
		Autoliv (1997)	$64.51	12.9%	
57	262	American Broadcasting Co. — Capital Cities ABC (1986) — Walt Disney Co. (1996)	$493.89	100.0%	14.16%
58	304	Storer Broadcasting — Private (1985)	$493.21	100.0%	14.16%
59	453	Royal Crown Cola — Private (1984)	$489.91	100.0%	14.14%
60	435	Spiegel — Beneficial Financial Corp (1965) > Beneficial (1998) — Household International (1998) HSBC Holdings (2003)	$478.56	100.0%	14.08%
61	372	Wesson Oil — Hunt Foods (1967) — Norton Simon (1968) — Esmark (1983) — Beatrice Foods (1984) — Private (1986)	$476.58	100.0%	14.07%
62	428	Howmet — Pechiney SA (1975)	$472.27	100.0%	14.05%
		Pechiney SA	$201.62	42.7%	
		Pfizer (1970)	$270.65	57.3%	
63	76	American Home Products > Wyeth (2002)	$461.19	100.0%	13.99%
64	241	Chicago Pneumatic Tool — Danaher Corp (1986)	$455.23	100.0%	13.96%
65	133	Safeway Stores — Private (1986) — Safeway Stores (1990)	$453.03	100.0%	13.95%
66	93	C.I.T. Financial — RCA (1980) — General Electric (1986)	$449.43	100.0%	13.93%
67	412	Merganthaler Linotype — Eltra (1963) — Allied (1979) — Honeywell International (1999)	$444.54	100.0%	13.90%
		Honeywell International	$420.43	94.6%	
		Henley Group (1986) — Wheelaborator Group (1989) — Waste Management (1998)	$13.01	2.9%	
		Fisher Scientific (1987) — Wheelaborator Group (1989) — Waste Management (1998)			
		Henley Manufacturing (1987) — Private (1989)	$11.09	2.5%	
68	437	Elliot Co. — Carrier Corp (1978) — United Technologies (1979)	$434.87	100.0%	13.85%
69	285	Sunshine Biscuits — American Tobacco (1966) > American Brands (1969) > Fortune Brands (1997)	$426.33	100.0%	13.80%
		Fortune Brands	$256.50	60.2%	
		Gallaher Group (1997)	$169.82	39.8%	
70	236	Columbia Broadcasting System > CBS Inc (1974) — Westinghouse (1995) — Viacom (2000)	$425.17	100.0%	13.80%
71	12	Royal Dutch Petroleum	$398.84	100.0%	13.64%
72	400	Mohasco Industries > Mohasco Corp. (1974) — Private (1989) — Mohawk Industries (1992)	$398.78	100.0%	13.64%

Rank Return	Rank Market Cap 1957	Original Name — 2003 Name (— Merger; > Name Change)	Total Accumulation	Percent Total	Annual Return
73	118	Texas Gulf Sulphur — Société Nationale Elf Aquitaine (1981) — Total Fina Elf (1991)	$395.86	100.0%	13.62%
74	322	Amstar — Private (1984)	$390.51	100.0%	13.59%
75	198	General Mills	$388.43	100.0%	13.58%
		General Mills	$297.78	76.7%	
		Kenner Parker Toys (1985) — Tonka (1987) — Hasbro (1991)	$6.12	1.6%	
		Crystal Brands (1985)	$0.00	0.0%	
		Darden Restaurants (1995)	$84.52	21.8%	
76	327	Beechnut Life Saver — Squibb Beechnut (1968) > Squibb (1971) — Bristol-Myers Squibb (1989)	$388.30	100.0%	13.58%
		Bristol-Myers Squibb	$308.99	79.6%	
		Zimmer Holdings (2001)	$68.43	17.6%	
		Westmark International (1987) > Advanced Tech Labs (1992) > ATL Ultrasound (1997) — Philips NV (1998) — Koninklijke Philips Elec (1999)	$8.04	2.1%	
		Spacelabs Medical (1992) — Instrumentarium (2002)	$2.33	0.6%	
		Sonosite (1998)	$0.51	0.1%	
77	252	McGraw-Hill	$386.60	100.0%	13.56%
78	132	Consolidation Coal — Continental Oil (1966) > Conoco (1969) — DuPont (1981)	$379.75	100.0%	13.52%
		DuPont	$293.18	77.2%	
		Conoco (1999) — Conoco Phillips (2002)	$86.57	22.8%	
79	354	Dixie Cup — American Can (1957) > Primerica (1987) — Primerica Corp New (1988) > Travelers (1994) > Travelers Group (1995) > Citigroup (1998)	$374.98	100.0%	13.49%
		Citigroup	$369.25	98.5%	
		Travelers Property Casualty (2002)	$5.73	1.5%	
		Transport Holdings (1995) — Conseco (1996)	$0.00	0.0%	
80	278	Melville Shoe > Melville (1976) > CVS (1996)	$370.66	100.0%	13.46%
		CVS	$365.33	98.6%	
		Footstar (1996)	$5.33	1.4%	
81	388	Magnavox — North America Philips (1975) — Philips NV (1987)	$367.19	100.0%	13.44%
82	478	Kayser Roth — Gulf & Western Industries (1975) > Paramount Communications (1989) — Viacom (1994)	$359.42	100.0%	13.39%
83	282	Worthington — Studebaker Worthington (1967) — McGraw Edison (1979) — Cooper Industries (1985)	$353.25	100.0%	13.35%
		Cooper Industries	$340.99	96.5%	
		Gardner Denver (1994)	$12.26	3.5%	
84	142	National Biscuit > Nabisco Brands (1971) — R.J. Reynolds Industries (1985) > RJR Nabisco (1986) — Private (1989) — RJR Nabisco Holdings (1991) — Philip Morris (2000) > Altria (2003)	$352.43	100.0%	13.34%
		Altria	$221.48	62.8%	
		R.J. Reynolds Tobacco (1999)	$125.22	35.5%	
		Sealand (1984) — CSX Corp (1986)	$5.74	1.6%	
85	240	Marathon — American Can (1957) > Primerica (1987) — Primerica New (1988) > Travelers (1994) > Travelers Group (1995) > Citigroup (1998)	$346.66	100.0%	13.30%
		Citigroup	$341.36	98.5%	

Rank Return	Rank Market Cap 1957	Original Name — 2003 Name (— Merger; > Name Change)	Total Accumu-lation	Percent Total	Annual Return
		Travelers Property Casualty (2002)	$5.30	1.5%	
		Transport Holdings (1995) — Conseco (1996)	$0.00	0.0%	
86	344	Amsted Industries — Private (1986)	$344.31	100.0%	13.28%
87	14	Shell Oil — Royal Dutch Petroleum (1985)	$323.96	100.0%	13.14%
88	367	Masonite — US Gypsum (1984) > USG (1984)	$322.67	100.0%	13.13%
		USG	$0.57	0.2%	
		AP Green (1988) — Global Industrial Techs (1998) — RHI (2000)	$105.85	32.8%	
		Timber Realization (1982) — Private (1983)	$216.25	67.0%	
89	402	Canada Dry — Norton Simon (1968) — Esmark (1983) — Beatrice Foods (1984) — Private (1986)	$329.28	100.0%	13.18%
90	13	Socony Vacuum Oil > Mobil (1966) — ExxonMobil (1999)	$322.41	100.0%	13.13%
91	307	Beatrice Foods — Private (1986)	$312.98	100.0%	13.05%
92	286	Motorola	$310.30	100.0%	13.03%
93	79	American Can > Primerica (1987) — Primerica New (1988) > Travelers (1994) > Travelers Group (1995) > Citigroup (1998)	$309.07	100.0%	13.02%
		Citigroup	$304.35	98.5%	
		Travelers Property Casualty (2002)	$4.72	1.5%	
		Transport Holdings (1995) — Conseco (1996)	$0.00	0.0%	
94	405	Daystrom Inc. > Schlumberger (1962)	$308.05	100.0%	13.02%
		Schlumberger	$216.87	70.4%	
		Transocean Sedco Forex (1999) > Transocean (2002)	$91.18	29.6%	
95	426	Hall Printing — Mobil (1979) — ExxonMobil (1999)	$305.35	100.0%	12.99%
96	141	North American Aviation > North American Rockwell (1967) > Rockwell Int'l (1973) Rockwell Int'l New (1996) > Rockwell Automation (2002)	$300.60	100.0%	12.96%
		Rockwell Automation	$129.97	43.2%	
		Meritor Automovtive (1997) > Arvinmeritor (2000)	$24.11	8.0%	
		Conexant Systems (1999)	$41.14	13.7%	
		Rockwell Collins (2001)	$105.38	35.1%	
97	336	Cannon Mills — Private (1982)	$300.28	100.0%	12.95%
98	77	RCA — General Electric (1986)	$300.01	100.0%	12.95%
99	156	Parke Davis — Warner-Lambert (1970) — Pfizer (2000)	$299.80	100.0%	12.95%
100	389	Miami Copper — Tennesse (1960) — Cities Services (1963) — Occidental Petroleum (1982)	$298.52	100.0%	12.94%
		Occidental Petroleum	$296.63	99.4%	
		IBP (1991) — Tyson Foods (2001)	$1.89	0.6%	
101	310	Equitable Gas > Equitable Resources (1984)	$291.07	100.0%	12.88%
102	442	Cream of Wheat — National Biscuit (1971) > Nabisco Brands (1971) — R.J. Reynolds Industries (1985) > RJR Nabisco (1986) — Private (1989) — RJR Nabisco Holdings (1991) — Philip Morris (2000) > Altria (2003)	$288.85	100.0%	12.86%
		Altria	$181.52	60.5%	
		R.J. Reynolds Tobacco (1999)	$102.63	35.5%	
		Sealand (1984) — CSX Corp (1986)	$4.70	1.6%	
103	16	Standard Oil of Indiana > Amoco (1985) — BP Amoco (1998)	$285.31	100.0%	12.83%
		BP Amoco	$262.02	91.8%	
		Standard Oil of New Jersey (1957–1963) > Exxon (1972) > ExxonMobil (1999)	$20.02	7.0%	

Rank Return	Rank Market Cap 1957	Original Name — 2003 Name (— Merger; > Name Change)	Total Accumu-lation	Percent Total	Annual Return
		Cyprus Minerals (1985) >Cyprus Amax (1993) >Phelps Dodge (1999)	$3.27	1.1%	
104	460	Bayuk Cigars — Private (1982)	$282.73	100.0%	12.81%
105	362	Associated Dry Goods — May Department Stores (1986)	$279.05	100.0%	12.78%
		May Department Stores	$249.50	82.0%	
		Payless Shoe Source (1996)	$29.55	9.7%	
106	107	Borg Warner — Private (1987) — Borg Warner Automotive (1993) > Borg Warner (2000)	$278.99	100.0%	12.78%
		Borg Warner	$265.64	95.2%	
		York International (1986) — Private (1988) — York Int'l New (1991)	$13.35	4.8%	
107	266	ACF Industries — Private (1984)	$278.81	100.0%	12.78%
108	173	Deere	$276.78	100.0%	12.76%
109	422	United Electric Coal — General Dynamics (1966)	$274.78	100.0%	12.74%
		General Dynamics	$274.76	100.0%	
		Houston Natural Gas (1968) — Internorth (1985) > Enron (1986)	$0.02	0.0%	
110	174	Household Finance > Household International Inc. (1981) — HSBC Holdings (2003)	$271.70	100.0%	12.71%
		HSBC Holdings	$255.77	94.1%	
		Schwitzer (1989) — Kuhlman (1995) — Borg Warner Automotive (1998) > Borg Warner (2000)	$10.56	3.9%	
		Scottsman Industries (1989) — Private (1999)	$3.89	1.4%	
		Enljer Industries (1989) — Zurn Industries (1997) — US Industries (1998)	$1.49	0.5%	
111	209	Rockwell Standard — North American Rockwell (1967) — Boeing (1986)	$270.13	100.0%	12.70%
112	281	Pitney Bowes	$268.50	100.0%	12.68%
		Pitney Bowes	$253.08	94.3%	
		Imagistics Ineternational (2001)	$15.42	5.7%	
113	101	Kimberly-Clark	$267.58	100.0%	12.68%
114	184	Otis Elevator — United Technologies (1976)	$266.20	100.0%	12.66%
115	311	Twentieth-Century-Fox — United Television (1981) — News Corporation (2001)	$264.41	100.0%	12.65%
116	91	Tidewater Oil — Getty Oil (1967) — Texaco (1984) — Chevron Texaco (2001)	$261.66	100.0%	12.62%
117	315	ArcherDaniels-Midland	$258.35	100.0%	12.59%
		ArcherDaniels-Midland	$245.53	95.0%	
		National City Bancorporation (1980) — Marshall & Isley (2001)	$12.82	5.0%	
118	423	Spencer Kellogg — Textron (1961)	$258.28	100.0%	12.59%
119	176	American Standard — Private (1987)	$255.54	100.0%	12.57%
120	2	Standard Oil of New Jersey > Exxon (1972) > ExxonMobil (1999)	$254.00	100.0%	12.55%
121	181	Beneficial — Household International (1998)	$250.03	100.0%	12.51%
122	283	Columbian Carbon — Cities Service (1962) — Occidental Petroleum (1982)	$247.76	100.0%	12.49%
		Occidental	$246.19	99.4%	
		IBP (1991) — Tyson Foods (2001)	$1.57	0.6%	
123	245	Eaton	$246.36	100.0%	12.48%
		Eaton	$223.07	90.5%	

Rank Return	Rank Market Cap 1957	Original Name — 2003 Name (— Merger; > Name Change)	Total Accumu- lation	Percent Total	Annual Return
		Axcelis Technologies Inc (2001)	$23.30	9.5%	
124	106	Consolidated Natural Gas — Dominion Resources (2000)	$242.17	100.0%	12.44%
125	414	American Brake Shoe > ABEX — Illinois Central RR (1968) — Illinois Central Industries > Whitman (1988) > PepsiAmericas (2001)	$241.77	100.0%	12.43%
		PepsiAmericas	$25.43	10.5%	
		PetInc (1991) — Grand Metropolitan (1995) > Diageo (1997)	$100.38	41.5%	
		Illinois Central (1990) — Canadian National Railway (1998)	$64.28	26.6%	
		Hussman International (1998) — Ingersoll Rand (2000)	$36.58	15.1%	
		Midas (1998)	$9.12	3.8%	
		Prospect Group (1989) — Private (1997)	$1.34	0.6%	
		Banctec (1990) — Private (1999)	$1.39	0.6%	
		Sylvan Food Holdings (1990) > Sylvan (1994)	$0.62	0.3%	
		Knowledge Universe (1992) *	$2.38	1.0%	
		Forschner Group (1990) > Swiss Army Brands (1990) — Victorinox (2002)	$0.25	0.1%	
126	411	Bliss EW — Gulf & Western Industries (1968) — Paramount Communications (1989) — Viacom (1994)	$241.52	100.0%	12.43%
		Viacom	$240.29	99.5%	
		GW Land (1969) *	$1.23	0.5%	
127	292	Cutler-Hammer — Eaton (1979)	$238.77	100.0%	12.40%
		Eaton	$216.19	90.5%	
		Axcelis Technologies Inc (2001)	$22.58	9.5%	
128	73	Montgomery Ward — Marcor (1968) — Mobil (1976) — ExxonMobil (1999)	$238.57	100.0%	12.40%
129	94	Southern Pacific — Santa Fe Southern Pacific (1984) — Burlington Northern Santa Fe (1995)	$233.80	100.0%	12.35%
		Burlington Northern Santa Fe	$143.71	61.5%	
		Santa Fe Energy — Devon Energy (1997)	$11.56	4.9%	
		Catellus Development (1990)	$11.30	4.8%	
		Monterey (1995) — Texaco (1997) > ChevronTexaco (2001)	$25.53	10.9%	
		Santa Fe Gold (1994) — Newmont Mining (1997)	$41.70	17.8%	
130	29	Minnesota Mining & Manufacturing > 3M (2002)	$233.78	100.0%	12.35%
		3M	$229.61	98.2%	
		Imation (1996)	$4.16	1.8%	
131	305	Marshall Field — Private (1982)	$233.62	100.0%	12.35%
132	200	National Gypsum — Private (1986)	$233.00	100.0%	12.34%
133	28	Continental Oil > Conoco (1979) — DuPont (1981)	$232.96	100.0%	12.34%
		DuPont	$179.85	77.2%	
		Conoco (1999) — Conoco Phillips (2002)	$53.11	22.8%	
134	116	Boeing	$229.29	100.0%	12.31%
135	401	Admiral — Rockwell International (1974) > Rockwell Automation (2002)	$225.04	100.0%	12.26%
		Rockwell Automation	$94.83	42.1%	
		Meritor Automovtive (1997) > Arvinmeritor (2000)	$17.59	7.8%	
		Conexant Systems (1999)	$24.50	10.9%	
		Mindspeed Technologies (2003)	$11.24	5.0%	

Rank Return	Rank Market Cap 1957	Original Name — 2003 Name (— Merger; > Name Change)	Total Accumu- lation	Percent Total	Annual Return
		Rockwell Collins (2001)	$76.88	34.2%	
136	225	Martin-Marietta — Lockheed Martin (1995)	$223.83	100.0%	12.25%
137	314	Yale & Towne — Eaton Manufacturing (1963)	$222.01	100.0%	12.23%
		Eaton	$201.02	90.5%	
		Axcelis Technology (2001)	$20.99	9.5%	
138	5	General Electric	$220.04	100.0%	12.21%
139	162	Associates Investments — Gulf & Western Industries (1969) — Paramount Communications (1989) — Viacom (1994)	$217.92	100.0%	12.18%
		Viacom	$216.80	99.5%	
		GW Land (1969) *	$1.11	0.5%	
140	232	Crucible Steel — Colt Industries (1968) — Private (1988)	$217.31	100.0%	12.18%
141	6	Gulf Oil > Gulf — Chevron (1984) > Chevron-Texaco (2001)	$214.12	100.0%	12.14%
142	261	Denver Rio Grande — Western Rio Grande Industries (1970) — Private (1984)	$211.30	100.0%	12.11%
143	464	American Crystal Sugar — Private (1973)	$208.44	100.0%	12.08%
144	92	Atlantic Richfield — BP Amoco (2000) > BP (2001)	$205.97	100.0%	12.05%
145	64	Continental Can — Continental Group (1976) — Private (1984)	$203.54	100.0%	12.02%
146	375	St. Louis–San Francisco — Burlington Northern (1980) > Burlington Northern Santa Fe (1995)	$201.93	100.0%	12.00%
		Burlington Northern Santa Fe	$121.79	60.3%	
		Burlington Resources (1989)	$73.71	36.5%	
		El Paso Natural Gas (1992) > El Paso Energy (1998) > El Paso (2001)	$6.43	3.2%	
147	189	Illinois Central RR — Illinois Central Industries (1964) > IC Industries (1975) > Whitman (1988) > PepsiAmericas (2001)	$199.64	100.0%	11.97%
		PepsiAmericas	$21.46	10.7%	
		PetInc (1991) — Grand Metropolitan (1995) > Diageo PLC (1997)	$84.71	42.4%	
		Illinois Central (1990) — Canadian National Railway (1998)	$54.24	27.2%	
		Hussman International (1998) — Ingersoll Rand (2000)	$30.87	15.5%	
		Midas (1998)	$2.94	1.5%	
		Prospect Group (1989) — Private (1997)	$1.13	0.6%	
		Banctec (1990) — Private (1999)	$1.17	0.6%	
		Sylvan Food Holdings (1990) > Sylvan (1994)	$0.52	0.3%	
		Knowledge Universe*	$2.38	1.2%	
		Forschner Group (1990) > Swiss Army Brands (1990) — Victorinox AG (2002)	$0.21	0.1%	
148	339	Gimbel Brothers — Private (1973)	$198.90	100.0%	11.96%
149	233	Westinghouse Air Brake — American Standard (1968) — Private (1988)	$198.58	100.0%	11.96%
150	272	American Stores — Albertsons (1999)	$197.99	100.0%	11.95%
151	205	Pullman — Wheelabrator Frye (1980) — Allied (1983) — Honeywell Int'l (1999)	$197.65	100.0%	11.95%
		Honeywell International	$178.81	90.5%	
		Henley Group (1986) — Wheelaborator Group (1989) — Waste Management (1998)	$5.53	4.3%	
		Fisher Scientific (1987) — Wheelaborator Group (1989) — Waste Management (1998)			
		Henley Manufacturing (1987) — Private (1989)	$4.72	2.4%	
		Pullman Transportation (1982) > Pullman Peabody (1985) >			

Rank Return	Rank Market Cap 1957	Original Name — 2003 Name (— Merger; > Name Change)	Total Accumu- lation	Percent Total	Annual Return
		Pullman (1987) — Private (1988)	$8.59	2.8%	
152	196	Square D — Private (1991)	$197.51	100.0%	11.95%
153	340	Beckman Instruments — SmithKline Beckman (1982) — SmithKline Beecham (1989) — Glaxo SmithKline (2000)	$197.13	100.0%	11.94%
		Glaxo SmithKline	$172.02	86.6%	
		Allergan (1989)	$11.46	5.8%	
		Allergan Specialty Therapy (1998) — Allergan (2001)			
		Advanced Medical Optics (2002)	$0.65	0.3%	
		Beckman Instruments New (1989) > Beckman Coulter (1998)	$13.01	6.6%	
154	11	International Business Machines	$196.50	100.0%	11.94%
155	382	South Puerto Rico Sugar — Gulf & Western Industries (1967) — Paramount Communications (1989) — Viacom (1994)	$196.31	100.0%	11.93%
		Viacom	$195.30	99.5%	
		GW Land (1969) *	$1.00	0.5%	
156	90	United Aircraft > United Technologies (1975)	$195.65	100.0%	11.93%
157	488	Firth Carpet — Mohasco Industries (1962) — Private (1989) — Mohawk Industries (1992)	$193.17	100.0%	11.89%
158	46	Monsanto Chemical > Pharmacia (2000) — Pfizer (2003)	$192.72	100.0%	11.89%
		Pharmacia	$174.95	83.9%	
		Monsanto New (2002)	$17.49	8.4%	
		Solutia (1997)	$0.28	0.1%	
159	335	Scovill Manufacturing — First City Industries (1985) — Private (1989)	$191.91	100.0%	11.88%
160	349	Raytheon	$189.77	100.0%	11.85%
161	295	Armour Co.— Greyhound (1970) > Dial (1991) > Viad (1996)	$188.27	100.0%	11.83%
		Viad	$86.61	43.8%	
		Dial New (1996)	$98.94	50.1%	
		G F C Financial (1992) > Finova Group (1995)	$2.73	1.4%	
162	493	Condé Nast — Private (1965)	$187.16	100.0%	11.82%
163	288	Mack Truck — Signal Oil & Gas (1967) — Signal (1968) — Allied Signal (1985) — Honeywell Int'l (1999)	$186.47	100.0%	11.81%
		Honeywell International	$176.36	94.6%	
		Henley Group (1986) — Wheelaborator Group (1989) — Waste Management (1998)	$5.46	2.9%	
		Fisher Scientific (1987) — Wheelaborator Group (1989) — Waste Management (1998)			
		Henley Manufacturing (1987) — Private (1989)	$4.65	2.5%	
164	54	Consolidated Edison	$185.54	100.0%	11.80%
165	271	Schenley Industries — Glen Alden (1971) — Rapid American (1972) — Private (1981)	$184.29	100.0%	11.78%
166	351	Laclede Gas	$182.54	100.0%	11.76%
167	150	International Telephone & Telegraph > ITT Corp (1983)	$181.81	100.0%	11.75%
		ITT Industries	$48.96	26.0%	
		ITT Hartford Group (1995) > Hartford Financial Services (1997)	$80.12	42.6%	
		ITT Nev (1995) — Starwood Hotels (1998)	$38.74	20.6%	
		Rayonier (1994)	$13.99	7.4%	
168	212	Texas Gulf Producing — Sinclair Oil (1964) — Atlantic Richfield (1969) — BP Amoco (2000)	$178.78	100.0%	11.71%

Rank Return	Rank Market Cap 1957	Original Name — 2003 Name (— Merger; > Name Change)	Total Accumu- lation	Percent Total	Annual Return
169	223	Foremost Dairies — McKesson (1994)	$174.67	100.0%	11.65%
170	36	Ford Motor	$173.49	100.0%	11.64%
		Ford	$102.53	59.1%	
		Associates First Capital (1998) — Citigroup (2000)	$63.43	36.6%	
		Travelers Property Casualty (2002)	$2.80	1.6%	
		Visteon (2000)	$4.73	2.7%	
171	353	Studebaker Packard — Studebaker Worthington (1967) — McGraw Edison (1979) Cooper Industries (1985)	$173.44	100.0%	11.64%
		Cooper Industries	$167.42	96.5%	
		Gardner Denver (1994)	$6.02	3.5%	
172	356	Moore McCormack Resources — Southdown (1988) — Cemex (2000)	$173.42	100.0%	11.64%
173	10	Standard Oil of California > Chevron (1984) > ChevronTexaco (2001)	$172.29	100.0%	11.62%
174	41	American Cyanamid >American Home Products (1994) > Wyeth (2002)	$171.49	100.0%	11.61%
		Wyeth	$163.51	95.3%	
		Cytec Industries (1994)	$7.98	4.7%	
175	301	Brooklyn Union Gas — Keyspan Energy (1998)	$170.23	100.0%	11.59%
176	98	Campbell Soup	$169.47	100.0%	11.58%
		Campbell Soup	$169.47	100.0%	
		Vlasic Foods International (1998)	$0.00	0.0%	
177	364	Ruberoid — General Aniline & Film Corp (1967) > GAF Corp (1968) — Private (1989)	$169.44	100.0%	11.58%
178	385	American Enka > Akzona (1970) — Akzo (1989) > Akzona Nobel (1994)	$167.75	100.0%	11.56%
179	416	Bath Iron Works — Bath Industries (1968) — Congoleum (1975) — Private (1980)	$166.06	100.0%	11.53%
180	387	Clevite Corp. — Gould (1969) — Nippon Mining (1988)	$164.62	100.0%	11.51%
181	153	Peoples Gas Light Coke > Peoples Gas (1968) > Peoples Energy (1980)	$163.89	100.0%	11.50%
		Peoples Energy	$105.63	64.4%	
		Midcon (1981) — Occidental Petroleum (1986)	$57.60	35.1%	
		IBP (1991) — Tyson Foods (2001)	$0.67	0.4%	
182	477	Diamond T Motor Car > DTM (1958)	$163.23	100.0%	11.49%
		Oliver (1960) > Cletrac (1960) — Hess Oil and Chemical (1960) > Amerada Hess (1969)	$29.58	18.1%	
		Murray (1960) > Wallace Murray (1965) — Household International (1981) HSBC Holdings (2003)	$125.81	77.1%	
		Schwitzer (1989) — Kuhlman (1995) — Borg Warner Automotive (1998) > Borg Warner (2000)	$5.19	3.2%	
		Scottsman Industries (1989) — Private (1999)	$1.91	1.2%	
		Enljer Industries (1989) — Zurn Industries (1997) — US Industries (1998)	$0.73	0.4%	
183	363	Cooper Industries	$163.09	100.0%	11.49%
		Cooper Industries	$156.75	96.1%	
		Gardner Denver (1994)	$6.34	3.9%	
184	452	Crown Cork & Seal	$159.18	100.0%	11.43%
185	125	Florida Power > Florida Progress Group (1982) — CPL			

Rank Return	Rank Market Cap 1957	Original Name — 2003 Name (— Merger; > Name Change)	Total Accumulation	Percent Total	Annual Return
		Energy (2000) > Progress Energy (2000)	$158.05	100.0%	11.42%
186	123	Bendix — Allied (1983) > Allied Signal (1985) > Honeywell Int'l (1999)	$156.45	100.0%	11.39%
		Honeywell International	$147.47	94.3%	
		Henley Group (1986) — Wheelaborator Group (1989) — Waste Management (1998)	$4.56	2.9%	
		Fisher Scientific (1987) — Wheelaborator Group (1989) — Waste Management (1998)			
		Henley Manufacturing (1987) — Private (1989)	$3.89	2.5%	
		Facet Enterprises (1976) — Pennzoil Company (1988) > Pennzenergy (1998) — Devon Energy (1998)	$0.24	0.2%	
		Pennzoil Quaker State (1998) — Royal Dutch Petroleum (2002)	$0.28	0.2%	
187	58	Atchison, Topeka, Santa Fe — Santa Fe Industries (1970) — Santa Fe Southern Pacific (1984) — Burlington Northern Santa Fe (1995)"	$154.55	100.0%	11.36%
		Burlington Northern Santa Fe	$95.00	61.5%	
		Santa Fe Energy (1991) — Devon Energy (1997)	$7.64	4.9%	
		Catellus Development (1990)	$16.87	10.9%	
		Monterey (1995) — Texaco (1997) > ChevronTexaco (2001)	$7.47	4.8%	
		Santa Fe Gold (1994) — Newmont Mining (1997)	$27.56	17.8%	
188	15	Sears Roebuck	$151.51	100.0%	11.32%
		Sears	$33.59	22.2%	
		Dean Witter Discover (1993) — Morgan Stanley (1997)	$60.44	39.9%	
		Allstate (1995)	$57.48	37.9%	
189	53	Cities Service — Occidental Petroleum (1982)	$150.72	100.0%	11.30%
		Occidental Petroleum	$149.77	99.4%	
		IBP (1991) — Tyson Foods (2001)	$0.95	0.6%	
190	294	Oklahoma Natural Gas > Oneok (1980)	$150.53	100.0%	11.30%
191	390	Mercantile Stores — Dillards (1998)	$149.82	100.0%	11.29%
192	126	Southern Railway — Norfolk Southern (1982)	$146.25	100.0%	11.23%
193	291	Gardner-Denver — Cooper Industries (1979)	$146.07	100.0%	11.23%
		Cooper Industries	$141.00	96.5%	
		Gardner Denver (1994)	$5.07	3.5%	
194	469	Emerson Radio & Phonograph — Nat'l Union Electric (1966) — Electrolux AB (1975)	$145.66	100.0%	11.22%
		Electrolux AB	$131.72	90.4%	
		SAPA AB (1997)	$13.94	9.6%	
195	404	Federal Paper Board — International Paper (1996)	$144.80	100.0%	11.21%
196	290	Missouri Pacific — Mississippi River Fuel > Missouri Pacific (1976) — Union Pacific (1982)	$143.16	100.0%	11.18%
		Union Pacific	$117.22	81.9%	
		Anadarko Petroleum (1995)	$25.93	18.1%	
197	155	May Department Stores	$143.09	100.0%	11.18%
		May Department Stores	$127.94	89.4%	
		Payless Shoe Source (1996)	$15.15	10.6%	
198	461	Intertype — Harris Seybold (1957) > Harris Intertype (1957) > Harris (1974)	$143.01	100.0%	11.18%

Rank Return	Rank Market Cap 1957	Original Name — 2003 Name (— Merger; > Name Change)	Total Accumulation	Percent Total	Annual Return
		Harris	$128.89	90.1%	
		Harris Computer Systems (1994) > Cyberguard (1996)	$12.45	8.7%	
		Lanier Worldwide (1999) — Ricoh (2001)	$1.68	1.2%	
199	352	Peninsular Telephone — GTE (1957) — Verizon Communications (2000)	$141.73	100.0%	11.16%
200	498	Jacob Ruppert — Private (1963)	$137.84	100.0%	11.09%
201	211	Texas Pacific Coal & Oil — Private (1963)	$137.72	100.0%	11.09%
202	358	Continental Baking — International Telephone & Telegraph (1968) > ITT (1983)	$136.42	100.0%	11.07%
		ITT Industries	$36.73	26.9%	
		ITT Hartford Group (1995) > Hartford Financial Services (1997)	$60.12	44.1%	
		ITT Nev (1995) — Starwood Hotels (1998)	$29.07	21.3%	
		Rayonier (1994)	$10.49	7.7%	
203	337	Washington Gas Light > WGL Holdings (2000)	$135.16	100.0%	11.04%
204	369	Harris Seybold > Harris Intertype (1957) > Harris (1974)	$134.79	100.0%	11.04%
		Harris	$121.48	90.1%	
		Harris Computer Systems (1994) > Cyberguard (1996)	$1.58	1.2%	
		Lanier Worldwide (1999) — Ricoh (2001)	$11.74	8.7%	
205	85	Southern	$134.18	100.0%	11.03%
		Southern	$133.57	99.5%	
		Mirant (2001)	$0.61	0.5%	
206	182	New England Electric System — National Grid Transco (2001)	$132.61	100.0%	11.00%
207	38	Pittsburgh Plate Glass > PPG Industries (1968)	$129.00	100.0%	10.93%
208	134	Liggett Group — Private (1979) — Grand Metropolitan (1991) > Diageo (1997)	$128.81	100.0%	10.93%
209	256	Combustion Engineering — Private (1989)	$128.78	100.0%	10.93%
210	8	Texas Co > Texaco (1959) — ChevronTexaco (2001)	$128.63	100.0%	10.93%
211	149	Baltimore Gas & Electric — Constellation Energy Group (1999)	$126.93	100.0%	10.90%
212	398	Alco Products > Citadel Industries (1965) — Private (1965)	$126.84	100.0%	10.89%
213	102	Public Service Electric and Gas — Public Service Enterprise (1986)	$126.18	100.0%	10.88%
214	202	Dayton Power & Light > DPL (1986)	$126.15	100.0%	10.88%
215	56	Olin	$126.06	100.0%	10.88%
		Olin	$26.47	21.0%	
		Squibb Beechnut (1968) > Squibb (1971) — Bristol-Myers Squibb (1989)	$74.90	59.4%	
		Westmark International (1987) > Advanced Tech Labs (1992) > ATL Ultrasound (1997) Philips (1998) — Koninklijke Philips Elec (1999)	$1.95	1.5%	
		Spacelabs Medical (1992) — Instrumentarium (2002)	$0.56	0.4%	
		Sonosite (1998)	$0.12	0.1%	
		Zimmer Holdings (2001)	$16.59	13.2%	
		Primex Technologies (1997) — General Dynamics (2001)	$5.47	4.3%	
216	323	Philco — Ford (1961)	$122.49	100.0%	10.81%
		Ford	$71.02	58.0%	
		Associates First Capital (1998) — Citigroup (2000)	$46.01	37.6%	
		Travelers Property Casualty (2002)	$2.03	1.7%	
		Visteon (2000)	$3.43	2.8%	

Rank Return	Rank Market Cap 1957	Original Name — 2003 Name (— Merger; > Name Change)	Total Accumu- lation	Percent Total	Annual Return
217	158	Seaboard Oil — Texaco (1958) — ChevronTexaco (2001)	$121.32	100.0%	10.79%
218	171	Cincinnati Gas & Electric > Cinergy (1994)	$120.60	100.0%	10.77%
219	20	Phillips Petroleum > Conoco Phillips (2002)	$119.61	100.0%	10.76%
220	399	Celotex — Jim Walter Corp (1964) — Private (1988) — Walter Industries	$119.04	100.0%	10.74%
221	50	Union Pacific Railroad > Union Pacific (1971)	$118.20	29.6%	10.73%
		Union Pacific	$96.79	81.9%	
		Union Pacific Resources (1995) — Anadarko Petroleum (2000)	$21.41	18.1%	
222	74	Philadelphia Electric > Peco Energy (1993) > Exelon (2000)	$117.70	100.0%	10.72%
223	480	Cuneo Press — Private (1974)	$117.69	100.0%	10.72%
224	484	Servel — Clevite (1967) — Gould (1969) — Nippon Mining (1988)	$115.98	100.0%	10.68%
225	445	Smith-Douglas — Borden (1965) — Private (1995)	$115.04	100.0%	10.66%
226	122	Virgina Electric — Dominion Resources (1983)	$114.75	100.0%	10.66%
227	61	General Telephone & Electric > GTE(1982) — Verizon Communications (2000)	$112.19	100.0%	10.60%
228	199	Sylvania Electric Products — General Telephone & Electric (1959) >GTE (1982) Verizon Communications (2000)	$112.13	100.0%	10.60%
229	89	Union Oil of California > Unocal (1985)	$111.62	100.0%	10.59%
230	21	Dow Chemical	$111.51	100.0%	10.59%
231	144	Freeport Sulphur > Freeport Minerals (1971) — Freeport McMoran (1981) — IMC Global (1997)	$110.88	100.0%	10.58%
		IMC Global	$5.46	4.9%	
		Freeport McMoran Energy Partner (1985) — Freeport McMoran (1990) — IMC Global (1997)			
		Freeport McMoran Gold (1985) — Minorco (1990) — Anglo-American (1999)	$6.86	6.2%	
		FM Properties (1992) — Stratus Properties (1998)	$1.24	1.1%	
		McMoran Oil & Gas (1994) > McMoran Exploration (1998)	$1.04	0.9%	
		Freeport McMoran Copper & Gold (1994, 1995)	$96.29	86.8%	
232	78	General Dynamics	$110.71	100.0%	10.57%
		General Dynamics	$110.70	100.0%	
		Houston Natural Gas Corp (1968) — Internorth (1985) > Enron (1986)	$0.01	0.0%	
233	138	Great Northern — Burlington Northern (1970) > Burlington Northern Santa Fe (1995)	$110.39	100.0%	10.57%
		Burlington Northern Santa Fe	$66.58	60.3%	
		Burlington Resources (1989)	$40.30	36.5%	
		El Paso Natural Gas (1992) > El Paso (2001)	$3.51	3.2%	
234	237	New York, Chicago & St. Louis — Norfolow & Western Railway (1964) — Norfolk Southern (1982)	$109.72	100.0%	10.55%
235	35	Caterpillar Tractor Inc. > Caterpillar (1986)	$109.65	100.0%	10.55%
236	326	Grand Union — Private (1977)	$108.86	100.0%	10.53%
237	414	United Biscuit of America > Keebler (1966) — Private (1974) — United Biscuits (1998)	$107.62	100.0%	10.51%
238	1	American Telephone & Telegraph > AT&T (1994)	$107.16	79.9%	10.50%
		AT&T	$2.04	1.9%	
		U.S. West (1984) > MediaOne Group (1998) — AT&T (2000)	$1.89	1.8%	
		U.S. West (New) (1998) — Qwest (2000)	$1.24	1.2%	

Rank Return	Rank Market Cap 1957	Original Name — 2003 Name (— Merger; > Name Change)	Total Accumu- lation	Percent Total	Annual Return
		Southwestern Bell (1984) >SBC Communications (1994)	$12.72	11.9%	
		American Info. Tech. (1984) > Ameritech (1991) — SBC Communications (1999)	$17.33	16.2%	
		Pacific Telesis (1984) — SBC Communications (1997)	$6.66	6.2%	
		AirTouch Communications (1994) — Vodafone (1999)	$8.53	8.0%	
		Bell Atlantic (1984) — Verizon Communications (2000)	$12.13	11.3%	
		NYNEX (1984) — Bell Atlantic (1997) — Verizon (2000)	$9.97	9.3%	
		Bell South (1984)	$19.99	18.6%	
		Lucent (1996)	$1.03	1.0%	
		Agere Systems (2002)	$0.30	0.3%	
		Avaya (2000)	$0.53	0.5%	
		NCR (1997)	$0.66	0.6%	
		AT&T Wireless (2001)	$2.42	2.3%	
		AT&T Broadband Services (2002) — Comcast (2002)	$9.75	9.1%	
239	459	Wayne Pump — Wayne Symington (1966) — Dresser Industries (1968) — Halliburton (1998)	$102.55	100.0%	10.39%
		Halliburton	$97.27	94.8%	
		Indresco (1992) — Global Industrial Techs (1995) — RHI (2000)	$5.28	5.2%	
240	190	McGraw Edison — Cooper Industries (1985)	$102.43	100.0%	10.39%
		Cooper Industries	$98.87	96.5%	
		Gardner Denver Co (1994)	$3.56	3.5%	
241	33	Sinclair Oil — Atlantic Richfield (1969) — BP Amoco (2000)	$101.57	100.0%	10.37%
242	219	Mississippi River — Missouri Pacific (1976) — Union Pacific (1982)	$101.38	100.0%	10.37%
		Union Pacific	$83.02	81.9%	
		Anadarko Petroleum (1995)	$18.37	18.1%	
243	287	Brown Group	$100.68	100.0%	10.35%
244	165	Northern Pacific — Burlington Northern (1970) > Burlington Northern Santa Fe (1995)	$100.16	100.0%	10.34%
		Burlington Northern Santa Fe	$62.05	94.5%	
		Burlington Resources (1989)	$34.83	53.1%	
		El Paso Natural Gas (1992) > El Paso (2001)	$3.27	5.0%	
245	230	St. Joseph Lead — St. Joe Minerals (1970) — Flour (1982) > Massey (2001)	$99.95	100.0%	10.33%
		Massey New	$34.32	34.3%	
		Flour (2001)	$65.63	65.7%	
246	121	American Natural Gas > American Natural Resources (1976) — Coastal — El Paso (2001)	$98.48	100.0%	10.30%
		El Paso	$42.30	42.4%	
		Wisconsin Gas (1975) — Wicor (1980) — Wisconsin Energy (2000)	$30.32	30.4%	
		Michigan Consolidated Gas (1988) > MCN Energy (1997) — DTE Energy (2001)	$18.99	19.1%	
		Primark (1982) — Thomson (2000)	$6.87	6.9%	
247	137	Middle South Utilities > Entergy (1989)	$97.81	100.0%	10.28%
248	220	New York State Electric & Gas > Energy East Corp (1998)	$96.28	100.0%	10.24%
249	413	Dome Mines — Placer Dome (1987)	$93.58	100.0%	10.18%
250	257	Magma Copper — Newmont Mining (1969)	$93.34	100.0%	10.17%

Rank Return	Rank Market Cap 1957	Original Name — 2003 Name (— Merger; > Name Change)	Total Accumu-lation	Percent Total	Annual Return
		Newmont Mining	$73.84	79.1%	
		Magma Copper New (1987) — Broker Hill Properties (1996) > BHP (2000)	$19.50	20.9%	
251	96	Southern California Edison > SCE (1988) > Edison Int'l (1996)	$92.49	100.0%	10.15%
252	136	Union Bag Camp Paper > Union Bag Camp (1966) — International Paper (1999)	$92.36	100.0%	10.15%
253	297	Jewel Tea > Jewel (1966) — American Stores (1984) — Albertsons (1999)	$91.05	100.0%	10.11%
254	444	Waukesha Motors — Bangor Punta (1968) — Lear Siegler (1984) — Private (1987)	$90.16	100.0%	10.09%
255	27	Pacific Telephone & Telegraph — AT&T (1983)	$89.18	100.0%	10.06%
		AT&T	$1.70	1.9%	
		U.S. West (1984) > MediaOne Group (1998) — AT&T (2000)	$1.57	1.8%	
		U.S. West (New) (1998) — Qwest (2000)	$1.03	1.2%	
		Southwestern Bell (1984) >SBC Communications (1994)	$10.58	11.9%	
		American Info. Tech. (1984) > Ameritech (1991) — SBC Communications (1999)	$14.42	16.2%	
		Pacific Telesis (1984) — SBC Communications (1997)	$5.55	6.2%	
		AirTouch Communications (1994) — Vodafone (1999)	$7.10	8.0%	
		Bell Atlantic (1984) — Verizon Communications (2000)	$10.09	11.3%	
		NYNEX (1984) — Bell Atlantic (1997) — Verizon (2000)	$8.29	9.3%	
		Bell South (1984)	$16.63	18.6%	
		Lucent (1996)	$0.85	1.0%	
		Agere Systems (2002)	$0.25	0.3%	
		Avaya (2000)	$0.44	0.5%	
		NCR (1997)	$0.55	0.6%	
		AT&T Wireless (2001)	$2.01	2.3%	
		AT&T Broadband Services (2002) — Comcast (2002)	$8.12	9.1%	
256	7	Union Carbide & Carbon > Union Carbide (1957) — Dow Chemical (2001)	$86.20	100.0%	9.98%
		Dow Chemical	$44.46	51.6%	
		Praxair (1992)	$41.74	48.4%	
257	381	Beaunit — El Paso Natural Gas (1967) > El Paso (1974) — Burlington Northern (1983) > Burlington Northern Santa Fe (1995)	$85.11	100.0%	9.95%
		Burlington Northern Santa Fe	$39.38	46.3%	
		Northwest Pipeline (1974) > Northwest Energy (1975) — Williams (1983)	$19.82	23.3%	
		Williams Communications Group (2001)		0.0%	
		Burlington Resources (1989)	$23.84	28.0%	
		El Paso Natural Gas (1992) > El Paso (2001)	$2.08	2.4%	
258	427	Lerner Stores — McCrory Stores (1962) — Rapid American (1976) — Private (1981)	$84.74	100.0%	9.94%
		Lerner Stores (1965) — McCrory Stores (1973)			
259	263	Deleware Power & Light > Delmarva Power & Light (1966) > Conectiv (1998) — Pepco Holdings (2002)	$83.31	100.0%	9.90%
260	494	Fajardo Sugar — Private (1958)	$82.29	100.0%	9.87%
261	140	Northern States Power Minn. > XCEL Energy (2000)	$82.23	100.0%	9.87%
262	394	General Signal — SPX (1998)	$82.11	100.0%	9.87%

Rank Return	Rank Market Cap 1957	Original Name — 2003 Name (— Merger; > Name Change)	Total Accumu- lation	Percent Total	Annual Return
263	168	Sterling Drug — Eastman Chemical (1988)	$81.92	100.0%	9.86%
264	203	Lockheed Aircraft > Lockheed (1977) > Lockheed Martin (1995)	$80.67	100.0%	9.83%
265	40	Commonwealth Edison > Unicom (1994) > Exelon (2000)	$80.60	100.0%	9.83%
		Exelon	$77.62	96.3%	
		Northern Illinois Gas (1970) > Nicor (1976)	$2.99	3.7%	
266	110	Panhandle Eastern > Panenergy (1996) — Duke Energy (1997)	$80.44	100.0%	9.82%
		Duke Energy	$36.97	46.0%	
		Anadarko Petroleum (1986)	$43.47	54.0%	
267	466	Reliance Manufacturing — Puritan Fashions (1965) — Private (1983)	$79.78	100.0%	9.80%
		Private	$75.27	94.3%	
		Technical Tape (1965) — Bieresdorf (1988)	$4.52	6.0%	
268	81	Ingersoll-Rand	$79.49	100.0%	9.79%
269	26	Kennecott Copper > Kennecott (1980) — Standard Oil of Ohio (1981) — BP (1987) — BP Amoco (1999)	$79.40	100.0%	9.79%
270	312	International Minerals & Chemicals > IMCERA (1990) > Mallinckrodt Group (1994) — Tyco International (2000)	$76.95	100.0%	9.72%
271	214	Winn-Dixie Stores	$76.04	100.0%	9.69%
272	175	Air Reduction (1970) — Airco (1977) — BOC (1978)	$75.65	100.0%	9.68%
273	407	Endicott Johnson — McDonough (1970) — Hansen (1981)	$75.11	100.0%	9.66%
		Hansen	$14.94	19.9%	
		US Industries New (1995)	$1.29	1.7%	
		Imperial Tobacco (1996)	$41.08	54.7%	
		Millennium Chemicals (1996)	$2.95	3.9%	
		Energy Co (1997) — Texas Utilities (1998) > TXU (2000)	$14.85	19.8%	
274	135	Borden — Private (1995)	$75.10	100.0%	9.66%
275	75	Scott Paper — Kimberly-Clark (1995)	$74.76	100.0%	9.65%
276	177	Louisville & Nashville — Seaboard Coast Line Industries (1971) — CSX Corp (1981)	$74.55	100.0%	9.64%
277	104	Central & South West — American Electric Power (2000)	$73.39	100.0%	9.61%
278	206	Dana	$72.81	100.0%	9.59%
279	330	United States Lines — Kidde Walter (1969) — Hansen PLC (1987)	$67.76	100.0%	9.42%
		Hansen	$13.48	19.9%	
		US Industries New (1995)	$1.16	1.7%	
		Imperial Tobacco (1996)	$37.07	54.7%	
		Millennium Chemicals (1996)	$2.66	3.9%	
		Energy Co. (1997) — Texas Utilities (1998) > TXU (2000)	$13.40	19.8%	
		Interim Systems (1987) — H&R Block (1991)	$2.52	3.7%	
280	300	Industrial Rayon — Midland Ross (1961) — Private (1985)	$70.00	100.0%	9.50%
281	415	Bond Stores > Bond Industries (1969) — Private (1981)	$68.74	100.0%	9.45%
282	69	Detroit Edison > DTE Energy Co. Holdings (1997)	$68.28	100.0%	9.44%
283	430	CNW (Chicago & North Western) > Northwest Industries (1968) — Lone Star Steel (1985)	$67.54	100.0%	9.41%
284	213	Clark Equipment — Ingersoll Rand (1995)	$67.10	100.0%	9.40%
285	451	Central Aguirre Sugar > Aguirre (1968) — Private (1978)	$66.59	100.0%	9.38%
286	221	Mead — Meadwestvaco (2002)	$66.20	100.0%	9.37%
287	34	Pacific Gas & Electric > P G & E Corp (1997)	$66.08	100.0%	9.36%

Rank Return	Rank Market Cap 1957	Original Name — 2003 Name (— Merger; > Name Change)	Total Accumu- lation	Percent Total	Annual Return
288	86	United Gas — Pennzoil (1968) > Pennzenergy (1998) — Devon Energy (1998)	$65.31	100.0%	9.33%
		Devon Energy	$13.02	19.9%	
		United Gas Corp (1974) — Midcon Corp (1985) — Occidental Petroleum (1986)	$34.02	52.1%	
		IBP (1991) — Tyson Foods (2001)	$0.22	0.3%	
		Battlemountain Gold (1985) — Newmont Mining (2001)	$2.94	4.5%	
		Pennzoil Quaker State (1998) — Royal Dutch Petroleum (2002)	$15.11	23.1%	
289	270	Cerro De Pasco > Cerro (1960) — Private (1976)	$64.98	100.0%	9.32%
290	100	Columbia Gas System > Columbia Energy Group (1998) — Nisource (2000)	$64.42	100.0%	9.30%
291	397	McCrory Stores — Rapid American (1976) — Private (1981)	$64.41	100.0%	9.30%
		Lerner Stores (1965) — McCrory Stores (1973)			
292	246	Atlantic Coast Line — Seaboard Coastline (1967) — CSX Corp (1980)	$63.87	100.0%	9.28%
293	264	Becor Western — Bucyrus Erie (1988) > Bucyrus International (1997) — Private (1997)	$63.81	100.0%	9.28%
294	84	United States Gypsum > USG (1984)	$63.48	100.0%	9.27%
		USG	$0.34	0.5%	
		AP Green (1988) — Global Industrial Techs (1998) — RHI (2000)	$63.14	99.5%	
295	67	Chesapeake & Ohio Railway > Chessie System (1973) — CSX (1980)	$63.45	100.0%	9.27%
296	128	St. Regis — Champion International (1984) — International Paper (2000)	$62.93	100.0%	9.25%
297	30	Westinghouse Electric > CBS (1997) — Viacom (2000)	$62.68	100.0%	9.24%
298	284	Seaboard Finance — AVCO (1969) — Textron (1985)	$62.65	100.0%	9.24%
299	418	National Sugar Refining — Private (1969)	$62.21	100.0%	9.22%
300	119	Halliburton	$59.73	100.0%	9.13%
301	152	United States Rubber > Uniroyal (1967) — Private (1985)	$59.52	100.0%	9.12%
302	49	Anaconda Copper Mining — Atlantic Richfield (1977) — BP-Amoco (2000)	$58.55	100.0%	9.08%
303	380	Acme Cleveland — Danaher Group (1996)	$57.59	100.0%	9.04%
304	392	Curtis Publishing — Private (1986)	$57.54	100.0%	9.04%
305	166	Thompson Products > Thompson Ramo Woodrige (1958) > TRW (1965) — Northrup Grumman (2002)	$57.32	100.0%	9.03%
306	97	Libbey-Owens-Ford > Trinova (1986) > Aeroquip Vickers (1997) — Eaton (1999)	$56.28	100.0%	8.99%
		Eaton	$50.96	90.5%	
		Axcelis Technologies Inc (2001)	$5.32	9.5%	
307	242	General Cable > G.K. Technologies (1979) — Penn Central (1981) > American Financial Underwriters (1994)	$55.81	100.0%	8.97%
		American Financial Underwriters	$48.16	86.3%	
		Sprague Technologies (1987) > American Annuity Group (1992) > Great American Financial Resources (2000)	$6.12	11.0%	
		General Cable (1992) — Private (1994)	$1.53	2.7%	
308	159	Westvaco Corp. > Meadwestvaco (2002)	$55.44	100.0%	8.95%
309	131	Cleveland Elec. Illuminating — Centerior Energy (1986) — Firstenergy (1997)	$54.87	100.0%	8.93%
310	105	General Public Utilities > GPU (1996) — Firstenergy (2001)	$54.70	100.0%	8.92%
311	45	American Gas & Electric > American Electric Power (1958)	$53.43	100.0%	8.87%

Rank Return	Rank Market Cap 1957	Original Name — 2003 Name (— Merger; > Name Change)	Total Accumu-lation	Percent Total	Annual Return
312	496	Divco Wayne — Boise Cascade (1968)	$52.66	100.0%	8.83%
313	160	Pacific Enterprises — Sempra Energy (1998)	$50.09	100.0%	8.72%
314	113	Curtiss-Wright	$50.06	100.0%	8.71%
315	331	Lowenstein & Sons — Springs Industries (1985) — Private (2001)	$49.78	100.0%	8.70%
316	318	McIntyre Porcupine > Mines McIntyre Mines (1974) — Private (1989) — Falconbridge (1998)	$48.11	100.0%	8.62%
317	377	Chicago Milwaukee St. Paul Pacific — Chicago Milwaukee (1972) — Private (1990)	$46.60	100.0%	8.55%
		Private	$45.30	97.2%	
		Heartland Partners (1990)	$1.30	2.8%	
318	103	National Cash Register > NCR (1974) — AT&T (1991)	$46.48	100.0%	8.54%
		AT&T	$8.71	18.7%	
		Lucent (1996)	$4.39	9.4%	
		Agere Systems (2002)	$1.26	2.7%	
		Avaya (2000)	$2.28	4.9%	
		NCR (1997)	$2.83	6.1%	
		AT&T Wireless (2001)	$5.36	11.5%	
		AT&T Broadband Services (2002) — Comcast (2002)	$21.65	46.6%	
319	146	Duquesne Light > D Q E (1990)	$45.91	100.0%	8.51%
320	145	West Penn Electric > Allegheny Power Systems (1960) > Allegheny Energy (1997)	$45.51	100.0%	8.49%
321	231	Link Belt — FMC (1967)	$45.15	100.0%	8.48%
		FMC	$20.77	46.0%	
		FMC Technologies (2001)	$24.38	54.0%	
322	490	DWG Cigars >DWG (1967) > Triarc Companies (1993)	$44.41	100.0%	8.44%
		Triarc	$15.72		
		Triarc B Shares (2003)	$28.69		
323	425	Cuban American Sugar > North American Sugar Industries (1963) — Borden (1971) — Private (1995)	$43.49	100.0%	8.39%
324	161	W.R. Grace — W.R. Grace New (1996) — Sealed Air New (1998)	$43.26	100.0%	8.38%
		Sealed Air (New)	$26.29	60.8%	
		Fresenius Medical Care (1996)	$14.64	33.8%	
		W.R. Grace New (1998)	$2.33	5.4%	
325	429	American Zinc Lead & Smelting > American Zinc (1966) — Private (1978)	$42.73	100.0%	8.35%
326	172	Dresser Industries — Halliburton (1998)	$42.66	100.0%	8.34%
		Halliburton	$40.46	94.8%	
		Indresco (1992) — Global Industrial Techs (1995) — RHI (2000)	$2.20	5.2%	
327	258	American Machine & Foundry > AMF (1970) — Minstar (1985) — Private (1988)	$42.15	100.0%	8.32%
328	47	J.C. Penney	$42.06	100.0%	8.31%
329	4	E.I. DuPont de Nemours	$41.82	100.0%	8.30%
		DuPont	$23.42	56.0%	
		Conoco (1999) >Conoco Phillips (2002)	$6.92	16.5%	
		General Motors (1962,1963, 1964)	$9.06	21.7%	
		Delphia Automotive Systems (1999) > Delphi (1999)	$1.03	2.5%	
		Raytheon (1997)	$0.48	1.2%	

Rank Return	Rank Market Cap 1957	Original Name — 2003 Name (— Merger; > Name Change)	Total Accumu-lation	Percent Total	Annual Return
		Electronic Data Systems (1996) >EDS	$0.48	1.2%	
		GM H Class (1985)	$0.43	1.0%	
330	3	General Motors	$41.47	100.0%	8.28%
		General Motors	$33.41	80.6%	
		Delphia Automotive Systems (1999) > Delphi (1999)	$3.79	9.1%	
		Raytheon (1997)	$1.54	3.7%	
		Electronic Data Systems (1996) >EDS	$1.78	4.3%	
		GM H Class (1985)	$0.96	2.3%	
331	147	Nat'l Dist. & Chem — Quantum Chem (1988) — Hansen PLC (1993)	$41.26	100.0%	8.27%
		Hansen PLC	$8.21	19.9%	
		US Industries New (1995)	$0.71	1.7%	
		Imperial Tobacco (1996)	$22.57	54.7%	
		Millennium Chemicals (1996)	$1.62	3.9%	
		Energy (1997) — Texas Utilities (1998) > TXU (2000)	$8.16	19.8%	
332	82	Owens Illinois Glass — Private (1987) — Owens Illinois Glass (1991)	$40.59	100.0%	8.23%
333	472	Ward Baking > Ward Foods (1964) — Private (1981)	$40.48	100.0%	8.22%
334	386	H.L. Green — McCrory Stores (1961) — Rapid American (1976) — Private (1981)	$40.44	100.0%	8.22%
335	316	Bridgeport Brass — Nat'l Dist. & Chem (1961) — Quantum Chem (1988) — Hansen PLC (1993)	$40.29	100.0%	8.21%
		Hansen PLC	$8.01	19.9%	
		US Industries New (1995)	$0.69	1.7%	
		Imperial Tobacco (1996)	$22.04	54.7%	
		Millennium Chemicals Co. (1996)	$1.58	3.9%	
		Energy Co (1997) — Texas Utilities (1998) > TXU (2000)	$7.96	19.8%	
336	88	F.W. Woolworth > Venator Group (1998) > Foot Locker (2001)	$39.86	100.0%	8.19%
337	87	Corning Glassworks > Corning (1989)	$39.19	100.0%	8.15%
		Corning	$20.27	51.7%	
		Covance (1997)	$5.07	12.9%	
		Quest Diagnostics (1997)	$13.84	35.3%	
338	112	El Paso Natural Gas > El Paso (1974) — Burlington Northern (1983) > Burlington Northern Santa Fe (1995)	$39.11	100.0%	8.14%
		Burlington Northern Santa Fe	$18.09	46.3%	
		Northwest Pipeline (1974) > Northwest Energy (1975) — Williams (1983)	$9.10	23.3%	
		Williams Communications Group (2001)		0.0%	
		Burlington Resources (1989)	$10.95	28.0%	
		El Paso (1992)	$0.95	2.4%	
339	260	Marquette Cement Manufacturing >Marquette (1975) — Gulf & Western Industries (1976) > Paramount Communications (1989) — Viacom (1994)	$38.34	100.0%	8.10%
340	371	Sutherland Paper > Kvp Sutherland (1960) — Brown (1966) — James River (1980) > Ft. James (1997) — Georgia Pacific (2000)	$37.85	100.0%	8.07%
		Georgia Pacific	$37.85	100.0%	
		Crown Vantage (1995) — Georgia Pacific (1999)			
341	17	Aluminum Company of America > Alcoa (1999)	$37.74	100.0%	8.06%

Rank Return	Rank Market Cap 1957	Original Name — 2003 Name (— Merger; > Name Change)	Total Accumu- lation	Percent Total	Annual Return
342	62	Phelps Dodge	$37.43	100.0%	8.04%
343	446	Bullard Co. — White Consolidated Inds (1968) — AB Electrolux (1986) > Aktiebolaget Electrolux (1989)	$36.63	100.0%	7.99%
		Aktiebolaget Electrolux	$33.13	90.4%	
		SAPA AB (1997)	$3.51	9.6%	
344	313	Blaw Knox — White Consolidated Industries (1968) — AB Electrolux (1986) > Aktiebolaget Electrolux (1989)	$36.46	100.0%	7.98%
		Aktiebolaget Electrolux	$32.97	90.4%	
		SAPA AB (1997)	$3.49	9.6%	
345	419	Universal Pictures — MCA (1966) — Matsushita Electric Industrial (1991)	$35.95	100.0%	7.95%
		Matsushita Electric Industrial	$35.95	100.0%	
		First Columbia Financial (1982 -1987)	$0.00	0.0%	
346	19	Eastman Kodak	$35.33	100.0%	7.91%
		Eastman Kodak	$25.23	71.4%	
		Eastman Chemical (1994)	$10.10	28.6%	
347	71	Texas Utilities > T X U (2000)	$35.09	100.0%	7.89%
348	324	American Bakeries — Private (1986)	$34.40	100.0%	7.85%
349	52	Chrysler — DaimlerChrysler (1998)	$34.13	100.0%	7.83%
350	338	Libby, McNeill & Libby — Nestlé (1976)	$34.01	100.0%	7.82%
351	357	Commercial Solvents — International Mineral & Chemical (1975) > Imcera (1990) > Mallinckrodt (1994) — Tyco (2000)	$32.63	100.0%	7.73%
352	208	General Portland Cement > General Portland (1972) — Private (1982) — Lafarge (1983)	$32.24	100.0%	7.70%
353	32	National Lead > NL Industries (1971)	$32.08	100.0%	7.69%
		NL Industries	$7.72	24.1%	
		Baroid (1988) > Tremont (1990) — Valhi (2003)	$6.61	20.6%	
		Baroid New (1990) — Dresser Industries (1994) — Haliburton (1998)	$17.75	55.3%	
354	24	International Paper	$31.97	100.0%	7.68%
355	424	Jefferson Lake Sulphur — Occidental Petroleum (1964)	$31.00	100.0%	7.61%
		Occidental Petroleum	$30.81	99.4%	
		I B P (1991) — Tyson Foods (2001)	$0.20	0.6%	
356	120	Douglas Aircraft — McDonnell Douglas (1967) — Boeing (1997)	$30.93	100.0%	7.60%
357	32	Allied Chemical & Dye > Allied Chemical (1958) >Allied (1981) > Allied Signal (1985) > Honeywell Int'l (1999)	$29.88	100.0%	7.52%
		Honeywell International	$28.26	94.6%	
		Henley Group (1986) — Wheelaborator Group (1989) — Waste Management (1998)	$0.87	2.9%	
		Fisher Scientific (1987) — Wheelaborator Group (1989) — Waste Management (1998)			
		Henley Manufacturing — Private	$0.75	2.5%	
358	269	Lilly Tulip — Owens Illinois Glass (1968) — Private (1987) — Owens Illinois Glass (1991)	$29.81	100.0%	7.52%
359	253	Indianapolis Power & Light > IPALCO Enterprises (1983) — A E S (2001)	$29.30	100.0%	7.48%
360	187	Climax Molybdenum — American Metal Climax (1957) > Amax (1974) — Cyprus Amax Minerals (1993) — Phelps			

Rank Return	Rank Market Cap 1957	Original Name — 2003 Name (— Merger; > Name Change)	Total Accumu-lation	Percent Total	Annual Return
		Dodge (1999)	$29.14	100.0%	7.47%
		Phelps Dodge	$6.90	23.6%	
		Alumax (1993) — ALCOA (1998)	$22.04	8.9%	
		AMAX Gold (1993) — Kinross Gold (1998)	$0.20	0.7%	
361	317	Anaconda Wire & Cable — Anaconda (1964) — Atlantic Richfield (1977) — BP Amoco (2000) > BP PLC (2001)	$29.08	100.0%	7.46%
362	42	Firestone Tire & Rubber > Firestone (1988) — Bridgestone-Firestone (1988)	$28.31	100.0%	7.40%
363	235	Baltimore & Ohio — Chesapeake & Ohio RR (1966) >Chessie Systems (1973) — CSX Corp. (1980)	$26.93	100.0%	7.28%
364	248	Island Creek Coal — Occidental Petroleum (1968)	$26.87	100.0%	7.28%
		Occidental Petroleum (1991)	$26.70	99.4%	
		IBP (1991) — Tyson Foods (2001)	$0.17	0.6%	
365	308	Newport News Shipbuilding — Tenneco (1968) — Tenneco New (1997) > Tenneco Automotive (1999)	$26.37	100.0%	7.24%
		Tenneco Automotive	$0.96	3.6%	
		Newport News Shipbuilding New (1996) — Northrup Grumman (2002)	$8.80	33.4%	
		Pactiv (1999)	$16.61	63.0%	
366	185	American Metal Climax > Amax (1974) — Cyprus Amax Minerals (1993) — Phelps Dodge (1999)	$25.95	100.0%	7.20%
		Phelps Dodge	$6.15	75.6%	
		Alumax (1993) — ALCOA (1998)	$19.62	23.7%	
		AMAX Gold (1993) — Kinross Gold (1998)	$0.17	0.7%	
367	247	Chicago R.I. & Pacific — Chicago Pacific (1984) — Maytag (1989)	$25.71	100.0%	7.18%
368	99	Niagara Mohawk Power > Niagara Mohawk Holdings (1999) — National Grid Group (2002)	$25.39	100.0%	7.15%
369	406	Oliver > Cletrac (1960) — Hess Oil & Chemical (1962) > Amerada Hess (1969)	$25.22	100.0%	7.13%
		Amerada Hess	$25.22	100.0%	
		White Motors (1960) — Northeast Ohio Axle (1980) > N E O A X (1986) > Envirosource (1989)	$0.00	0.0%	
370	448	Dayton Rubber > Dayco (1960) > Day International (1987) — M.A. Hanna (1987) — Polyone (2000)	$24.49	100.0%	7.07%
371	436	General Finance — C N A Financial (1968)	$24.42	100.0%	7.06%
372	280	National Tea — Private (1982)	$23.97	100.0%	7.02%
373	25	Aluminum > Alcan Aluminum (1966) > Alcan (2001)	$23.89	100.0%	7.01%
374	293	Homestake Mining — Barrick Gold (2001)	$23.52	100.0%	6.98%
375	194	Champion Paper — U S Plywood Champion (1967) > Champion Int'l (1972) — Int'l Paper (2000)	$22.99	100.0%	6.92%
376	491	Hercules Motors — HUPP (1961) — White Consolidated Industries (1967) — AB Electrolux (1986) > Aktiebolaget Electrolux (1989)	$22.65	100.0%	6.89%
		Aktiebolaget Electrolux	$20.48	90.4%	
		SAPA AB (1997)	$2.17	9.6%	
377	440	Reed Roller Bit > G.W. Murphy Industries (1967) > Reed Tool (1972) — Baker Oil Tools (1975) > Baker Int'l (1976) — Baker Hughes (1987)	$21.98	100.0%	6.82%
378	163	Walker Hiram Gooderham & Worts — Walker Hiram Consumers Home (1980) > Walker Resources (1981) — Gulf Canada (1986) —			

Rank Return	Rank Market Cap 1957	Original Name — 2003 Name (— Merger; > Name Change)	Total Accumu-lation	Percent Total	Annual Return
		Gulf Canada Resources (1987)	$21.67	100.0%	6.79%
379	191	Southern Natural Gas > Sonat (1982) — El Paso Energy (1999)	$21.10	100.0%	6.73%
380	319	American Chain & Cable — Private (1976) — Babcock (1990)	$20.71	100.0%	6.68%
381	273	First National Stores — Private (1974) — First National Supermarkets (1978) — Private (1985)	$20.59	100.0%	6.67%
382	192	Lehigh Portland Cement — Private (1977)	$19.38	100.0%	6.53%
383	265	Revere Copper & Brass — Private (1986)	$19.12	100.0%	6.50%
384	343	J.J. Newberry — McCrory (1972) — Rapid American (1976) — Private (1981)	$18.62	100.0%	6.44%
385	346	Erie Railroad > Erie Lackawanna RR (1960) — Norfolk & Western Railway (1968) — Norfolk Southern Corp. (1982)	$18.49	100.0%	6.43%
386	456	General Host — Private (1998)	$18.21	100.0%	6.39%
387	59	Reynolds Metal — Alcoa (2000)	$17.31	100.0%	6.28%
388	115	Hercules Powder > Hercules (1966)	$17.04	100.0%	6.24%
389	449	Cudahy Packing — General Host (1972) — Private (1998)	$16.44	100.0%	6.16%
390	368	Chain Belt Co. > Rex Chainbelt (1964) > Rexnord (1973) — Banner Industries (1987) — Fairchild (1990)	$15.88	100.0%	6.08%
		Fairchild	$14.80	93.2%	
		Global Sources Ltd. (2000)	$1.09	6.8%	
391	341	Royal McBee — Litton Industries (1965) — Northrup Grumman (2001)	$15.20	100.0%	5.98%
		Northrup Grumman	$9.78	64.4%	
		Western Atlas (1994) — Baker Hughes (1998)	$4.35	28.6%	
		Unova (1997)	$1.06	7.0%	
392	217	Fruehauf Trailer Corp. > Fruehauf Corp. (1963) — Varity (1989) — Lucasvarity (1996) — TRW (1999) — Northrup Grumman (2002)	$13.89	100.0%	5.78%
393	396	Falstaff Brewing — Private (1989)	$13.66	100.0%	5.74%
394	44	Amerada Petroleum — Amerada Hess (1969)	$13.54	100.0%	5.72%
395	167	Burroughs > Unisys (1986)	$13.23	100.0%	5.67%
396	43	Crown Zellerbach — James River (1986) — Ft. James (1999) — Georgia Pacific (2000)	$11.88	100.0%	5.43%
397	391	American Motors — Chrysler Corp (1987) — DaimlerChrysler (1998)	$11.53	100.0%	5.36%
398	51	Goodrich	$11.11	100.0%	5.28%
		Goodrich	$10.21	91.9%	
		ENPRO Industries (2002)	$0.90	8.1%	
399	457	Briggs Manufacturing — Jim Walter Corp. (1972) — Private (1988) — Walter Industries	$11.12	100.0%	5.28%
400	195	American Airlines > Amr Corp (1982)	$11.04	100.0%	5.26%
		AMR Corp	$4.98	45.1%	
		Sabre Group Holdings (2000)	$6.06	54.9%	
401	309	Alpha Portland Industries > Slattery Group (1985) — Private (1990)	$10.34	100.0%	5.12%
402	183	Illinois Power > Illnova Corp Holding (1994) > Dynegy (2000)	$9.93	100.0%	5.02%
403	124	American Smelting & Refining > Asarco (1975) — Grupo Mexico (1999)	$9.85	100.0%	5.00%
404	157	Babcock & Wilcox — J. Ray McDermott & Co. (1978) > McDermott (1980) — McDermott International (1983)	$9.67	100.0%	4.96%
405	384	Case (Ji) — Tenneco New — Tenneco Automotive (1996)	$9.50	100.0%	4.93%

Rank Return	Rank Market Cap 1957	Original Name — 2003 Name (— Merger; > Name Change)	Total Accumu- lation	Percent Total	Annual Return
		Tenneco > Tenneco Automotive (1999)	$0.35	3.6%	
		Pactiv Corp. (1999)	$5.98	61.9%	
		Northrup Grumman	$3.17	33.4%	
406	169	Enserch — Texas Utilities (1997) > TXU (2002)	$9.32	100.0%	4.88%
		TXU	$7.06	75.7%	
		Pool Energy Services (1990) — Nabors Industries (1999)	$1.04	11.1%	
		Enserch Exploration Partners (1986) — Newfield Exploration (2002)	$1.23	13.2%	
407	22	International Nickel Co. CDA > Inco (1976)	$9.30	100.0%	4.88%
408	9	U S Steel > USX (1986) > USX Marathon (1991) > Marathon Oil (2000)	$8.25	100.0%	4.61%
		Marathon Oil	$6.87	83.3%	
		United States Steel (1991)	$1.38	16.7%	
409	302	Copper Range — Louisiana Land and Exploration (1977) — LL&E Royalty Trust (1983)	$7.96	100.0%	4.53%
		LL&E Royalty Trust	$6.25	78.6%	
		Burlington Resources (1997)	$1.71	21.4%	
410	39	Goodyear Tire & Rubber	$7.93	100.0%	4.52%
411	365	Republic Aviation > RAC (1966) — Fairchild Hiller (1966) > Fairchild Industries (1971) — Banner Industries (1989) > Fairchild (1990)	$7.93	100.0%	4.52%
		Fairchild	$7.38	93.2%	
		Global Sources (2000)	$0.54	6.8%	
412	455	Bigelow-Sanford — Sperry & Hutchinson (1967) — Baldwin United (1981) — PHLCORP (1986) — Leucadia National (1992)	$7.66	100.0%	4.44%
413	57	Sperry Rand > Sperry (1979) — Unisys (1986)	$7.05	100.0%	4.26%
414	127	Distillers Corp Seagram > Seagram (1974) — Vivendi Universal (2000)	$5.95	100.0%	3.88%
415	438	Motor Wheel — Goodyear Tire & Rubber (1964)	$5.90	100.0%	3.86%
416	289	Cincinnati Milling Machine > Cincinnati Milacron (1970) > Milacron (1998)	$5.45	100.0%	3.69%
417	95	Consumers Power — CMS Energy (1987)	$5.34	100.0%	3.64%
418	373	Great Western Sugar — Great Western United (1968) — Hunt International Resources (1978) — Maxco (1979)	$5.25	100.0%	3.60%
419	154	Commercial Credit — Control Data (1968) > Ceridian Corp (1992)	$3.84	100.0%	2.91%
		C D S I Holdings	$0.00	0.0%	
420	420	Foster Wheeler	$3.64	100.0%	2.80%
421	465	Diana Stores — Daylin (1969) — W.R. Grace (1979) — W.R. Grace New (1996) — Sealed Air New (1998)	$3.55	100.0%	2.74%
		Sealed Air (New)	$2.16	33.8%	
		Fresenius Medical Care (1996)	$1.20	60.8%	
		W.R. Grace New (1998)	$0.19	5.4%	
422	321	Vanadium — Foote Minerals (1967) — Cyprus Minerals (1988) > Cyprus Amax Minerals (1993) — Phelps Dodge (1999)	$3.52	100.0%	2.73%
423	370	Walworth Co. — International Utilities (1972) — Echo Bay Mines (1983) — Kinross Gold (2003)	$3.47	100.0%	2.69%
		Kinross Gold Mines	$3.43	98.9%	
		Gotaas Larsen — Private (1988)	$0.04	1.1%	
424	332	Dan River — Private (1983) — Dan River GA (1997)	$3.44	100.0%	2.67%

Rank Return	Rank Market Cap 1957	Original Name — 2003 Name (— Merger; > Name Change)	Total Accumu- lation	Percent Total	Annual Return
425	495	Pfeiffer Brewing > Associated Brewing (1962) > Armada (1973) — Private (1990)	$3.01	100.0%	2.38%
426	80	Inland Steel — Ryerson Tull New (1999)	$2.51	100.0%	1.99%
427	492	Munsingwear > Premiumwear (1996) — New England Business Service (2000)	$2.05	100.0%	1.54%
428	306	Genesco	$2.01	100.0%	1.50%
429	250	Penn-Dixie Industries — Continental Steel	$2.00	100.0%	1.49%
430	55	Kaiser Aluminum > Kaisertech Inc. (1987) — Maxxam (1988)	$1.98	100.0%	1.47%
431	483	Missouri-Kansas-Texas — Katy Industries (1968)	$1.67	100.0%	1.10%
432	244	United Airlines > UAL Corp. (1969)	$1.65	100.0%	1.08%
433	333	Allied Supermarkets > Vons Companies (1987) — RMI Titanium (1997) > RTI International Metals (1998)	$1.63	100.0%	1.05%
434	207	Armstrong Cork > Armstrong World Industries (1980) > Armstrong Holdings (2000)	$1.62	100.0%	1.03%
435	325	Inspiration Consolidated Copper — Hudson Bay Mining & Smelting (1978) — Inspiration Resources (1983) — Terra Industries Inc. (1993)	$1.27	100.0%	0.52%
436	63	International Harvester > Navistar International (1986)	$0.96	100.0%	-0.09%
437	139	Lone Star Industries	$0.94	100.0%	-0.12%
438	70	S.H. Kress — Genesco (1964)	$0.75	100.0%	-0.62%
439	201	Kresge > Kmart (1977)	$0.74	100.0%	-0.63%
440	210	National Supply — Armco Steel (1958) — A K Steel (1999)	$0.59	100.0%	-1.11%
441	48	Armco Steel >Armco Inc (1978) — A K Steel (1999)	$0.56	100.0%	-1.21%
442	238	Allied Stores — Campeau Corp (1985)	$0.51	100.0%	-1.42%
443	109	Owens Corning	$0.50	100.0%	-1.45%
444	151	Federated Department Stores — Campeau (1988) — Camdev (1990)	$0.47	100.0%	-1.62%
445	186	American Viscose — Raybestos Manhattan (1981) > Raymark (1982) > Raytech (1986)	$0.44	100.0%	-1.73%
446	130	Penn Central > American Financial Underwriters (1994)	$0.40	100.0%	-1.92%
		American Financial Underwriters	$0.32	80.4%	
		Sprague Technologies (1987) > American Annuity Group (1992) > Great American Financial Resources (2000)	$0.04	8.8%	
		General Cable (1992) — Private (1994)	$0.04	10.8%	
447	111	Manville — Berkshire Hathaway (2001)	$0.40	100.0%	-1.95%
448	359	Cone Mills — Private (1984 – 1992) — Cone Mills NC (1992)	$0.39	100.0%	-1.99%
449	179	New York Central — Penn Central (1968) > American Financial Underwriters (1994)	$0.35	100.0%	-2.20%
		American Financial Underwriters	$0.28	80.2%	
		Sprague Technologies (1987) > American Annuity Group (1992) > Great American Financial Resources (2000)	$0.03	8.7%	
		General Cable (1992) — Private (1994)	$0.04	11.1%	
450	482	Holland Furnace — Athlone Industries (1964) — Private (1993)	$0.28	100.0%	-2.72%
		Athlone Industries (private)	$0.16	57.8%	
		Allegheny Ludlum (1993) — Allegheny Teledyne — Allegheny Technologies	$0.08	29.7%	
		Water Pik (1999)	$0.01	2.3%	
		Teledyne Technologies (1999)	$0.03	10.1%	
451	170	Northern Natural Gas > Internorth (1980) > Enron (1986)	$0.25	100.0%	-2.89%

Rank Return	Rank Market Cap 1957	Original Name — 2003 Name (— Merger; > Name Change)	Total Accumu- lation	Percent Total	Annual Return
452	222	Food Fair Stores — Pantry Pride (1983) > Revlon Group (1986) — Private (1987) — Revlon (1996)	$0.19	100.0%	-3.44%
453	462	Van Raalte — Cluett Peabody (1968) — West Point Pepperell (1986) — Westpoint Stevens (1993)	$0.16	100.0%	-3.87%
454	279	Stevens (JP) — West Point Pepperell (1988) — Westpoint Stevens (1993)	$0.16	100.0%	-3.89%
455	475	Aldens Inc. — Gamble Skogmo (1964) — Wickes Companies (1980) — Private (1989) — Collins & Aikman New (1994)	$0.15	100.0%	-4.01%
456	379	Cluett Peabody — West Point Pepperell (1986) — Westpoint Stevens (1993)	$0.13	100.0%	-4.25%
457	320	Trans World Airlines — Transworld (1979) — Liquidated (1987)	$0.12	100.0%	-4.35%
		TW Services (1987) — TW Holdings (1989) > Flagstar Companies (1993) — Bankrupt (1997)		0.0%	
		UAL Corp. (1987) — Bankrupt (2002)	$0.12	100.0%	
458	114	Jones & Laughlin Steel — LTV (1974) — Ling Temco Vought New (1993)	$0.09	100.0%	-5.02%
		Ling Temco Vought New		0.0%	
		Wilson Foods (1981) — Dockosil Companies (1989) > Foodbrands America (1995) — IBP (1997) — Tyson Foods (2001)	$0.09	100.0%	
459	383	American Export Lines > American Export Isbrandtsen Lines (1964) > American Export Industries (1967) > AEICOR (1978) > Doskocil Cos. (1983) > Foodbran Americas (1995) — IBP Inc (1997) —Tyson Foods (2001)	$0.08	100.0%	-5.18%
460	410	Lees & Sons — Burlington Industries (1960) > Private (1987) — Burlington Industries Equity Inc. (1992) — Burlington Industries Inc. New (1994)	$0.06	100.0%	-5.71%
461	108	Youngstown Sheet & Tube — Lykes Youngstown Corp. (1969) — LTV (1978) — Ling Temco Vought New (1993)	$0.06	100.0%	-5.98%
		Ling Temco Vought New		0.0%	
		Foods (2001)	$0.06	100.0%	
462	347	Warner Brothers — Warnaco Inc. (1967) — Private (1986) — Warnaco New (1992)	$0.05	100.0%	-6.04%
463	395	Wilson Co. — Ling Temco Vought Inc. (1967) — Ling Temco Vought New (1993)	$0.05	100.0%	-6.34%
		Ling Temco Vought New		0.0%	
		Wilson Foods (1981) — Dockosil Companies (1989) > Foodbrands America (1995) — IBP (1997) — Tyson Foods (2001)	$0.05	100.0%	
464	251	Burlington Industries — Private (1987) — Burlington Industries Equity (1992) > Burlington Industries New (1994)	$0.04	100.0%	-6.46%
465	129	Allis Chalmers	$0.03	100.0%	-6.97%
466	361	Reading Co. > Reading Entertainment Co. (1996)	$0.02	100.0%	-7.95%
467	408	Publicker Industries — Publicard Inc. (1998)	$0.02	100.0%	-8.07%
468	350	Family Finance > Aristar (1973) — Gamble Skogmo (1979) — Wickes Companies (1980) — Private (1989) — Collins & Aikman Corp New (1994)	$0.02	100.0%	-8.55%
469	243	Wheeling Steel Corp. — Wheeling-Pittsburgh Steel Corp. (1968) > W H X Corp. (1994)	$0.01	100.0%	-8.72%
470	468	Republic Pictures — Triton Group (1985) — Intermark (1990) — Triton Group (1993) > Alarmguard Holdings (1997) — Tyco International (1999)	$0.00	100.0%	-11.50%
471	18	Bethlehem Steel	$0.00	100.0%	-13.54%
472	224	Addressograph Multigraph > A M International (1979)	$0.00	100.0%	-100%

Rank Return	Rank Market Cap 1957	Original Name — 2003 Name (— Merger; > Name Change)	Total Accumu- lation	Percent Total	Annual Return
473	476	American Shipbuilding	$0.00	100.0%	-100%
474	254	Colorado Fuel & Iron > CF&I Steel (1966)	$0.00	100.0%	-100%
475	470	Cornell-Dubilier — Federal Pacific Electric Co. (1960) — U V Industries (1972) — Sharon Steel Co. (1980)	$0.00	100.0%	-100%
476	366	Eagle Picher > Eagle Picher Industries (1966)	$0.00	100.0%	-100%
477	228	Eastern Airlines — Texas Air (1986) > Continental Airlines Holdings (1990)	$0.00	100.0%	-100%
478	489	Goebel Brewing	$0.00	100.0%	-100%
479	268	W.T. Grant	$0.00	100.0%	-100%
480	497	Guantanamo Sugar	$0.00	100.0%	-100%
481	463	Holly Sugar — Imperial Sugar Co. (1988) — Bankrupt (2001)	$0.00	100.0%	-100%
482	204	International Shoe > Interco (1966)	$0.00	100.0%	-100%
483	431	Jaeger Machine	$0.00	100.0%	-100%
484	229	Joy Manufacturing — Private (1987) — Joy Technologies (1991) — Harnischfeger Industries (1993)	$0.00	100.0%	-100%
485	499	Manati Sugar	$0.00	100.0%	-100%
486	486	Manhattan Shirt > Manhattan Industries (1968) — Salant (1988)	$0.00	100.0%	-100%
487	479	Monarch Machine Tool > Genesis Worldwide (1999)	$0.00	100.0%	-100%
488	450	Minneapolis Moline > Motec Industries (1961)	$0.00	100.0%	-100%
489	276	G.C. Murphy — Ames Department Stores (1985)	$0.00	100.0%	-100%
490	68	National Steel > National Intergroup (1983) > Foxmeyer Health (1994) > Avatex (1997)	$0.00	100.0%	-100%
491	454	New York, New Haven & Hartford	$0.00	100.0%	-100%
492	249	Pan American World Airways > Pan Am (1984)	$0.00	100.0%	-100%
493	37	Republic Steel — L T V (1984)	$0.00	100.0%	-100%
494	193	Sunbeam — Allegheny International Inc. (1982)	$0.00	100.0%	-100%
495	500	Artloom Carpet > Artloom Industries (1958) > Trans United Industries (1959)	$0.00	100.0%	-100%
496	417	U.S. Hoffman Machinery	$0.00	100.0%	-100%
		Lionel	$0.00		
497	393	United States Smelting and Refining > U V Industries (1972) — Sharon Steel (1980)	$0.00	100.0%	-100%
498	434	Vertientes-Camaguey Sugar	$0.00	100.0%	-100%
499	355	White Motors — Northeast Ohio Axle Co. (1980) > N E O A X (1986) > Envirosource Inc. (1989)	$0.00	100.0%	-100%
500	360	Zenith Radio > Zenith Electronics (1984)	$0.00	100.0%	-100%

NOTES

2: Creative Destruction or Destruction of the Creative?

1. Richard Foster and Sarah Kaplan, *Creative Destruction: Why Companies That Are Built to Last Underperform the Market, and How to Successfully Transform Them* (New York: Random House, 2001), 8.
2. This undertaking would have been impossible without the superb work of my research assistant, Jeremy Schwartz.
3. Ironically, the S&P Composite Index excluded the largest stock in the world at that time, American Telephone & Telegraph, so as not to let one firm dominate the index.
4. At that time, the firms in the S&P 500 Index accounted for about 85 percent of the value of all NYSE-listed stocks.
5. From S&P's Web site, http://www2.standardandpoors.com/spf/pdf/index/500factsheet.pdf.
6. Since 1993, new additions to the index have averaged slightly more than 5 percent of the index's market value.
7. When a firm went private, I assumed the funds from the privatization were put into an index fund whose returns matched the updated S&P 500 Index. If a privatized firm went public again, I assumed that the firm was repurchased with the funds that were put into the index fund. Privatized firms constituted only about 3 percent of the value of these portfolios.
8. This assumes there are not enough sellers, including short sellers, to offset the automatic increase in demand.
9. In March 2004 Standard & Poor's announced that starting in 2005 the firm would weight the stock in its index by the amount of "float," or shares that are available to outside investors, instead of by the total number of shares. This would reduce shares in the index when shares are closely held by owners (as is the case with Wal-Mart) and may moderate the price movements in the stocks upon addition and deletion from the index.

10. See "Index Effect Redux," Standard and Poor's, September 8, 2004. The impact on the prices of stocks added by S&P has been reduced in recent years, but this is partly due to speculators bidding up the price of stocks before the announcement. See also Roger J. Bos, "Event Study: Quantifying the Effect of Being Added to an S&P Index," Standard and Poor's, September 2000.
11. The Baby Bells were Southwestern Bell, Bell South, Bell Atlantic, NYNEX, Pacific Telesis, Ameritech, and US West Communications. In 2004 the surviving firms are SBC Communications (Southwestern, Ameritech, and Pacific Telesis), Bell South, Verizon (Bell Atlantic and NYNEX), and Qwest (US West).
12. If the dividend yield on the Total Descendants portfolio is significantly higher than the other portfolios, this is a tax disadvantage, but this effect was not significant for the portfolios we analyzed.
13. There are a few cases where a stock distribution is considered a taxable event by the IRS.

3: The Tried and True: Finding Corporate El Dorados

1. Richard Foster and Sarah Kaplan, *Creative Destruction*, 9.
2. The firm retained its ticker symbol, MO, or "Big Mo," as traders affectionately call Philip Morris.
3. S&P deleted this company from its index only five months after the index was launched. Although the firm was one of the smallest in the index ($6 million capitalization), inquiries to S&P have come up with no reason why the firm was deleted.
4. See the Heinz Web site, http://heinz.com/jsp/about.jsp; Associated Press, "Heinz Enters Talks to Acquire European Company," December 20, 2000; Nikhil Deogun and Jonathan Eig, "Heinz Is Close to a Deal to Buy CSM's Grocery Products Unit," *Wall Street Journal Europe*, December 20, 2000.
5. When we add Kroger, a consumer staples firm, eighteen, or 90 percent, of the firms are in either consumer staples or health care. Chapter 4 describes the evolution of these industries.
6. Firms with zero or negative earnings were put into the high-P/E-ratio quintile. Returns were calculated from February 1 to February 1 so that investors could put actual instead of projected earnings in for the fourth quarter.
7. If the firm repurchases its shares in lieu of paying a cash dividend, the same positive effect on returns will be realized. See Chapter 9 for a discussion of share repurchases.
8. Peter Lynch with John Rothchild, *One Up on Wall Street* (New York: Simon & Schuster, 1989), 198–99.
9. Charles Munger. "A Lesson on Elementary, Worldly Wisdom as It Relates to Investment Management and Business," 1994 speech at the USC business school.

10. Jeremy Siegel, "The Nifty Fifty Revisited: Do Growth Stocks Ultimately Justify Their Price?" *Journal of Portfolio Management* 21, 4 (1995), 8–20.
11. Peter Lynch with John Rothchild, *Beating the Street* (New York: Simon & Schuster, 1994), 139.
12. Warren Buffett, "Mr. Buffett on the Stock Market," *Fortune*, November 22, 1999.

4: Growth Is Not Return: The Trap of Investing in High-Growth Sectors

1. Qi Zeng, "How Global Is Your Industry," U.S. and the Americas Investment Perspectives, Morgan Stanley, New York, June 30, 2004.
2. For reference, see the weekly publication "Sector Strategy: Where to Invest Now," Goldman Sachs Equity Research, New York.
3. Formerly stocks were classified by SIC, or Standard Industrial Classification, a system developed by the government. In 1997 the SIC codes were expanded to include firms in Canada and Mexico and renamed NAICS, North American Industrial Classification System.
4. "Oil-Gas Drilling and Services Current Analysis," Standard and Poor's Industry Surveys, August 14, 1980, O103.
5. As of March 2004 only Delta and Southwest belong to the S&P 500 Index. TWA, Eastern, Pan Am, and United went bankrupt.
6. Real energy prices fell about 30 percent from 1977 through 1997 after adjusting for inflation.

5: The Bubble Trap: How to Spot and Avoid Market Euphoria

1. Alan Greenspan, opening remarks at the symposium "Rethinking Stabilization Policy," sponsored by the Federal Reserve Bank of Kansas City, Jackson Hole, Wyoming, August 29–31, 2002.
2. Robert Shiller, *Irrational Exuberance*, 2nd ed. (Princeton: Princeton University Press, 2005), 87.
3. Ralph C. Merkle, "Nanotechnology: What Will It Mean?" *IEEE Spectrum*, January 2001.
4. Gregory Zuckerman, "Nanotech Firms Turn Tiny Fundamentals into Big Stock Gains," *Wall Street Journal*, January 20, 2004.
5. This and all other articles that I wrote can be accessed through http://www.jeremysiegel.com.
6. Bloomberg News mentioned that Mary Meeker, the Internet guru from Morgan Stanley, had also warned about Internet stocks in an article in the *New Yorker*.
7. Shorting is the strategy of selling shares you do not own by effectively "bor-

rowing" them from someone else. The short seller hopes to make a profit by replacing the borrowed shares by buying them back at a lower price. Clearly if the stock price rises, the short seller loses.

6: Investing in the Newest of the New: Initial Public Offerings

1. About one-third of these firms survived in their current corporate form through December 31, 2003. If they did not, I substituted the return on the Ibbotson small stock index (see note 2 for this chapter).
2. The small stock index consists of the smallest quintile of stock traded on the New York and Nasdaq exchanges and is reported by Ibbotson.
3. Jay Ritter, "The 'Hot Issue' Market of 1980," *Journal of Business* 57, 2 (1984), 215–40.
4. Jay Ritter, "Big IPO Runups of 1975–September 2002," available at http://bear.cba.ufl.edu/ritter/RUNUP750.pdf.
5. TheGlobe.com subsequently traded as low as 2 cents a share, VA Linux at 54 cents.
6. Burton G. Malkiel, *A Random Walk Down Wall Street,* 8th ed. (New York: W.W. Norton, 2003), 77.
7. Christopher Palmeri and Steven V. Brull, "If You've Got It, Spend It: Gary Winnick Is Spreading His Millions Around with Gusto," *Business Week,* October 16, 2000.
8. Denis Berman, "Dialing for Dollars," *Wall Street Journal,* August 12, 2002, A1.
9. Ibid.
10. Randall E. Stross, *eBoys: The First Inside Account of Venture Capitalists at Work* (New York: Crown Business, 2000).
11. Ariana Eunjung Cha, " 'Johnny Appleseed' for a Risky Field," *Washington Post,* November 13, 2002.
12. See Jay Ritter, "Some Factoids about the 2003 IPO Market," August 2004, 9, available on his website at http://bear.cba.ufl.edu/ritter/IPOs2003.pdf.
13. Benjamin Graham, *The Intelligent Investor* (New York: HarperCollins, 1984).
14. Charles Mackay, *Extraordinary Popular Delusions and the Madness of Crowds,* Martin Fridson, editor (New York: John Wiley & Sons, 1996).
15. Ibid.
16. This was worth $10,000, or about $150,000 in today's dollars.
17. Edward Chancellor, author of *Devil Take the Hindmost,* claims that MacKay's recounting of this secret enterprise is apocryphal. Nevertheless, I fully agree with Jason Zweig, who e-mailed me that although the anecdote is ahistorical, "It's a darn shame, it's such a good . . . reminder of the danger of 'blind pools,' " investment vehicles where the use of the funds is not specified. These were sold to the public in the 1920s but are now outlawed.
18. I thank Michael Lewis, who brought this firm to my attention through *Bloomberg News* to its subscribers.
19. Malkiel, *A Random Walk Down Wall Street,* 56.

7: Capital Pigs:
Technology as Productivity Creator and Value Destroyer

1. Scott Thurm, "Costly Memories, Behind TiVo, iPod, and Xbox: An Industry Struggles for Profits," *Wall Street Journal,* October 14, 2004, A1.
2. Yochi J. Dreazen, "Telecom Carriers Were Driven by Wildly Optimistic Data on Internet's Growth Rate," *Wall Street Journal,* September 26, 2002, B1.
3. *Wall Street Journal,* op cit.
4. "The Great Telecom Crash," *The Economist,* July 18, 2002.
5. This and other data were reported in Dennis K. Berman, "Behind the Fiber Glut—Innovation Outpaced the Marketplace," *Wall Street Journal,* September 26, 2002, B1.
6. Dennis K. Berman, "Telecom Investors Envision Potential in Failed Networks," *Wall Street Journal,* August 14, 2003, 1.
7. "Too Many Debts; Too Few Calls," *The Economist,* July 20, 2002, 59.
8. While exact Internet usage numbers are hard to come by, highly regarded estimates for traffic growth were 107 percent in 2001, 87 percent in 2002, and 76 percent in 2003. See Andrew Odlyzko, "Internet Traffic Growth: Sources and Implications," n.d., available at http://www.dtc.umn.edu/~odlyzko/doc/itcom.internet.growth.pdf.
9. "The Great Telecom Crash," *The Economist,* July 18, 2002, 59.
10. Dennis K. Berman, "Technology Races Far Ahead of Demand and the Workplace," *Wall Street Journal,* September 26, 2002.
11. See http://www.bankruptcydata.com.
12. Berman, "Telecom Investors Envision Potential in Failed Networks."
13. See Dreazen, "Telecom Carriers Were Driven by Wildly Optimistic Data"; "Too Many Debts; Too Few Calls"; Odlyzko, "Internet Traffic Growth."
14. Chairman's letter, Berkshire Hathaway annual report, 1985.
15. Ibid.
16. Morgan Stanley did a similar study over a shorter period in "Watch Their Feet, Not Their Mouths," U.S. and the Americas Investment Perspectives, New York, October 7, 2002.
17. Mark Odell, "Carriers Relish Some Big Net Savings," *Financial Times,* July 24, 2000.
18. Scott McCartney, "Web Effect Is Greater on Airline Revenue Than Costs," *Wall Street Journal,* October 17, 2002, B2.
19. Jim Collins, *Good to Great: Why Some Companies Make the Leap . . . and Others Don't* (New York: HarperBusiness, 2001), 163.

8: Productivity and Profits:
Winning Managements in Losing Industries

1. PBS Home Video, "Warren Buffett Talks Business," filmed in 1994 at the Keenan Flagler Business School at the University of North Carolina.
2. Berkshire Hathaway annual report, 1996.
3. Jim Corridore, *Industry Surveys: Airlines,* Standard & Poor's, New York, May 20, 2004.
4. Berkshire Hathaway annual report, 1999, in reference to why he avoided technology stocks.
5. Sam Walton, *Sam Walton: Made in America* (New York: Bantam, 1993), 91.
6. Branford Johnson, "Retail: The Wal-Mart Effect," *McKinsey Quarterly,* 2002, no. 1.
7. Walton, *Sam Walton: Made in America,* 262.
8. Jim Collins, *Good to Great,* 155–56.
9. Ibid., 156.
10. Ibid.
11. Ken Iverson, *Plain Talk* (New York: Wiley, 1997), 54–59.
12. Pankaj Ghemawat and Henricus Stander, "Nucor at a Crossroads," case study 9-793-039, Harvard Business School, 1992 (revised 1998), 7.
13. *Fortune,* December 13, 1988, 58, cited in Ghemawat and Stander, "Nucor at a Crossroads," 9.
14. Jim Collins, *Good to Great,* 138.

9: Show Me the Money:
Dividends, Stock Returns, and Corporate Governance

1. The 1871–2003 period is analyzed because this is when data on dividends, available from the Cowles Foundation studies, become very reliable. Jeremy Siegel, *Stocks for the Long Run,* 3rd ed. (New York: McGraw-Hill, 2002).
2. Andy Kessler, "I Hate Dividends," *Wall Street Journal,* December 30, 2002.
3. Sara B. Moller, Frederik Schlingemann, and Rene Stulz, "Wealth Destruction on a Massive Scale? A Study of Acquiring-Firm Returns in the Recent Merger Wave," NBER working paper no. 10200, December 2003.
4. Jarrad Harford, "Corporate Cash Reserves and Acquisitions," School of Business Administration, University of Washington, November 1998, quote from abstract.
5. As related by Roger Lowenstein in his book *Buffett: The Making of An American Capitalist* (New York: Random House, 1996), 133n.
6. *Nightline,* ABC News, May 21, 2003.
7. Berkshire Hathaway annual report, 1999, 17.

8. Jeremy Siegel, "The Dividend Deficit," *Wall Street Journal,* February 19, 2001.
9. Raj Chetty and Emmanuel Saez, *Dividend Taxes and Corporate Behavior: Evidence from the 2003 Dividend Tax Cut,* NBER Working Paper, 10841.
10. Blaine Harden, "For Years, Many Microsoft Millionaires Hit the Options Key," *Washington Post,* August 5, 2003.
11. *The Financial Economists Roundtable,* of which I am a member, meets every year to discuss important issues facing financial institutions and our economy. In 2003, the topic was "executive compensation," and we concluded that the excessive issuance of stock options were distorting management incentives and the income statements of firms, and called for the repeal of section 162 (m) of the Internal Revenue Code.

10: Reinvested Dividends: The Bear Market Protector and Return Accelerator

1. The level of earnings in 1954 turned out to be almost exactly what would have been predicted by drawing a trend line through real per-share earnings growth from 1871 through 1929.
2. Hubert B. Herring, "Marlboro Man Rides a Bit Lower in the Saddle," *New York Times,* April 4, 1993.
3. The only close call occurred in Rose Cippoline's lawsuit against Philip Morris in 1988. This was the first case a tobacco company lost. Cippoline had smoked cigarettes since age seventeen, and the jury awarded Cippoline's husband $400,000 in damages. But upon appeal the verdict was overturned.
4. The total punitive damages were $145 billion, and Philip Morris was assessed about half of that level, since it sells about half of the cigarettes in the United States.
5. James Glassman, a financial writer, claimed that John Slatter, a Cleveland investment advisor and writer, invented the Dow 10 system in the 1980s. Harvey Knowles and Damon Petty popularized the strategy in their book *The Dividend Investor: A Safe, Sure Way to Beat the Market* (Chicago: Probus, 1992), as did Michael O'Higgins with John Downes in *Beating the Dow: A High-Return, Low-Risk Method for Investing in the Dow Jones Industrial Stocks with as Little as $5,000* (New York: HarperCollins, 1991). See John R. Dorfman, "Study of Industrial Averages Finds Stocks with High Dividends Are Big Winners," *Wall Street Journal,* August 11, 1988, C2.
6. See Alon Braz, John R. Graham, Campbell R. Harvey, and Roni Michaely, "Payout Policy in the 21st Century," NBER working paper no. 9657, April 2003, and Franklin Allen and Roni Michaely, "Payout Policy," Wharton Financial Institutions Center, April 2002.

7. Byron Wien and Frances Lim, "Lessons from Buyback and Dividend Announcements," October 4, 2004.
8. As a result of this exemption, the dividends they pay are not subject to the new 15 percent federal tax on dividends.

11: Earnings: The Basic Source of Shareholder Returns

1. Forbes debate with Robert Arnott, April 29, 2004. Ira Carnahan, "Should You Still Be a Bull?," *Forbes*, April 19, 2004.
2. Earnings filed with the IRS may differ from these.
3. It was partly the reaction of investors themselves that spurred management to increase write-offs. In the 1990–91 recession, investors bought firms that had large write-offs under the assumption that they would drop losing divisions and become more profitable.
4. Berkshire Hathaway annual report, 1992.
5. Bear Sterns Research, "Stock Option Valuation: Evolving to Better Valuation Models," June 2004.
6. David Stires, "The Breaking Point," *Fortune*, February 18, 2003.
7. Tim Carvell, "The Year in Ideas: Core Earnings," *New York Times Magazine*, December 15, 2002, 76.
8. Open letter from Warren Buffett to David Blitzer, managing director of Standard & Poor's, dated May 15, 2002.
9. "Do Stock Prices Reflect Information in Accruals and Cash Flows About Future Earnings?" Richard Sloan, *The Accounting Review*, 71, 1996.
10. "Do Analysts and Auditors Use Information in Accruals," Richard Sloan, Mark T. Bradshaw, and Scott A. Richardson, *Journal of Accounting Research*, 39, 2001.
11. Leonard Nakamura, "What Is the U.S. Gross Investment in Intangibles: (At least) One Trillion Dollars a Year," Working Paper no. 01-15, Federal Reserve Bank of Philadelphia, October 2001.

12: Is the Past Prologue?
The Past and Future Case for Stocks

1. Jeremy Siegel, *Stocks for the Long Run*, 3rd ed. (New York: McGraw-Hill, 2002), 13.
2. See S. J. Brown, W. N. Goetzmann, and S. A. Ross, "Survival," *Journal of Finance* 50, 1995, 853–73.
3. Adapted from Elroy Dimson, Paul Marsh, and Mike Staunton, *Triumph of the Optimists: 101 Years of Global Investment Returns* (Princeton: Princeton University Press, 2002).
4. Elroy Dimson, Paul Marsh, and Mike Staunton, "Global Investment Returns Yearbook 2004," ABN-AMRO, February 2004.
5. Elroy Dimson, Paul Marsh, and Mike Staunton, *Triumph of the Optimists*, 175.

In fact, *Triumph of the Optimists* may have actually understated long-term international stock returns. The U.S. stock markets, and other world markets for which we have data, did very well in the thirty years prior to 1900, when their study begins. U.S. returns measured from 1871 outperform those returns taken from 1900 by 32 basis points. Data from the United Kingdom show a very similar pattern.

6. Ibid.
7. Robert Arnott in Ira Carnahan, "Should You Still be a Bull?" *Forbes,* April 19, 2004.

13: The Future That Cannot Be Changed: The Coming Age Wave

1. Peter Peterson, *Gray Dawn: How the Coming Age Wave Will Transform America—and the World* (New York: Three Rivers Press, 2000), cover of book.
2. Ibid., 18.
3. These data are taken from Peter Drucker's essay "The Next Society," *The Economist,* November 3, 2001, page 5 of survey.
4. Assume people begin working at age twenty and retire at sixty-five, so the ratio is the number of people between twenty and sixty-four divided by the number of people sixty-five and over.
5. Cited in Paul Wallace, *Agequake: Riding the Demographic Rollercoaster Shaking Business, Finance, and Our World* (London: Nicholas Brealey Publishing, 1999), 31.
6. Peterson, *Gray Dawn,* 20.
7. Gary Becker, in Wallace, *Agequake,* 135–144.
8. Wallace, Ibid., 21.
9. James Vaupel, "Setting the Stage: A Generation of Centenarians?" *Washington Quarterly* 23, 3 (2000): 197–200.
10. Gina Kolata, "Could We Live Forever?" *New York Times,* November 11, 2003.
11. Testimony before the Senate Special Committee on Aging, Hearing on "The Future of Human Longevity: How Important Are Markets and Innovation?" June 3, 2003.
12. "Forever Young," *The Economist,* March 27, 2004, 6.
13. *National Vital Statistics Reports* 51, 3 (2002), Centers for Disease Control and Prevention, National Center for Health Statistics.
14. Peterson, *Gray Dawn,* 34.
15. Although the Social Security system is gradually raising the age at which full benefits are being paid—to sixty-seven from sixty-five—from 2002 through 2027, the minimum age at which benefits are being paid, sixty-two, has not been increased.
16. "Forever Young," op. cit., 15.
17. Nicholas Vanston, "Maintaining Prosperity," *Washington Quarterly* 23, 3 (2000): 225–38.

18. Pauline Givord, "The Decline in Participation Rates Among the Older Age Groups in France," paper presented at the conference "Ageing, Skills and Labour," sponsored by the European Network of Economic Policy Research Institutes, Nantes, France, September 7–8, 2001.

19. The tax rates used to fund Social Security are shared equally by the employer and the employee up to a given level of income, which is about twice the national average. In 2004, the total Social Security tax rate is 12.4 percent on earned income up to $87,900.

20. Paul Samuelson, "Social Security," *Newsweek,* February 13, 1967.

21. If the Fed tries to stop this inflation by tightening the money supply, this will cause wages to fall dramatically, again setting the stage for generational conflict.

14: Conquering the Age Wave: Which Policies Will Work and Which Won't

1. Peter Peterson, *Running on Empty* (New York: Farrar, Straus and Giroux, 2004), 195.

2. Productivity throughout will refer to labor productivity. There are other productivity measures that correct for the quantity and quality of labor and capital.

3. One of the important exceptions is Great Britain's public pension system, which changed its policy in 1995 to pay benefits that are only indexed to inflation, not to the general level of wages. As a result, Great Britain's pension system is also one of the few in the developed world that is solvent on a long-term basis. But this solvency comes at the cost that those retiring years from now will receive a benefit far lower than the wages they received before retirement.

4. See Robert M. Solow, "A Contribution to the Theory of Economic Growth," *Quarterly Journal of Economics* 70 (1956): 65–94.

5. Albert Ando, Dimitrios Christelis, and Tsutomu Miyagawa, "Inefficiency of Corporate Investment and Distortion of Savings Behavior in Japan," NBER working paper no. 9444.

6. Paul S. Hewitt, "The Gray Roots of Japan's Crisis," Asia Program Special Report, Woodrow Wilson International Center for Scholars, January 2003.

7. "A Shrinking Giant," *The Economist,* January 8, 2004.

8. Pierre Sicsic and Charles Wyplosz, "French Post-War Growth from (Indicative) Planning to (Administered) Market," Centre for Economic Policy Research, discussion paper no. 1023, 1994.

9. The trustees of the Social Security System have measured the sensitivity of their revenue and cost equations to the rate of productivity growth. The increase in productivity needed to balance Social Security over the next seventy-five years is far more modest, but this understates the productivity needed to balance the system by midcentury since it includes all the surpluses the system will accrue over the next two decades.

10. Remarks by Chairman Alan Greenspan, at the Securities Industry Association annual meeting, Boca Raton, Florida, November 6, 2003.

11. Edward Prescott, "Why Do Americans Work So Much More Than Europeans," *Federal Reserve Bank of Minneapolis Quarterly Review* 28, 1 (2004): 2–13.

12. Jeremy Rifkin, *The European Dream: How Europe's Vision of the Future Is Quietly Eclipsing the American Dream* (New York: Penguin Books, 2004), 14.

13. Steven J. Davis and Magnus Henrekson, "Tax Effects on Work Activity, Industry Mix and Shadow Economy Size: Evidence from Rich-Country Comparisons," NBER working paper series no. 10509.; National Bureau of Economic Research, 2004.

14. *Helvering vs. Davis* (1937) and *Fleming vs. Nestor* (1960).

15: The Global Solution: The True New Economy

1. Joel Mokyr, *The Lever of Riches: Technological Creativity and Economic Progress* (New York: Oxford University Press, 1990), 20.

2. Ibid., 29.

3. Michael Kremer, "Population Growth and Technological Change: 1,000,000 B.C. to 1990." *Quarterly Journal of Economics,* 108 (August 1993): 681–716.

4. William D. Nordhaus, "Do Real Output and Real Wage Measures Capture Reality? The History of Lighting Suggests Not," in Timothy F. Bresnahan and Robert J. Gordon, eds., *The Economics of New Goods* (Chicago: University of Chicago Press, 1997), 29–66.

5. Roy Porter, "The Eighteenth Century," in Lawrence Konrad et al., eds., *The Western Medical Tradition, 800 BC to AD 1800* (Cambridge: Cambridge University Press, 1995).

6. Michael Hart, *The 100: A Ranking of the Most Influential Persons in History* (New York: Citadel Press, 1994), 38.

7. Quoted in Julian Simon, *The Ultimate Resource 2: People, Materials, and Environment* (Princeton: Princeton University Press, 1996), Chapter 26.

8. See Applied History Research Group, University of Calgary, "The Ming Dynasty's Maritime History," available at http://www.ucalgary.ca/applied_history/tutor/eurvoya/ming.html.

9. The work has survived only thanks to a Japanese reprint.

10. Charles Jones, *Introduction to Economic Growth,* 2nd ed. (New York: W. W. Norton & Company, 2002), 16.

11. E. Einstein, *The Printing Press as Agent of Change: A Communications and Cultural Transformation in Early Modern Europe* (Cambridge: Cambridge University Press, 1979), 11.

12. Michael Rotschild, *Bionomics* (New York: Henry Holt, 1990), 8–9.

13. Hume, quoted in Simon, *Ultimate Resource 2*, Chapter 26.

14. Jared Diamond, *Guns, Germs, and Steel: The Fates of Human Societies* (New York: W.W. Norton, 1997), 412.

15. Jones, *Introduction to Economic Growth*, 88.
16. Letter to Robert Hooke, 5th February 1676.
17. Lee Gomes, "A Beautiful Mind from India Puts Internet on Alert," *Wall Street Journal*, November 4, 2002.
18. Quoted in Thomas Friedman, "Is Google God?" *New York Times*, June 29, 2003.
19. Ministry of Information Industry, *Tenth Five-Year Plan (2001–2005)*, available in English at http://www.trp.hku.hk/infofile/china/2002/10-5-yr-plan.pdf.
20. Mary Meeker, Lina Choi, Yoshiko Motoyama, "The China Internet Report," April 14, 2004, Morgan Stanley Research, 6.
21. Vogelstein, Fred, "How Intel Got Inside," *Fortune*, October 4, 2004, 134.
22. Thomas Friedman, "Origin of Species," *New York Times*, March 14, 2004.
23. These relative incomes are quoted on a purchasing power parity (PPP) basis.
24. Yasheng Huang, "China Is Just Catching Up," *Financial Times*, June 7, 2004.
25. Dominic Wilson and Roopa Purushothaman, "Dreaming with BRICs: The Path to 2050," Global Economics Research Paper no. 99, Goldman Sachs, October 1, 2003.
26. Michael Shari, "Indonesia: Consumer Heaven?" *Business Week*, March 24, 2003.
27. Thomas Hout and Jim Hemerling, "China's Next Great Thing," *Fast Company*, March 2004; Dennis Eng, "Levi's, Pillowtex Deals Worth Billions to Li & Fung," *The Standard: Great China's Business Newspaper*, January 9, 2004.
28. See Gabriel Kahn, "Chinese Firms Buy Rights to Famous Trademarks," *Wall Street Journal*, December 26, 2003.
29. See George Wehrfritz, "China: Going Global," *Newsweek International*, March 1, 2004, and Clay Chandler, "Inside the New China," *Fortune*, October 4, 2004, 98.
30. See Constance Sorrentino and Joyanna Moy, "U.S. Labor Market Performance: International Perspective," *Monthly Labor Review* (Bureau of Labor Statistics), June 2002, and Bureau of Labor Statistics, "Comparative Civilian Labor Force Statistics: Ten Countries, 1959–2003," June 2004.
31. See Bureau of Labor Statistics, "Occupational Employment and Wages, 2002."
32. Matthew Spiegelman and Robert H. McGuckin III, "China's Experience with Productivity and Jobs," report R-1352-04-RR, The Conference Board, New York, June 2004.
33. Allan Blinder, "Free Trade," *The Concise Encyclopedia of Economics*, available at http://www.econlib.org/library/Enc/FreeTrade.html.
34. Thomas Friedman, "What Goes Around . . ." *New York Times*, February 26, 2004.

16: Global Markets and the World Portfolio

1. Eighteen of these firms had B shares that were available to overseas investors.
2. Marc Levinson, "China's Now the Straw That Stirs the Asian Drink," *Newsweek*, December 13, 1993.

3. I first showed this negative relation between economic growth for both developed and emerging countries in *Stocks for the Long Run* (New York: McGraw-Hill, 1998), Figures 9-2, 130.

4. Elroy Dimson, Paul Marsh, and Michael Staunton, *Triumph of the Optimists*. They have no ready explanation for this phenomenon and suggest that some of the early GDP data were of poor quality and that fast-growing countries did not have strong institutions that protected shareholder rights.

5. Alison Rogers, "China's Stock Market Crush," *Fortune*, September 7, 1992, 8.

6. Charles P. Thomas, Francis E. Warnock, and Jon Wongswan, "The Performance of International Portfolios," Federal Reserve Working Paper 2004-817, September 2004.

7. Qi Zeng, "How Global Is Your Industry," U.S. and the Americas Investment Perspectives, Morgan Stanley, New York, June 30, 2004.

8. The global sectors and their corresponding ticker symbols are energy (IXC), financial (IXG), health care (IXJ), technology (IXN), and telecom (IXP). These sectors are based on the S&P Global 1200, which approximates the 1,200 largest stocks in the world market.

9. John Maynard Keynes, *The General Theory of Employment, Interest and Money* (London: Macmillan, 1936), 158.

10. Furthermore, if everyone fails, the government may come to the rescue. A severe bear market in U.S. stocks, which is apt to precipitate a recession, is more likely to induce governmental tax relief than a bear market in foreign stocks, which impacts relatively few domestic investors. The reduction in the dividend and capital gains tax followed the severe bear market of 2000–2002, but the bear markets that hit Japan after their bubble burst in 1989 did not result in beneficial legislation for U.S. investors.

11. See John Bogle, *Common Sense of Mutual Funds* (New York: John Wiley and Sons, 1999); John Bogle, *John Bogle on Investing* (New York: McGraw-Hill, 2001); Jeremy Siegel, *Stocks for the Long Run*, 3rd ed. (New York: McGraw-Hill, 2002).

12. Developed Europe covers Austria, Belgium, Denmark, Finland, France, Germany, Ireland, Italy, Netherlands, Norway, Portugal, Spain, Sweden, Switzerland, and the United Kingdom. These proportions are quoted as of April 30, 2004, and will vary over time.

13. Japan and developed Asia, which includes Australia, New Zealand, Hong Kong, and Singapore.

14. Because the Morgan Stanley indexes target 80 percent of the market value of each country, they naturally hold the largest stocks in each country. This means that the indexes are subject to the same distortions that impact the S&P 500 or the Russell 2000. In 2002 Morgan Stanley took steps to reduce the turnover of shares in its index to minimize this distortion.

15. The following funds can be purchased separately. The European fund costs 0.32 percent per year, the Pacific fund 0.29 percent, and the emerging-markets fund 0.53 percent.

16. Vanguard does not literally hold all the stocks in the Wilshire Index, but uses sophisticated statistical techniques to replicate its returns. As a result, there is some small tracking error in the returns on this fund, but its tracking error has gone down significantly in recent years.
17. Although in some aspects it is more restrictive than Standard & Poor's indexes by excluding the Bermuda-based firms Tyco and Schlumberger.
18. In recent years the Russell 2000 index has been subject to the same "gaming" problems that have plagued the S&P 500 Index, as speculators have bought and sold stocks ahead of the changes in the index capitalization.

17: Strategies for the Future: The D-I-V Directives

1. The Reward-Risk ratios are the Sharpe Ratios, developed by William Sharpe, and represent the expected return on the strategy (the arithmetic mean) minus the risk-free rate divided by the risk, or standard deviation of the strategy. See William Sharpe, "The Sharpe Ratio," *Journal of Portfolio Management*, Fall 1994.
2. E. Dimson, P. March, and M. Staunton, *Global Investment Returns Yearbook 2004*, ABN-AMRO, February, 2004, p. 34.
3. Quoted in David Eisner, "It Works: Buying $1 for 40 cents," *Chicago Tribune*, December 8, 1985, section 7, 1.

Appendix

1. Thatcher Glass actually saw the end of the milk bottle coming and diversified into plastics and glass bottles for drugs, which is a major reason Rexall purchased it in 1966.
2. Nabisco was founded as the National Biscuit Company in 1898.
3. Under the procedures for calculating the returns of the Total Descendant portfolio, an investor takes the cash from a privatization and places it in an S&P 500 Index fund. If and when the privatized firm is resold to the public, the accumulation from the index fund is used to purchase these newly issued shares.
4. In July 2004, it was reported that KKR finally sold Borden Chemical, the last piece of its investment in RJR Nabisco. The investors in its 1987 fund reportedly lost $730 million on the buyout but, because of other successful investments, the fund had a compound return of about 10 percent, which matched the S&P Index over that period. See "A Long Chapter Ends for Kohlberg Kravis: Fund Books Loss on RJR after 15 Years," *International Herald Tribune*," July 9, 2004.

ACKNOWLEDGMENTS

There is no question that an author is reliant on many individuals in the production of a book such as this. But I can honestly say that one person, Jeremy Schwartz, stands above all others in importance. Jeremy, a 2003 graduate of the Wharton School, not only has extraordinary skills in research and computing, but also the rare ability to organize and express ideas in a way that is accessible to both professional and nonprofessional readers.

Jeremy's capacity to work hard is as great as mine. He not only convinced me that tracing through the returns on all the original S&P 500 firms from 1957 forward was possible, but he obtained all the data and created the algorithms that carried all these calculations to completion. Using our laptop computers, we stayed in constant contact through many long evenings, on weekends, and during my heavy travel schedule. I continually relied on being able to filter both my ideas and rough drafts through his superb judgment. I can say without hesitation that without Jeremy's involvement over the last three years, this book would never have come to fruition.

John Mahaney, my editor, also played an extremely important role in encouraging me to emphasize the bottom line of my ideas to the reader. It is not easy for an editor with no professional training in finance or economics to guide an author who already has written a bestselling book on the subject. But John did it with extraordinary skill and finesse, and the book is unquestionably better because of his guidance. I also wish to thank Wes Neff, my agent, who not only led me to the right publisher but also kept my spirits up when the effort needed to synthesize the research and complete the manuscript seemed insurmountable.

My gratitude also goes to those who have read early versions of the book and provided extremely important feedback. Professor Jay Ritter of the University of Florida, the leading expert on initial public offerings, provided invaluable advice and detailed comments on the manuscript. Randy

Kessler of Lazard Freres provided early feedback that helped organize and bring out the major ideas of the book. Dan Rottenberg and David Conti also made invaluable suggestions on early versions of the manuscript.

My close friend and colleague, Robert Shiller of Yale University, author of the bestselling *Irrational Exuberance,* was an enthusiastic supporter of the thesis of this book. Bob and I often sparred on the stage, I taking the bullish and he taking the bearish position on the stock market. But after reading a draft of this book, he exclaimed that our ideas about how investors should approach the market, particularly avoiding stocks with high valuations, are far closer than many realize.

I am blessed to have access to such talented Wharton students to assist with the massive research needed to complete this book. Leonard Lee, a 2002 graduate, did some of the very early work on long-term returns from 1950 onward. Particular credit goes to Ryan Hinkle, a 2003 Wharton undergraduate who did a superb job of programming the demographic model of world consumption that enabled me to evaluate the solutions to the age wave crisis. I also wish to thank Jason Spindel and Stephanie Weiss, who helped gather and evaluate the original S&P 500 firms, and Shaun Smith, Ana Nekhamkin, Andrew Rosner, and Bonnie Schein, who worked and commented on various parts of the manuscript.

I am also indebted to Howard Silverblatt, Howard Bernheim, and Andy Halula from Standard and Poor's Corporation, who have been extraordinarily helpful at providing us with data that helped us calculate these long-run returns. David Blitzer and Robert Friedman filled me in on the background and details of the formulation of "core earnings," a breakthrough concept in achieving uniformity and clarity in corporate earnings.

One's family is always a part of the book-writing process, both in providing encouragement and tolerance of the long hours needed to research and compile this project. Like a family on a long car trip asking "Are we there yet?" I often received the question "Are you done yet?" My wife, Ellen, and my sons, Andrew and Jeffrey, reminded me that I could always work a bit longer to perfect the manuscript, but there was a time to lay down the pen (or in our twenty-first century, close our laptops) and declare the project done. I hope what I produced is worthy of their love and forbearance.

INDEX

ABOUT THE AUTHOR

JEREMY J. SIEGEL is the Russell E. Palmer Professor of Finance at the Wharton School of the University of Pennsylvania. Dr. Siegel received his Ph.D. in economics from M.I.T. and is the author of the classic and influential *Stocks for the Long Run*. Professor Siegel writes and lectures about the economy and financial markets and has appeared frequently on CNN, CNBC, NPR, and other networks. He is a regular columnist for *Kiplinger's* and has contributed op-eds and articles to the *Wall Street Journal, Barron's,* the *Financial Times,* and other national and international news media.